WELCOME UNREASON

A study of 'madness' in the novels of Marguerite Duras

RAYNALLE UDRIS

CIP-GEGEVENS KONINKLIJKE BIBLIOTHEEK, DEN HAAG

Udris, Raynalle

Welcome unreason / Raynalle Udris. — Amsterdam - Atlanta, GA 1993 :
Rodopi. — (Faux titre, ISSN 0167-9392 ; 66)
Met lit. opg., reg.
ISBN: 90-5183-444-6
Trefw.: Duras, Marguerite (werken) / Franse letterkunde ;
geschiedenis ; 20e eeuw.

©Editions Rodopi B.V., Amsterdam - Atlanta, GA 1993
Printed in The Netherlands

ACKNOWLEDGEMENTS

This study is particularly indebted to the following individuals for their various forms of help and support:

Ninette Bailey

Madeleine Renouard

Janis Udris

the staff of Birkbeck College Library, Malet Street, London

CONTENTS

LIST OF ABBREVIATIONS

Throughout this study the following abbreviations will be used in reference to the particular texts:

AO   *L'Anti-Oedipe* (Deleuze & Guattari, Minuit, 1972)
HF   *Histoire de la Folie* (Foucault, Gallimard 1972)
TF   *Territoires du Féminin* (Marini, Minuit 1977)

Texts by Duras

VT   *La Vie Tranquille* (1944)
BCP   *Un Barrage Contre le Pacifique* (1950)
MG   *Le Marin de Gibraltar* (1952)
PCT   *Les Petits Chevaux de Tarquinia* (1953)
S   *Le Square* (1955)
MOCA   *Moderato Cantabile* (1958)
DHSE   *Dix Heures et Demie du Soir en Eté* (1960)
HMA   *Hiroshima mon Amour* (1960)
AMA   *L'Après-midi de Monsieur Andesmas* (1962)
RLVS   *Le Ravissement de Lol V.Stein* (1964)
VC   *Le Vice-consul* (1965)
DDE   *Détruire, Dit-elle* (1969)
A   *L'Amour* (1971)
FG   *La Femme du Gange* (1973)
P   *Les Parleuses* (1974)
L   *Les Lieux* (1977)
HAC   *L'Homme Assis dans le Couloir* (1980)
YV   *Les Yeux Verts* (1980)
MM   *La Maladie de la Mort* (1982)
HA   *L'Homme Atlantique* (1982)
AT   *L'Amant* (1984)
YB   *Les Yeux Bleus, Cheveux Noirs* (1986)
VM   *La Vie Matérielle* (1987)
EL   *Emily-L* (1987)

LIST OF TABLES   pp.

INTRODUCTORY REMARKS

"L'homme de nos jours n'a de vérité que dans l'énigme du fou qu'il est et qu'il n'est pas."[1]

"On nous a appris depuis l'enfance que tous nos efforts devaient tendre à trouver un sens à l'existence qu'on mène, à celle qu'on nous propose. Il faut en sortir. Et que ce soit gai."[2]

Madness constitutes a recurrent feature of Duras' texts and of Durasian production in general. From her early writings, the lexical leitmotifs of 'fou' and 'folie' metaphorically establish a semantic contamination which pervades the narratives and later becomes associated with sexuality or alcohol in *Les Yeux Bleus, Cheveux Noirs* or *La Vie Matérielle*. The seme of madness is further echoed and significantly reinforced by the presence of 'mad' characters, mostly women, who from text to text gradually move

---

[1] Michel Foucault, *Histoire de la Folie* (NRF Paris, 1972) p.548 (HF P.548). Throughout this thesis, references to novels and other texts by Marguerite Duras and to some other important sources will not, for the most part, be footnoted. Initials for the texts, with page numbers, will follow citations of such work. For a list of initials used for particular texts, cf. p.10 above.

[2] Marguerite Duras, *Outside* (POL Paris, 1984) p.176

from a secondary to a central position in the narrative: from the mention, for instance, of "la vieille folle" in *Dix Heures et Demie du Soir en Eté*, the episodic appearance of Louis the sailor in *Le Marin de Gibraltar* or even the obsessive presence/absence of Valerie in *L'Après-midi de Monsieur Andesmas*, to Lol's madness later found in the woman of *L'Amour* or the disturbing presence of the vice-consul, etc. Moreover, places associated with madness also recur from text to text, be it the forest in *Détruire Dit-elle* or *Emily-L*, the beach or the sea-wall in *L'Amour* or the many references to "les passages" by the sea in *Emily-L* and *Les Yeux Bleus, Cheveux Noirs*. Throughout Duras' writing, madness enters into a series of symbolic equivalences whereby 'les fous' equal the lepers or the beggars (*Le Vice-consul*), the Jews (*Aurélia Steiner, La Douleur*), hungry or abandoned dogs (*L'Après-midi de Monsieur Andesmas, L'Amour*), seagulls (*L'Amour, Emily-L*), and, especially, women (particularly in *Le Ravissement de Lol V.Stein, La Maladie de la Mort, Le Vice-consul, Emily-L*). The significance of such explicit or metaphorical references to madness is further reinforced by Duras' self-confessed fear of becoming mad. (P p.199)

Madness nevertheless remains an ambiguous and vague concept and my initial assumption, according to which madness, and especially unreason, constitutes a key element in the Durasian world, cannot be completely free of 'parti-pris'.[3]

However, Duras' writing explores so many limit-zones of human experience that it is difficult to imagine not working in relation to mental illness, to the uncertainty of the subject and of

---

[3]This is a bias which cannot be avoided, in spite of Borgamano's stated position against any unifying critical approach, according to which one must not exchange "l'ambivalence destructive [des textes de Duras] contre un sens unique" ('Le Corps et le Texte' in D.Bajomé & R.Heyndels, *Ecrire, Dit-elle*, Université de Bruxelles, 1983, p.61). Such an attractive position only hides another pitfall. Indeed Borgamano acknowledges: "On peut évidemment reconnaître dans le corps-texte écartelé, les maladies du corps social: *le texte durassien n'échappe pas toujours aux pièges du miroir*" (my emphasis). This passage reveals a conception of the text as pure form which in effect operates a reduction as significant as that of the unifying position. Each critical approach must indeed face and endorse the risks of its own limitations. Aware of the fundamental ambiguity of its own task, the critical venture needs to remain conscious of its limitations by which each specific reading remains just an added dimension in an already enormous corpus of interpretations. Such knowledge promotes the fundamental doubt and modesty which remain the guarantee of critical integrity.

his/her position in society and in the world in general. Marguerite Duras' texts indeed remain in touch with the problematic of their time insofar that they articulate a sociological and philosophical modernity linked to the meaning of madness and unreason. Madness constitutes the most disturbing experience of humanity: it is beyond definition in that it escapes understanding and cannot be said or thought:

> "Depuis des siècles, médecins et philosophes se sont penchés sur le problème de la 'folie' sans réussir à savoir exactement ce que c'est. On a supposé qu'aucun homme n'y échappait, on a parlé d'une 'folie' nécessaire, voire de la nécessité pour chacun d'avoir la 'folie' de tout le monde."[4]

Madness constitutes such a threat to reason that, as Foucault shows in *L'Histoire de la Folie*, its presence has since the classical age remained orchestrated and partly neutralised by society. This dominance of reason may lead one to forget that "le discours du psychotique c'est l'affaire de tous. C'est le symptôme de toute appartenance à la totalité, de toute inscription dans le corps social."[5]

As Sheridan stresses,

> "We must abandon any notion that we now possess the truth about madness. Indeed, we must set aside anything we think we know about it, any temptation to analyze, order, classify madness from some retrospective standpoint."[6]

In the following chapters I examine to what extent Duras' prose, and the novels of the cycle of Lol V.Stein[7] in particular, are

---

[4]Maud Mannoni, in *Le Psychiatre, son Fou et la Psychanalyse* (Points, Paris 1971) p.37

[5]Armando Verdiglione, *La Folie dans la Psychanalyse* (Payot, Paris 1977) p.25

[6]Alan Sheridan, *Michel Foucault: the Will to Truth* (Tavistock, London 1981) p.14

[7]Jean Pierrot recalls that the expression 'cycle of Lol V.Stein' was first used by Dominique Noguez in 'Les India Songs of Marguerite Duras' in *Cahiers du XXème Siècle* (1977). It refers to the constellation of works referring to *Le Ravissement de Lol V.Stein*, *Le Vice-consul* and *L'Amour* and their filmic equivalents *La Femme du Gange* and *India Song* (*Marguerite Duras*, Corti 1986, p.201)

situated in this perspective. Durasian writing, with the central presence of the absent female figures of Lol and Anne-Marie Stretter, or the anonymous women of the later texts, does not allow the acquisition of any obvious truth; but as Michel de Certeau mentions,

> "Cet art se détache absolument des stratégies qui spécifient, par exemple, les démarches philosophiques: il n'entre pas dans la production d'un sens ou d'une parole; il n'articule aucune méthode qui permettrait l'acquisition d'une vérité."[8]

In creating such texts, Marguerite Duras situates herself in "cet affrontement au dessous du langage de la raison". But

> "Vers quoi pourrait nous conduire une interrogation qui ne suivrait pas la raison dans son devenir horizontal, mais chercherait à retracer dans le temps, cette verticalité constante, qui, tout au long de la culture européenne, la confronte à ce qu'elle n'est pas, la mesure à sa propre démesure? Vers quelle région irions-nous, qui n'est ni l'histoire de la connaissance, ni l'histoire tout court, qui n'est commandée ni par la téléologie de la vérité, ni par l'enchaînement rationnel des causes, lesquels n'ont valeur et sens qu'au delà du partage? Une région, sans doute, où il serait question plutôt des limites que de l'identité d'une culture."[9]

The danger of such literature resides in the reader's possible misrecognition of its signifying enterprise. But in spite of the disturbance of discourse which reflects the loss of mastery or the absence of the subject, the recurrent presence of the enunciative voice, epitomised in the title of *Détruire Dit-elle* or in the repeated "il dit (...) elle dit" in some of the most enigmatic, rarefied texts such as *L'Amour*, clearly indicates that even if the subject appears lost, there still remains a "prise de parole". The ambivalence of the presence/absence of the subject remains in the line of the dilemma confronted by Foucault and indeed by all those who have an experience of madness: how can madness be apprehended outside

---

[8] Michel de Certeau, 'Marguerite Duras: On Dit' in *Ecrire Dit-elle* pp.259-260
[9] M. Foucault, *Histoire de la folie*, Plon 1961 p.iii (original preface)

reason? How can meaning exist without excluding madness by the same token? How is it possible to include both sides of the original cogito, reason and the silence of madness, without the internment of one or the other? We are indeed confronted with the problem of language and meaning: can madness and Unreason challenge Reason from the inside of Reason itself? This constitutes an insurmountable dilemma which nevertheless remains, as Marguerite Duras' writing shows, the very source of creativity.

To conduct the investigation of madness and unreason in Marguerite Duras' prose, I first assess how the madness described in the Durasian text has to do with the "délire cliniquement parfait" mentioned by Jacques Lacan in relation to *Le Ravissement*,[10] and what effect such a characteristic has on the reader's reception of Duras' text. I later examine how the evolution of the concept of madness reflected in the titles of the three texts of the cycle, from the reference to Lol's individual experience in *Le Ravissement*, to that of social exclusion in *Le Vice-consul* and to the more universal sphere of *L'Amour*, is closely related to the social contexts in which madness is pictured. I finally analyse the link between love and unreason in Marguerite Duras' prose from *Le Ravissement* onwards. I ultimately argue that unreason preexists any social context and is in fact an integral part of the logic of Duras' writing.

Throughout this study, and especially when dealing with the vice-consul's state of abnormality, I shall alternately use the terms 'unreason' and 'madness'. The term 'unreason', if one follows the distinction made by Foucault, refers to the liberation of imaginary powers, inscribed in an atemporal dimension and marked by repetition: "le retour de la déraison prend l'allure d'une répétition massive, qui renoue avec elle-même par delà le temps." (HF p.383). The term 'madness' is more circumscribed and linked to a modern apprehension:

> "la conscience de la folie s'accompagne au contraire d'une certaine analyse de la modernité, qui la situe

---

[10]Lacan's declaration is reported by Marguerite Duras during an interview with Rivette and Narboni in *Cahiers du Cinéma* 1969, quoted by Pierrot op.cit. p.204.

d'entrée de jeu dans un cadre temporel, historique et social." (HF p.383)[11]

My investigation will principally concentrate on the texts of the 'cycle of Lol V.Stein', since not only are they chronologically central to Marguerite Duras' production but they also constitute a turning-point in her mode of writing:

"J'ai commencé à écrire avec ça, avec *Le Ravissement de Lol V.Stein*, *L'Amour* et *La Femme du Gange*" (L p.90)

It is mostly from this constellation of texts, echoed by filmic versions, that madness becomes most clearly stated and that its presence operates a transformation of the narrative texture to reflect "ce plaisir *fou*, un peu hagard d'écrire" (my emphasis)[12] which translates what Marguerite Duras describes as "cet inconnu de moi-même".[13]

---

[11]The reactions to both 'unreason' and 'madness' have differed historically. From the 19th century onwards, the fear of unreason has been very emotional: "prise presque dans son entier dans le mouvement des résurrections imaginaires (...) la déraison devenant ainsi, par excellence, le contretemps du monde" (ibid. p.383). Madness has remained more precisely situated in the chronology of nature and history.

[12]'La Vie Duras', in *Libération* 11.1.90 p.21

[13]ibid. p.20

SECTION I

LA FOLIE EST FEMME

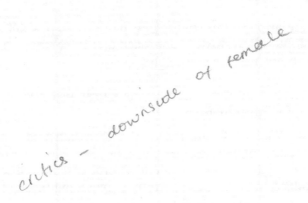

Chapter 1

LA MISE EN SCÈNE DE LA FOLIE

Duras' central figures from *Un Barrage Contre le Pacifique* to *Emily-L* are mostly female, with the possible exceptions of the vice-consul and of Mr Andesmas. Their male centrality is in any case signalled in the titles of the narratives, though it could be argued that Valerie is in fact the central focus of *L'Après-midi de Monsieur Andesmas*.

Duras' early novels, in which madness was just thematically alluded to and did not itself constitute a major concern of the narrative, referred to more concrete situations. In *Un Barrage Contre le Pacifique*, for instance, madness constituted an extra element in the family relationships, poverty and boredom experienced by Suzanne, the main protagonist. Female characters in Duras' early fictions were often pictured as in touch with reality and able to act on the world, be it the woman narrator in *Le Boa*, Francine in *La Vie Tranquille* or Maria in *Dix Heures et Demie du Soir en Eté*. Gradually, and especially from *Le Ravissement de Lol V. Stein* to *L'Amour*, the active female position becomes eroded. An evolution takes place in Duras' writing; the female characters' desire becomes so overwhelmingly symptomatic of another reality that these characters remain passive, locked in their fantasy. And one can wonder at this point if in the texts of the Indian cycle, namely *Le Ravissement de Lol V. Stein*, *Le Vice-consul* and *L'Amour*, the female symptomatic behaviour can be identified as clinical madness, and if so examine what conclusions can be drawn in relation to this study. To explore these possibilities I propose to adopt an intertextual approach and to compare the Durasian text to other narrative accounts.

1 Delirium of madness in the Duras text and in some accounts of clinical madness

The confrontation of the Durasian text with other female accounts of madness like those of Mary Barnes, Emma Santos, and Unica Zürn[1] makes evident several common, disturbing features. Indeed in all of these narratives, including those of Duras, one can find:

> a similar origin of the psychic trauma.
> a related symptomatology.
> similar descriptive and stylistic elements.

Similar origin of the psychic trauma

⌐The texts examined consistently indicate that madness in its clinical sense stems from separation from the love object and from an irremediable need to be united, or reunited, with that specific other which most often appears to be the mother.⌐

For Emma Santos in *La Loméchuse*, the immediate psychic trauma originates from her parting from her lover. Her refusal to accept the separation from the other and her fantasy of fusion into one feed her subsequent aspiration to a physical fusion with her doctor Elisabeth. The merging of the 'I' into the 'you' is reflected in the nominal amalgamation 'Elisabemma', and signals a brief episode of regressive satisfaction:

> "Elles sont dépouillées de leur corps, vont l'une vers l'autre, elles sont nues (...) elles porteront l'enfant (...) elles sont échappées de leur prison intérieure et elles sourient à leur médiocrité".[2]

Mary Barnes' inner conflict is situated at the level of her desire for the body of the Other, mostly that of the mother. "A la

---

[1]Emma Santos, *La Loméchuse* and *L'Itinéraire Psychiatrique* (Femmes, 1978 & 1977) Unica Zürn, *L'Homme Jasmin* (Gallimard 1970) Mary Barnes and Jo Berke, Mary Barnes: Two accounts of a Journey Through Madness. (Mac Gibbon and Kee, London, 1971)

[2]Santos op.cit. (*La Loméchuse*) p.108

limite de la mort physique, elle donna à voir que son désir était désir du corps de l'autre".[3] She experiences a prolonged period of autogenic primitivism: the return to the intra-uterine phase expresses the desire to be the child or the phallus inside the mother's body.

With Unica Zürn, we encounter the same type of desire with the need to enter a state of pre-existence:

> "Quel bonheur d'être avant le commencement! Rien ne peut nous arriver parce que nous ne pouvons pas nous arriver à nous-mêmes."[4]

Unica Zürn is completely absorbed in her fantasy dreams of being united with ' l'homme jasmin', the man who haunts her hallucinations.

In most of Duras' texts, including her most recent, madness is also linked to the impossibility of fusion with the Other, signalled by the recurrence of 'le cri':

> "Un cri.On a crié vers la digue.
> Le cri a été proféré et on l'a entendu dans l'espace tout entier" (A p.12)
> "On a crié un nom d'une sonorité insolite, trou-blante..."
> "Ce cri ne venait pas du hall mais de beaucoup plus loin, il était chargé d'échos de toutes sortes, de passé, de désir..." (YB pp.11 & 37)[5]

For Lol the need for fusion takes on the form of a refusal of the separation from the couple of Michael Richardson and Anne-Marie Stretter during the episode of the ball; the beggar-woman in *Le Vice-consul* exemplifies the search for the mother. Madness in her case originates from the radical rejection and exile from the motherland:

---

[3] Maud Mannoni op. cit. p.189

[4] Zürn op.cit. p.14

[5] "Lorsque le désir se rend visible, le cri revient, rappel essentiel. Convergences des complicités de désir (*Le Vice-consul*). Ou indice d'un désir amoureux perdu, éloigné (*Moderato Cantabile, Hiroshima Mon Amour*). L'immanence du désir. Le cri dépasse les présences, il remémore des situations. Le cri affirme qu'il n'y a pas de fusion, qu'il n'y en a pas eu" confirms France Théoret in 'La Lenteur, le Cri, l'Autonomie', in *Marguerite Duras à Montréal* (Spirale, Montréal 1981) p.92

> "Exclue, hors de ses origines, de son entourage, enfermée dans son ombre, dans sa langue maternelle désaimantée, son dedans est intolérable, rempli de faims".[6]

For Anne-Marie Stretter and the vice-consul the quest for fusion takes on the appearance of a "chassé-croisé" in which the vice-consul endeavours to be united with Anne-Marie Stretter, herself a highly significant figure who is the very symbol of Origin, and whose desire is to identify with India and with the beggar-woman.

Because most of the protagonists are female, it is hardly surprising that madness takes on some specific common characteristics, in the multiple references to childbearing. Mary Barnes moulds her excrements into imaginary babies. Female fecundity becomes a magic power which the 'witch-woman' sees as a special attribute. For Emma Santos, to be pregnant corresponds to a compensation, a rebellion against society. She dreams of covering the earth with her abnormal offspring in order to produce a new race which would invade the town. Unica Zürn also imagines giving birth to her town:

> "Ce désir devient si excessif qu'elle éprouve les douleurs de l'enfantement, les mêmes symptomes qu'à la naissance de ses enfants. Elle ne sait pas comment il est possible de se sentir enceinte d'une ville toute entière".[7]

This birth also resembles a revenge, both in fantasy and biologically, in so far as women, because of their historical social exclusion from the symbolic order of language, find it difficult to transform their inner turmoil into a work of art. Whereas the writer Hermann Melville can translate into writing his emotional trauma, Unica "sent douloureusement les limites, l'étroitesse, la monotonie qui sont parfois celle de la vie d'une femme. Des rêves éveillés - sans avoir le pouvoir de les exprimer dans une oeuvre."[8]

Whatever happens, the woman in those texts can only show her power in choosing the side of madness:

---

[6] Sylvie Gagné, 'L'Ombilic des Indes' in *Marguerite Duras à Montréal* p.104
[7] Zürn op.cit. p.33.
[8] ibid. p.66

"La folle hurle. Le fou se tait sauf les homosexuels. Le fou montre la coupure avec le monde dans un grand silence. L'homme a eu la parole avant sa naissance. La femme doit la conquérir en passant souvent par les chemins de la folie et le cri".[9]

The Durasian text also centres around female characters affected by madness and often apprehended in their symptoms by men; such are the cases, for instance, of Lol V.Stein and the beggar-woman, respectively observed by J.Hold and P.Morgan. The reference to the female figures' fecundity does not, however, take on a meaning of personal rebellion in Duras, but remains above all biological; the beggar-woman is one example. Another is the woman in *L'Amour*, who at the end of her animal peregrination fills the town with her children behind the sea-wall: "Ses enfants sont là-dedans (...) elle les fait, elle leur donne (...) la ville en est pleine, la terre" (A p.52).

Madness in those texts thus originates in a parting from the other, in the impossibility of union with the love object and the desire to go beyond these limitations. The female psychic conflict stems from the forced removal from the origin, and indeed Duras situates her writing at the "point originaire de l'inconscient psychique, comme point de certitude où s'enracinent langage et folie".[10] It appears moreover that madness in the Durasian text can be compared to the symbiotic transference mentioned by Mannoni.[11] Such a transfer is situated at the level of the most primitive forms of identification. It corresponds to the lack of differentiation between a subject and its object, with the subject attempting to recover her/himself through the representation of the lost object - the lost object being the mother. After the loss of the object, an image is substituted.

"Au cours de sa vie l'individu a affaire à des substituts d'images. Le sujet est dès lors en relation non tant avec un objet qu'avec le signe de sa perte, de sa trace".[12]

---

[9]Santos op.cit. (*L'Itinéraire Psychiatrique*) p.127.

[10]Ruth Menahem op. cit. p.167

[11]Mannoni op.cit. p.134

[12]ibid p.135

The Other becomes an image of ideal "suppléance", yet access to symbolisation does not occur. In Lacanian theory, psychosis stems from the absence of the symbolic. The mirror identification can only take place if 'language' has made it possible for the subject to recognize her/his own image. In the symbiotic transfer, such recognition is absent, and the subject only sees in him/herself the presence of castration; hence the absence of the imaginary in relation to the Other. By the irruption of a self-image, the imaginary order has introduced a gap in which the subject cannot dissociate the Other from her/himself. It can be argued that the Durasian phenomenon has to do with a disturbance of the symbolic through the absence of a satisfactory mirror identification. The state of primitive non-differentiation and subsequent depersonalisation can be found in Lol V.Stein's identification with Michael Richardson's couple or in Anne-Marie Stretter's identification with India-as-origin.

In *L'Amour*, however, the state of love and desire is such that no mediation is required. Identification no longer occurs with the Other but with desire itself. The Durasian text is unique in that, in a kind of "retournement" of desire on itself, the very idea of desire tends for the characters to replace desire itself.

The related symptomatology

A certain symptomatology can be seen to be common to the various womens' accounts of madness and to the Durasian text, and finds itself translated in various features.

a) *Loss of self-awareness*

The loss of a sense of self occurs through the distantiation of the characters in relation to their physical existence. The body is experienced as a burden, as something which has to be got rid of. Via a process of mental distantiation, Emma Santos has become absent from her body since childhood: "Ce n'est pas facile d'avoir un corps à diriger, des jours elle perd la tête".[13] Physical distancing is more concrete for Mary Barnes, who abandons her body to her doctor; a body close to physical death since she refuses to feed it and has to be force-fed for a time. She becomes

---

[13]Santos op.cit. (*La Loméchuse*) p.13

"morceau charnel coupé de son corps".[14] Unica Zürn experiences her body through hallucinations, as if "des ailes immatérielles" went right through it, as if she had become bodiless.[15] Her dreams of fusion with the man of her hallucinations corresponds to a vision of incorporation:

> "elle croit, par expérience personnelle, à la possibilité pour un corps d'en habiter un autre de manière éthérée."[16]

The characters of *L'Amour* are constantly objectified in their physical existence, in that they tend to lose their physical boundaries and become assimilated to their environment. In the incessant movement of his ambulatory activity, for instance, the walker is pictured as topographically linked to the sea, as if he had become part of it (A pp.9-10, 11). Similarly the woman's white body can be associated with the town of S.Thala. The characters' physical dispossession is also evident in the recurrent absence of personal pronouns or possessive markers:

> "ne sait pas être vue. Ne sait pas être regardée. Se tient face à la mer. Visage blanc. Mains à moitié enfouies dans le sable, immobiles comme le corps."(A p.10)

b) The body apprehended in its biological dimension

In her fantasy world, Emma Santos expresses a need to go below or beyond her human shell:

> "Elle était la vie, une petite partie de la vie, le monde, une partie indispensable (...) Etre vie dans la vie. Animal. Plante. Air. Soleil. Eau. Tout. Vie. Vie. Vie."[17]

Through her fantasies she experiences repeated metamorphoses, which take her through different stages of animality: "elle est insecte, puis carnivore, mammifère, elle allaite ses petits." The need for a biological experience is very strong: "La fête aux urines se prépare secrète".[18] She acquires power in the

---

[14]Mannoni op.cit. p.189
[15]Zürn op.cit. p.29
[16]ibid. p.69
[17]Santos op.cit. (*La Loméchuse*) p.49
[18]ibid p.54

activity of sleeping as a contrast to the passivity of her life: "Elle crie dans son sommeil sa puissance infinie et subit éveillée sa vie de muette." As for Mary Barnes, she recovers from her "années de descente" via the biological experience and the need to be milk-fed, and to play with her excrement. The woman's biological existence is most evident in *L'Amour*. Pregnant, she can be identified as animal when she walks towards the sea wall: "elle fonce, bestiale". (A p.73) She can later be assimilated to a plant in a tropistic movement: "dans un movement indiscernable tant il est lent, tout entier, le corps suit les yeux (...) il se place dans la direction de la lumière naissante..." (A pp.141-142). Sleep dominates her physical existence. The beggar-woman of *Le Vice-consul* is similarly comparable to the woman of *L'Amour*.

c) The common thematic

For Emma Santos in particular, the union of the opposite categories of birth/life and death signals a desire to return to her biological origins. She carries a suitcase filled with dolls, a suitcase which symbolically becomes both a womb and a coffin. In Duras' texts, the equation between life and death is also obvious: in the Durasian logic to be alive is paradoxically presented as the equivalent of being dead. The traveller of *L'Amour*, for instance, no longer needs to kill himself, since in his existence with the woman on the beach he has already died to himself.

With this succinct establishment of intertextual links, we can point to the existence in the texts referred to of a loss of self-identity and of physical wholeness; such symptoms translate a need to come closer to the essence of life, in the very folds of the biological.

Comparison of descriptive and stylistic elements

Several stylistic connections can be identified between the other womens' texts and those of Duras' 'Indian Cycle':

a)   the strong presence of the referential, and the use of geometry and colour.

b)   the similarity of various descriptive elements.

c)   the disturbance of the syntactic.

a) The referential and the use of geometry and colour

In all the texts considered, referential reality tends to lose its social dimension for the women involved. These characters experience a distantiation in relation to their environment. Their sensations take over and strongly affect the ways in which they view their settings. In *La Loméchuse* in particular, this position is translated by a very strong symbolic activity of language. The medicine and the drink of Ricoré become "l'eau de vie" or "le rituel" and sensory impressions predominate. This constant direct contact with the environment and the strong presence of the referential are characteristics which can also be found in the text of *L'Amour*: the night becomes "la matière noire" (A p.23), the sea is "le gouffre de sel" (A p.27), while the town is described as "la masse de l'enchaînement continu" (A p.28) (etc.).

In *La Loméchuse*, the referential is largely perceived through geometrical shapes or coloured spots. Her doctor's flat is, alternatively, "océan vertical" or "carré turquoise". This kind of geometry recalls the schematised setting of *L'Amour*, in which space is often defined by the recurrence of geometrical patterns. The town described in *La Loméchuse* is striking in its colourful impact, and echoes very strongly the descriptions found in *L'Amour*:

- "la ville c'est une mosaïque de faïence bleue. Bleu, bleu, bleu"[19]
- "Elle montre devant elle, la mer, la plage, la ville bleue ..." (A p.14)

A predominance of primary colours can be observed in these texts. The main colours of *La Loméchuse* are blue, red, black and, especially, white. The blue town has already been mentioned, but we also find:

"le foetus rouge sur le bleu de la méditerranée (...) la première femme marchait vers le rouge de l'argile et eût l'envie de se décorer les lèvres pour être en accord avec le bleu du ciel".[20]

---

[19]Santos op.cit. (*La Loméchuse*) p.19
[20]ibid. p.16

Black is for Emma Santos the negative sign of her social identification, while white is seen as the favoured colour of the human being in touch with madness, as the colour of fantasy and void:

> "elle est heureuse parce qu'il n'y a pas de mots. C'est très loin avant le langage. Elle est bien dans le blanc. Les mots n'ont pas de sens. Elle est délivrée. Elle n'a pas à lutter avec une langue étrangère qu'elle ne comprend pas".[21]

For Unica Zürn, colours appear mainly in the description of her hallucinations: red, black or grey, and again white. White and red are the colours of madness, colours of 'l'homme jasmin', who represents the very personification of madness. White is his favourite colour, "la couleur de la dignité et de l'élection".[22] She also calls him "l'homme blanc":

> "comment pourrait-elle l'appeler autrement, lui qui émet les insoutenables rayons de l'inquiétante blancheur"[23]

Taken up in her desire to identify with him, she dresses in red and white with a "manteau blanc à doublure rouge".[24] She only absorbs white- or red-coloured food - wine, yoghourts or white bread - ,[25] and in order to associate with the colours of the white man, "elle verse un verre de jus de tomates sur son drap blanc".[26] Black corresponds to threat: "elle met un manteau blanc et ainsi vêtue elle se promène (...) dans une nouvelle et noire dépression".[27]

Similarly, in *L'Amour*, the colours mentioned are white, black and blue. The blue of the man's eyes in *L'Amour* is also present in one of Marguerite Duras' later texts, *Les Yeux Bleus, Cheveux Noirs*, where it belongs to a "jeune étranger". The blue of the sea takes on a sense of life, and connotes liberation from constraints.

---

[21]ibid. p.97
[22]Zürn op.cit. p.128
[23]ibid. p.104
[24]ibid. p.49
[25]ibid. p.118
[26]ibid. p.128
[27]ibid. p.124

The white of the woman of *L'Amour*, or of the town of S.Thala and of the seagulls, signals non-existence. White is a symbol of external disintegration, be it of S.Thala or of the woman's physical self-awareness; a necessary disintegration which allows access to another state of being. The black colour of the sea-wall, of smoke, of the sea which becomes rough and is seen as black mud, again connotes threat in Duras' text.

It appears therefore that in the texts examined white is associated with madness and liberation, while black recalls society or the negativity of madness. The fact that in most of the texts primary colours are referred to suggests, in my view, that the experience which takes place occurs at a fundamental level. Colours become symbols of life; blue is associated with liquidity, amniotic or otherwise, but red with blood. When they are presented through the binary opposition black versus white, they express the presence of a mental or social conflict, the antitheses of life/death, reason/unreason.[28]

b) Similarity of descriptive elements

A certain number of intertextual similarities can be established from one text to another at the level of descriptive activity. Unica Zürn is haunted by the male character who feeds her hallucinations. She repeatedly refers to him as "l'homme jasmin" or "l'homme blanc", in a fashion similar to that of Jacques Hold, who names Lol's fantasy "l'homme de T.Beach" or "l'homme de S.Tahla"; an appellation which later, in *L'Amour*, becomes simply "l'homme".

The description of Unica Zürn's return to Berlin recalls certain referential and thematic elements of *L'Amour*. Like S.Thala, which crumbles into ruins, Berlin is a half-destroyed town split in two: "déchirée". The characters' link to the town is particularly stressed in both texts. The woman of *L'Amour* walks in the town to renew her relationship with it. "S.Thala, mon S.Thala" she utters (A p.111), while Unica Zürn wants to have an instrumental role in the rebirth of a Berlin given back to its previous unity. The desire to give birth to the town, referred to above, can also be found in both texts. Unica Zürn feels pregnant

---

[28]If, in Mary Barnes, colours are not so much part of the narration, they nevertheless constitute a powerful therapeutic element in her recovery. Indeed she emerged from madness when she took up painting.

with the town[29] while the woman of *L'Amour* peoples the town with her successive births (A p.52). The whiteness mentioned in relation to the town, however, which can again also be found in both texts, can take on contradictory connotations. Unica Zürn disperses small white pieces of paper through a window, "oiseaux blancs de sa transfiguration"[30] in order to join in with the atmosphere of festivity in the town. The whiteness of S.Thala stresses, on the contrary, the crumbling away of a place and the obsessive enclosure of the characters.

c) Disturbance of the syntactic

In the text of *La Loméchuse*, the most 'written' of the 'clinical' accounts of madness, we find various accelerations of rhythm in the sudden passage from indirect to direct style, a fragmented style as in the "vie vie vie" already quoted, and various word enumerations which become the equivalent of an incantatory practice:

> "il faut vomir cracher rejeter projeter renvoyer repousser évacuer, expirer très fort, expulser, actionner la machine".[31]

We also meet a reiteration of sentences as in the scansion of the final chapter, punctuated in each paragraph by an "adieu Elisabeth", which stresses the end of Emma's relationship with her (female) doctor and signals the onset of a mental crisis. The unruly punctuation in many instances escapes the normalisation of the full stop or the comma. Such disturbances of the syntactic, which also give an emotional charge to the text, recall some instances of Jacques Hold's style in *Le Ravissement* (RLVS P.116). In *L'Amour*, however, the various stylistic devices of fragmentation tend to establish a semantic void, and allow the reader to approach more openly an ultimate meaning of the text; the primitivism dissimulated behind the emotional load of some passages of *Le Ravissement de Lol V.Stein* is confirmed in *L'Amour*.

The accounts of Unica Zürn, Mary Barnes, and Emma Santos carry the stamp of suffering and of the difficulty of living mental

---

[29]Zürn op.cit. p.33

[30]ibid. p.33

[31]Santos op.cit. (*La Loméchuse*) p.42

disturbance. A differentiation can however be established in which the two opposite poles of madness become evident: that of madness apprehended from the side of reason, as in the cases of Unica Zürn and Emma Santos, and the pole of madness lived as liberation, as in Mary Barnes' journey through madness.

When madness is apprehended from the side of reason, suffering and a feeling of ostracism unavoidably ensue. The presence of others constitutes a major obstacle to self- discovery in the account of *La Loméchuse*.

> "Elle deviendra folle quand l'entourage la jugera folle, puis criminelle (...) On lui impose le rôle d'assassin, on lui donne la place de débile mentale (...) elle va la prendre cette toute petite place pour réajuster ses mots à ton langage de médecin".[32]

Madness viewed in relation to society is an episode to be suppressed:

> "j'ai travaillé pour être acceptable, comme vous, désirée (...) Pour être acceptée de nouveau dans la société: la folie est quelque chose dont il faut se débarrasser dans une dernière métamorphose".[33]

Because social rehabilitation remains ultimately impossible, madness is experienced as an inescapable incarceration in this "palais gothique", through which the recuperated mad woman finally finds her social identity: "j'existe aux yeux de la société comme folle". For Unica Zürn, madness is linked to the limited scope of her female condition and to her inability to express her feelings through recognized artistic creation. She lives her madness as 'an enclosement in a circle or in a prison'.[34]

The second pole of madness leads to a liberation process. If in *La Loméchuse* a freeing dimension can also be discerned, it remains on the whole dominated by the social apparatus. For Emma Santos, madness is primarily seen, especially at the beginning of the narrative, as an escape from the mediocrity of everyday living, as an exultation of inner life:

---

[32]ibid. p.152
[33]ibid. p.110
[34]Zürn op.cit. p.124

"ceux qui acceptent se contentent des petites heures volées au travail dans un café, des plaisanteries sur les corps extérieurs, pour l'intérieur on n'a pas le temps (...) se tuer c'est supprimer son intérieur, devenir normale".[35]

An attempt at liberation takes place for Emma through several episodes of regression to childhood. She dances, sings, and covers herself in sand: "Femme boue, elle s'ouvre et se dégage du moule...elle vit".[36] She considers herself God and she watches the small human beings. However, because of the social imperative in which she finds herself trapped, Emma's liberation is abortive.

For Unica Zürn, the only liberating moments occur through her hallucinatory episodes:

"quelques jours extraordinaires, nuits pleines d'événements hallucinatoires, bouleversants, une brève envolée, la sensation d'être un personnage hors-série, et puis par là-dessus la chute, le retour à la réalité où elle reconnaît ses illusions".[37]

But from the moment when she is labelled by an institution, she loses this state of liberation and is left only with her symptoms of madness.

If the liberating dimension of madness cannot fully occur for Unica Zürn or for Emma Santos, it is mainly because a space has not been provided for them which would have allowed them to live their psychic conflict. The symbolisation which would enable them to overcome the internal conflicts cannot be carried out satisfactorily since, as Jo Berke mentions,

"the true function of the caves, or in modern terms, the retreat, must be to provide an appropriate setting, whereby the dis-ease or internal conflict can become personified or expressed in symbols".[38]

---

[35]Santos op.cit. (*La Loméchuse*) p.110

[36]ibid. p.16

[37]Zürn op.cit. p.109

[38]Jo Berke, *I Haven't Had to Become Mad Here* (Penguin 1979) p.129

For Mary Barnes in turn, the 'Laingian home' has offered her the necessary setting in which to live her delirium. The availability of a space has made it possible for her to stage her anguish of castration, with the joint orchestration of an audience which functions both as witness and as support for her delirium. "Par une longue marche vers l'insensé, elle a fini par retrouver la 'cause' d'un désir".[39] Similarly, if the liberatory dimension dominates in *L'Amour*, as opposed to *Le Ravissement de Lol V.Stein* or *Le Vice-consul*, this is due largely to the presence of a space, the beach, on which madness can be lived, against or parallel to the social system.[40] As for Zürn or Santos, with Lol V.Stein or the vice-consul, the social setting - be it bourgeois society for Lol or the powerful embassy circle for the vice-consul - circumscribes the characters' madness. The latter are still submitted to the order of reason, while madness tends to remain mediated by the other, such as J.Hold with his account of Lol's madness or the whites of the Embassy in relation to the vice-consul.

In this analysis of some clinical aspects of madness, many features have been found to be shared between various accounts of madness by female writers and the Durasian text. Psychoanalytic considerations have revealed the presence of a common root of the characters' inner conflict. This tends to be expressed by an equivalent aetiology and by common symptoms, via a similar use of language. We can therefore conclude that Duras' texts of the 'Indian cycle', and *L'Amour* in particular, constitute an account of 'real madness' as it may be observed clinically.[41]

---

[39]Mannoni op.cit. p.189

[40]Similarly, female existence also acquires a liberating dimension in Duras' later *La Maladie de la Mort* and *Les Yeux Bleus, Cheveux Noirs*, through the presence of a staging apparatus; the lighted floor of the bedroom is the medium which allows the woman to regain her active role in relation to the man.

[41]One must, however, remain very cautious here. The language of the Durasian account cannot readily be assimilated to 'pathological' language, since language embodies both 'ordinary' and 'pathological' madness. In spite of extensive psychopathological research, it is not yet clear how pathology inscribes its discourse in the functioning of language. Nevertheless, as Ruth Menahem mentions in *Langage et Folie*, the linguists are very keen to use their normative linguistic techniques to describe a pathological language, to avoid the collusion between "sens et non-sens" (p. 137). Furthermore the reality-status of madness has to be relativised on two other accounts. First of all, and as Foucault has repeatedly pointed out, madness in its mental-alienation form becomes

2 Place and function of madness in the Durasian text.

What distinguishes Marguerite Duras' texts from other female accounts of madness resides primarily in her mastery of the signifier. Ruth Menahem exemplifies this point very appropriately for our concern here: "le poète utiliserait en les maîtrisant les procédés qui sont imposés par son fonctionnement psychique au schizophrène".[42] For those who experience madness as mental illness, language as a whole takes on a specific dimension, and it is beyond doubt that any nonsense or lack of meaning stems primarily from psychotic suffering. The writer in turn never escapes an intellectual play with language, and linguistic expression is not separable from the poetic discovery where the 'logic of meaning' can be found. For the psychotic, however, the organization of language becomes impossible, since the guarantee offered by the surface has disappeared:

> "le langage est à la fois passion et action, résorbé dans la profondeur. Il n'y a plus de sens, plus de grammaire ni de syntaxe à la limite."

---

meaningful only in relation to its immediate outside and complementary dimension: reason. Secondly, we have to remember the assumptions of culturalist theory and recall that we are dealing here with occidental madness. As Jaccard mentions, "la manière 'correcte' d'être fou diffère donc selon les cultures...le symptôme n'a pas d'existence en soi (...) il a une signification et une fonction pour le sujet et l'entourage auquel il est destiné." (*La Folie* (P.U.F. Paris 1979) p.32).

In quoting the conclusions of American anthropologist Ruth Benedict in *Anthropology and the Abnormal*, Jaccard recalls that what we consider in the west as pathological features are seen as quite normal in other societies: "la folie n'est pas une maladie, elle est une déviance par rapport à la norme sociale" (op.cit. 32). This said, it does not invalidate the fact that certain individual behaviours attributed to mental pathology do exist: "refuser de diminuer les individus par des diagnostics psychiatriques, ce n'est pas du même coup sous-estimer leurs différences morales, psychologiques et sociales. Il est important de garder à l'esprit que si la maladie mentale, stricto sensu, n'existe pas, cela ne signifie pas que certaines conduites personnelles attribuées à la maladie mentale n'existent pas." (op.cit. p.39).

[42]Ruth Menahem op. cit. p.163

For the writer in turn,

> "le salut vient de cette production des surfaces qui
> permettent de résister au vertige de la profondeur des
> corps."[43]

Similarly, in Duras' texts, even if there are recurrent
references to "le gouffre" which threatens to engulf Lol V.Stein, or
to the frightening depth of female sexuality in the later fictions, in
L'Homme Atlantique or in *Les Yeux Bleus, Cheveux Noirs*, language
nevertheless functions as mastery over madness. Even if madness
remains a dangerous temptation, learnt most certainly, as
mentioned in *L'Amant*, from the mother, Duras remains a
writer[44] for whom madness is a fascination. Rather than being "un
langage-affect", Durasian language offers an effect of language.
When she writes she does not, like the psychotic, try to reinstate
meaning and reason; she works to cast out the 'affect'.

> "Le fantasme de l'engloutissement dans le corps de la
> mère, dans la langue maternelle, qui menace le
> schizophrène, est conjuré grâce à la ligne de partage qui
> sépare le langage en surface des profondeurs de
> l'inconscient"[45]

Duras' writing practice is therefore an expression not so much
of various degrees of lived psychological suffering as of an
exploration of the limits of madness, of what constitutes for a
human being "the bearable", as if "she had already been there".

> "Il s'agit du déchiffrement de ce qui est déjà là et qui
> déjà a été fait par vous dans le sommeil de votre vie,
> dans son ressassement organique, à votre insu." (VM
> p.30)

What remains at stake in this linguistic mastery is the
movement of "partir du sens plein, en être submergé et arriver
jusqu'au non-sens" (VM p.30).

---

[43]ibid. p.165

[44]Menahem's reminder about Artaud also applies to Duras: "N'oublions pas que
Artaud reste poète quand il est fou et que les fous ne sont pas tous poètes."
(op.cit. 165)

[45]ibid. p.166

In comparison with the other womens' accounts of madness, Marguerite Duras' mastery of writing is primarily noticeable at two levels:

1. at the semantic level which deals with the resolution of inner conflict. We shall return to this in our study of *L'Amour* below.[46]
2. at a narrative level which contributes greatly to the coherence of Duras' writing.

To consider briefly this latter aspect, we can observe that the Durasian texts, and *L'Amour* in particular, go beyond the pure narrative biographical account and create, through the coherence of writing rather than through narration, an experience of reason rooted in a "pratique de la perte"; a practice of loss which can be read as a textualisation of the disintegration of reason and logos, as the substitution of another symbolic formation.

This practice penetrates many aspects of the text, through the extended and systematic disintegration of the fictional level, whereby the female characters in particular tend to lose their realistic status, empty themselves and lose their 'ego', as in *L'Amour*. The systematisation of the concept of void is established in the Durasian text by a fragmented stylistic - "mots troués", unfinished sentences, deceptive syntactic usages etc. - and by a thematic of the 'blanc', which evokes the void, what cannot be named in language and which is metaphorically alluded to by "le mot-trou" of Lol V.Stein. In spite of a tension towards truth detectable in the intensity of the enigmatic scope of the signifier, there is no discovery to be made in the text, no secret to be revealed. In its very disarticulation the text opens meaning to its maximum and returns us not to any concrete signification but to a concept of essentiality which can be apprehended as irrationality. The Durasian text escapes objective language, is not assimilated to the language of logos, and tries, like Foucault's but at a fictional rather than at a theoretical level,[47] to set up a language without

---

[46]cf. Chapter 6 for a study of the setting of *L'Amour* and the reconstruction of the end of the world.

[47]"...Foucault reconnaît, en effet, la nécessité de maintenir son discours dans ce qu'il appelle une 'relativité sans recours', c'est-à-dire sans appui à l'absolu d'une raison ou d'un logos. Nécessité et impossibilité à la fois de ce que Foucault appelle ailleurs 'un langage sans appui', c'est-à-dire refusant en principe sinon en

symbolic support. The politics of fragmentation, of disintegration of meaning, resists, in Duras' texts, the empire of the 'said' - of language - and finds itself very close to the essence of madness, to what Foucault has named "une archéologie du silence".[48] Madness is silence since any kind of discourse is always a carrier of meaning and therefore of reason insofar that it produces meaning. The text of *L'Amour* is inscribed in reason, and one can indeed assert that it is not at the level of the form as such that the text articulates madness, even if the disintegration of the syntax and the disjunction of meaning allude to madness, a madness trapped in the reason of senses. The text does, however, send us back to madness in a more direct 'real' fashion, by way of the void installed which refuses recourse to any message:

> "Et si la folie, c'est, en général, par-delà toute structure historique factice et déterminée, l'absence d'oeuvre, alors la folie est bien par essence et en général, le silence, la parole coupée, dans une césure et une blessure qui *entament* bien la vie comme *historicité en général*." (op. cit. p.84)[49] (original emphasis)

---

fait de s'articuler sur une syntaxe de la raison." (Jacques Derrida, *L'Ecriture et la Différence*, (Seuil 1967) p.60)
[48]As Derrida did recall, Foucault's project in *Histoire de la Folie* was to establish a link betwen silence and madness. And it is the history of the 'archeology' of this silence that he attempted to retrace.
"Et à travers tout le livre court ce thème qui lie la folie au silence, aux 'mots sans langage' ou 'sans sujet parlant', murmure obstiné d'un langage qui parlerait tout seul, sans sujet parlant et sans interlocuteur, tassé sur lui-même, noué à la gorge, s'effondrant avant d'avoir atteint toute formulation et retournant sans éclat au silence dont il ne s'est jamais reparti. Racine calcinée du sens'." (op. cit. p.57)
Derrida went on to show, however, the inaccuracy of the term "archéologie du silence" and the quasi impossibility of achieving such a project: "On ne peut sans doute pas écrire une histoire, voire une archéologie contre la raison, car, malgré les apparences, le concept d'histoire a toujours été un concept rationnel. (...) Une écriture excédant, à les questionner, les valeurs d'origine, de raison, d'histoire, ne saurait se laisser contenir dans la clôture métaphysique d'une archéologie." (op. cit. p.59)
[49]ibid. p.84

But whatever the philosophical consequences of such a practice of the loss may be, one of its oft-remarked-on immediate results is the reader's fascination[50] with Duras' texts. An interplay of void and aspiration to truth - the metaphor of madness itself, madness remaining according to Lacan in search of another signifier - is installed in the text and spreads the practice of the loss to the reader her/himself. Indeed since, despite the 'élan' of the text, final meaning is absent, the reader, far from being limited by any pre-established signification, can go beyond the text, establish a void and accept to be carried by the intertext; hence the proliferation of various types of writing generated by the Durasian text: "On n'écrit pas tellement sur l'écrivain mais plutôt par l'écrivain, c'est plus qu'une médiation: il s'agit d'une traversée".[51] The reader finds him/herself in an inner split which is not without danger:

> "Ne pas perdre de vue qu'il y a un risque, toujours, de se perdre, de ne plus pouvoir en sortir, de rester là, figés, comme lorsqu'on reste muet dans une rencontre fascinante".[52]

Indeed if the reader accepts to enter Marguerite Duras' texts, she/he accepts to be placed in a state of dispossession, in search of the secret of writing, of an Origin.

---

[50]"It seems that sentiments of gratitude, fascination or admiration permeate the writings of all those who want to write about Duras (...) Marguerite Duras has accrued the mystique of being someone more in touch with the fundamentals of human existence than other mortals" (Trista Selous, 'Evidence of Struggle - Problems with India Song' in *Undercut* no 3/4 p.4)

[51]André Roy, 'Ecrire Duras' in *Marguerite Duras à Montréal* p.81

[52]Gagné op.cit. ('L'Ombilic des Indes') p.101

Chapter 2

MADNESS AND WRITING

"J'ai commencé à écrire ce dont justement je sais
qu'il vous serait impossible de pressentir la raison,
d'apercevoir le devenir (...) c'est à votre
incompréhension que je m'adresse toujours." (HA
p.18)

The similarity between women's lived experiences of madness
and the fictional account of what happens chiefly to Duras' female
figures in terms of unreason contributes to explaining why Duras'
writing has often been regarded by feminist critics over the decades
as representing the woman's problematic.

The basic assumption shared by many French feminist writers
is a belief in the estrangement from language suffered by women.
Language is seen as masculine, based entirely on one fundamental
signifier: the Phallus. "Et on peut s'étonner (...) que la femme soit
assez aliénée pour parler 'le langage du Vir'".[1] Women are caught
in a real contradiction, and in the course of history have remained
mute, silenced by this linear and grammatical linguistic system, that
orders the symbolic, the superego, the Law. As Gauthier asserts,

"... si les mots 'pleins' appartiennent aux hommes,
comment parler 'autrement', à moins, peut-être, de

---

[1]Xavière Gauthier, 'Existe-t-il une Ecriture de Femmes?' in *Tel Quel* no.58
(Summer 1974) p.96

pouvoir faire entendre ce qui s'agite et souffre, muet, dans les *trous du discours*, dans le non-dit ou le non-sens." (*original emphasis*)[2]

Writing, for women, therefore becomes an inscription of femininity. It must escape, warns Hélène Cixous, the phallocentric tradition by which "presque toute l'histoire de l'écriture se confond avec l'histoire de la raison dont elle est à la fois l'effet, le soutien, et un des alibis privilégiés."[3] Female language hence has to emerge from the darkness of repression, and Duras' writing is apprehended as one possible exploration of this 'dark continent'. Duras, having chosen her own writing name to escape the 'name of the father',[4] herself proposes a translation of this unknown language, originating in darkness:

"I think 'feminine literature' is an organic, translated writing...translated from blackness, from darkness. Women have been in darkness for centuries. They do not know themselves. Or only poorly. And when women write, they translate the darkness...The writing of women is really translated from the unknown, like a new way of communicating rather than an already formed language."[5]

"Women", asserts Duras, "have never known what they were. So they aren't lost. Behind them, there is darkness."[6]

This belief in the 'unknowable' nature of women, which no doubt helps explain the enigma and often ungraspable desire of Duras' female characters - from Anne Desbaresdes in *Moderato Cantabile* to Lol and then The Woman of her later fictions -, also explains that for Duras, writing constitutes madness freely consented to, an expression for women of that part of themselves which suffocates and explodes. All women, she asserts, share the

---

[2]ibid. p.96

[3]Hélène Cixous, 'Le Rire de la Méduse' in *L'Arc* no.61 (1975) p.42

[4]Gauthier op.cit. Gauthier reminds the reader that the 'Name of the Father' is designated in psychoanalysis "comme ce qui détermine la soumission à la loi et au 'langage convenu'". (p.96)

[5]Marguerite Duras in an interview with Susan Husserl-Kapit in *Signs* Winter 1975, p.425

[6]ibid. p.428

same madness as Michelet's witches,[7] those women from the Middle Ages who lost touch with social reality in their osmosis with nature. "Madness" mentions Duras "has found other expressions but it is still there. It is still the same madness"[8] perhaps better known in modern times as neurosis.

When women escape their silencing they can only express themselves in a fragmented way, since they cannot find their language within the linear linguistic system. Fragmentation, recalls Kristeva, already to be found in the last century in the literary avant-garde from Mallarmé to Joyce and Artaud, is "... l'indice d'une pulsion qui n'a pas été saisie par le système linguistique et idéologique."[9] Fragmentation in a text calls into question the phallic position of the speaking subject, that of mastery. By such positioning the subject experiences sexual difference as a process of differentiation.[10] This explains that from the reader's point of view, Duras' writing, which includes so many ruptures, omissions, 'blanc' spaces and syntactic holes, can also be sensed as the translation of a female language which verges on madness.

> "Marguerite Duras quitte les sentiers battus du roman traditionnel qui s'écrit avec préméditation, avec intention, et se laisse lire dans sa transparence pour construire un univers irrationnel, aux limites de la folie."[11]

Non-sense moreover is present not only in Duras' mode of writing but can also be seen inscribed in the subject-matter of most of her novels. Sexuality, and especially female sexual desire,

---

[7]ibid. p.430. cf. Jules Michelet, *La Sorcière* (1862), "...a text that has been assimilated by many new French feminist writers, particularly Cixous, Clement and Gauthier. It is a part of their canon." (editors' note, Elaine Marks & Isabelle Courtivron (eds), *New French Feminisms* (Harvester Press 1981) p.175)

[8]in Husserl-Kapit, op.cit. p.432

[9]Julia Kristeva, 'Oscillation du Pouvoir au 'Refus'' in *Tel Quel* no.58 (Summer 1974) p.99

[10]The French feminists are on the whole more convinced than their American counterparts of the 'différence' between male and female, and are more imbued with notions of specificity.

[11]Sylvia Venet, 'Femme dans L'Ecriture - Marguerite Duras' in *La Chouette* no.6 (Sept.1981)

repeatedly and increasingly present in Duras' production, becomes the "non-sens qui multiplie le sens".[12]

Duras has often been received by modern criticism as articulating the 'feminine'. One could suggest that this is why Eric Marty, as a male reader, finds Duras' work intimidating. "L'oeuvre de Duras est intimidante, énigmatique (*pour moi*): il n'est pas aisé d'en saisir la clef..."[13] (my emphasis). But one could argue that the gender position of the reader is not as such a guarantee of 'understanding' of Duras' writing, and Marty indeed situates the problem at the level of the contemporaneity of the text itself. The culprits would be the readers of Duras' production:

> "...je crois ne guère supporter le public durassien tant il déforme de manière particulièrement fausse son oeuvre romanesque; par public, je n'entends pas les acheteurs nombreux et anonymes de ses livres, mais quelque chose de beaucoup plus éthéré et vague, cette sorte de rumeur complaisante et avide qui l'entoure."[14]

Ultimately Marty denounces a kind of Durasian feminist criticism as being at the root of such complaisance. In my view Marty is partly right in seeing, in this psychological manifestation of the contemporary critic, a succumbing to the narcissistic temptation which often shapes feminist criticism. Marty asserts of one of Marcelle Marini's instances of self-reflexivity:

> "Ce n'est pas la subjectivité qui me gêne...mais c'est le fait que cette subjectivité soit à ce point engluée dans le Moi et que ce Moi plutôt que de travailler ne reflète que lui-même."[15]

Duras' texts would become for feminist critics an excuse to expose one's inner problematic and Duras herself would be seen as a proponent of the feminist stand. This aspect can indeed be present in feminist criticism, but Marty's declared irritation with such a language of fascination ignores the valuable insights on

---

[12]Julia Kristeva op.cit. (*Tel Quel* 1974) p.99
[13]Eric Marty, 'Marguerite Duras: Hypothèses - Notations - Fragments', in *La Chouette* no.15 p.81
[14]ibid. p.81
[15]ibid. pp.81-82

sexual politics that a critical project justified in terms of the feminist perspective can bring. How could egotistic tendencies in feminist critical discourse be avoided? Is it not part of the feminist project to counteract the dominant trend by which the fact of women's subjectivity (as opposed to objectivity) has too often been erased, suppressed, or ignored?

Marty, as he himself notices, hardly avoids the same complicit bias when he recognizes in Duras' texts nothing less than "her voice". He also acknowledges that his own text, which he refers to as "hypothèse légère de lecture", stems similarly from a subjective problematic, "hypothèse d'autant plus légère que ce texte est tout entier brouillé par *l'humeur* d'un moment...".[16] Indeed one could also say of Marty's article that his writing, perhaps more 'retenu', certainly less openly subjective, is nevertheless misleading. He does write in abstract, almost mythical terms, about the pain of the perverse as "jouissance infinie du ridicule". He also mentions, in the intrusions of the vice-consul, "l'irruption d'un autre possible, d'un autre désir, d'un autre sexe";[17] he later asserts that "le non-humain de l'humain déborde dans les secousses du rire", without trying to allude to what this other 'possible' desire or non-human sexuality may be.

Discarding the feminine or feminist pathos too often stressed in Duras' texts, Marty gives exclusive (but no less subjective) priority to another Durasian element: laughter; he addresses himself to this "trivialité étrange du rire".[18] But the recognition of the extensive and recurrent use of perversion in this "rire du scandale" and "scandale du rire", particularly present in *Détruire Dit-elle*, read as a perverse farce, also falls under a similar criticism of reductionism. He gives priority to laughter, "ce rire énorme et incongru" which occurs at dramatic moments in Duras' narrations, be it in some passages of *La Douleur*, in *Détruire Dit-elle* or in the farcical figure of the Vice-consul, or indeed in *Les Yeux Bleus, Cheveux Noirs* or *Emily-L*. Laughter, however, is one among other elements of Duras' philosophy of despair, of this "gai désespoir" which shapes all Durasian production. Marty prefers to focus only on the semantics of the word 'gai' rather than on those of despair.

---

[16]ibid. p.81

[17]ibid. p.85

[18]ibid. p.83

Laughter is an element of limited importance, more present in some works than in others, possibly dominant in *Détruire Dit-elle* and also present in *Emily-L*, but alternatively replaced by tears in *L'Amour*, *Le Vice-consul* and, increasingly so, in Duras' latest productions such as *La Maladie de la Mort* and *Les Yeux Bleus, Cheveux Noirs*: "Ils rient. Se voir rire les rend fous de bonheur (...) Après avoir ri, ils pleurent ensemble comme chaque jour" (YB p.99). Laughter, which in Marty's terms can give way in Duras to the same harsh sadism as in Bataille but without the same jubilation, is in my view in Duras' texts only the manifestation of a wider perspective. Laughter is a distancing device which functions not only as a sign of an impossible desire or existence for the narrative figures, but also, or alternatively, as a sign of defiance and/or a symptom of unreason in relation to the social context. Rather than seeing in Duras' texts the triviality of a perverse game around the impossibility of desire, which would somehow exist for the sake of it, I would argue that such play with 'the limit', such an "impossibilité d'être" expressed through laughter, has more to do with a contemporary problematic, with the inescapability of the individual's dilemma, trapped in a social structure. To view laughter in isolation, and not in relation to its pathos, feminist or otherwise, is to operate a reduction which can in Marty's article be interpreted mainly as a 'counteractive move', un "mouvement d'humeur" - as he himself admits - in relation to modern feminist criticism.

In a more radical and elaborated approach,[19] Trista Selous not only dismisses modern feminist critics as making inconsistent claims when they see Duras' writing as politically subversive in terms of sexual politics, but also asserts that the fetishistic portrayal of women in Duras' fictions supports rather than subverts masculine dominant ideology.

Trista Selous examines the critical context in which Duras' work has been discussed, which supports the concept of women's culture and which stresses the 'feminine' qualities of works of fiction. Selous disregards the feminist assumptions which tend to

---

[19]Trista Selous, *A Study of the Novels of Marguerite Duras up to 1971, in the Light of Contemporary French Writers and Thinkers* (PhD Thesis, University of London, June 1985), published as *The Other Woman* (Yale University Press, Newhaven & London 1988)

equate femininity and femaleness, and resists the position which sees womanhood as the guarantor of the truth of the critics' position regarding femininity. Selous then also questions the claim, put forward by Marini and Irigaray for instance, according to which female language would have been suppressed by the masculinist order; she sees in Marini's critical position an attempt to take Duras' work as an illustration and a complement to Irigaray's theoretical account of the existence of a feminine language. Selous finds the feminist position difficult to sustain for theoretical reasons. She bases her argumentation on the Lacanian framework, which is also the starting-point for discussion used by French writers, and she asserts that the assumption of a specific, anatomically based feminine language is unsustainable. For Selous, the feminist position does not take into account the impersonal nature of language, or the pre-existent and "other" nature of language in relation to the subject who utters it. Selous also examines the feminist claim by which Duras would be subversive in terms of sexual politics and according to which her work would be a step towards the lifting of the oppression of women. Such a view maintains that female oppression consists in the silencing of women's true nature and language, in the denial of their specificity in a world dominated by men. We have already mentioned that Selous disputes the claim made by Marini and others, that

> "women's meanings have been excluded from language, that women are alienated into speaking, writing and understanding themselves in terms of someone else's definitions, those of a masculinist language".[20]

But she furthermore does not believe in the silencing of women's nature; she sees this view as itself a result of women's ideological oppression: "my own feminism would lead to a recognition of individuality and difference among women as among men",[21] and to see Duras' texts as a manifestation of the 'feminine' is, in her opinion, counterproductive. Selous does however recognize that women express themselves differently from men; this is due to their gender-position, she argues.

---

[20]ibid. p.18
[21]ibid. p.10

"I see the positions of feminine and masculine subjects as ideologically constructed gender positions as opposed to anatomically determined sexual characteristics"[22]

Therefore, asserts Selous, while one cannot avoid adopting a gendered subject-position in relation to meaning, that relationship does not necessarily conform to the anatomical sex of the individual. Furthermore, the workings of the unconscious in producing meanings make any position unstable:

"My view is that the possible meanings of gender are constantly being both reproduced and modified, and that texts such as those written by Duras have, like any other representations, a part to play in that process."[23]

Having established the lack of relevance and coherence in much of feminist criticism, Selous pursues her study with an examination of Duras' texts. She investigates the fantasy increasingly produced by Duras' later fiction - up to *L'Amour* - and she sees it as based on the production of the inarticulate, of "les blancs", variously present as narrative gaps, absent characters, lost moments...all contributing to this unsaid and unknowable in Duras' texts. Selous maintains, against various critical claims, that Duras' unusual use of language does not in fact break any grammatical rules, and that these "blancs" can easily be bridged by the reader. The blancs are thus those elements of the reader's fantasy produced implicitly by the text, "created through the operations of the reader's desire to make sense of the text...". The reader

"is not led to infer that the 'blancs' are the result of any deliberate omission of information. If things are left unsaid, it then seems that they are unsayable".[24]

This implies, according to Selous, a greater passivity on the part of the Durasian reader: "the reader must accept that there will be 'blancs' and even that these are part of the 'point'."[25]

In fact Selous reads in these "blancs" an increasing loss of the female figure as subject of desire. Instead, the woman character,

---

[22]ibid. p.10
[23]ibid. p.11
[24]ibid. p.119
[25]ibid. p.156

while retaining some kind of subjecthood, is increasingly constructed in Duras' fiction as an object to be watched by a male subject; her desire, however, is never understood or identified.

> "The fetishised woman figure is, I think, the most important element of the fantasy which Duras invites the reader to build around her texts (...) the fetishism of visual representations of women both draws on and produces a fetishism which is already built into the psychic organization of the spectator who responds to it."[26]

The woman reader in particular would identify with what could be herself: a woman presented as Phallus, in the inaccessibility of her own desire. The fascination of Duras' novels would for Selous reside in the lure of perceiving a woman that is both subject and object at the same time and still a subject "in so far as 'blancs' are produced where her desire should be."[27]

Selous' perspective indeed restores a balance in the reception of Duras' literature, which is often too easily assimilated to feminist works. But because she adopts a reader-centred approach and therefore keeps her analysis at the level of what can be perceived at first hand by a potential reader - a repetitive narrative structure where a woman figure is placed as object of desire for the male protagonist -, she arrives at the increasingly non-subversive and anti-feminist significance of Duras' texts.

On the other hand she tends to ignore the problem: who is the reader who indulges in reading Duras' novels? There is no study in Selous' work of actual reader reception of Duras' writing. Though a lot of Duras' fiction does have the ingredients of popular literature -love or murder story - one can assert with confidence that it is predominantly the more educated middle-class reader who, alerted by Duras' increasing fame or challenged by her elliptic, deceptive style, reads her books. And one would expect such a reader to be more alert and to create meanings which go beyond the surface structure of the narratives. Selous attacks Duras' works for their reinforcement of existing ideological notions of gender by which the woman is seen as passive, object rather

---

[26]ibid. p.211
[27]ibid. p.217

than subject. But such a reinforcement nevertheless remains unpredictable, on unconscious as well as conscious grounds, especially in view of what can be seen as the more distanciated Durasian reader. One could in fact adopt Selous' own argument to relativise her above claim in relation to Duras' writing. She asserts that 'possible' meanings of gender are "constantly both reproduced and modified" and I would in fact support this in so far as each reader, female as well as male, produces meanings and that these meanings, generated by Duras' texts, remain for each potential reader indeed "unstable and always modified."

In Selous' highly argumentative work, in which Marini, Irigaray, Cixous, Montrelay, Lacan - to name only a few -, and of course Duras herself,[28] end up being largely dismissed on grounds of misleading argumentation, incoherence or harmful representations, she herself seems to fall into a trap: that of her own theory of ideology. Her idea of a reader-centred approach in a study of gender-meanings generated by Duras' works does not lead her to engage with real readership. However

> "any features to which one could point as having occasioned this or that response are themselves the product of a particular interpretive framework... they are the result of the interpretive strategies one possesses."[29]

In spite of her strongly polemical study and of the sound premises by which masculinity and femininity are seen to be ideologically constructed rather than biologically determined, Trista Selous in the end only presents another interpretation of Duras' texts, based on her own ideological premises. Because Selous' argumentation stems from and wants to promote the welcome assumption that women as well as men can change language and the cultural presuppositions of our modern society,[30] Duras' viewpoint and narrative strategy are dismissed as being regressive, even harmful for the psychic and social health of the female

---

[28]Freud and Mitchell, whose views more directly support Selous' own project, would, however, constitute exceptions.

[29]Jane Tompkins, *Reader Response Criticism: From Formalism to Post-Structuralism* (John Hopkins U.P. Baltimore 1980) p.xxii

[30]"Women have to find a place within the patriarchal structure as well as men..." (Selous op.cit. p.212)

reader. I see in this position the refusal of a social awareness, an optimism which verges on idealism according to which women are seen as free subjects, hardly affected by the state of patriarchy. While it is undoubtedly also difficult for men to really find their status of subject - they also have been loaded with characteristics of their gender to conform to - the repression of women as subjects in Western society is historically proven as being extremely difficult to lift. Selous' view dismisses the power of the unconscious in its inhibiting force, by which Western women are still repeatedly seen as expressionless, forced to feel but also wishing to feel[31] more passive, locked into that position of woman as object rather than subject.

While appreciating the reasons for Selous' unease in relation to Duras' texts, I would argue that the mirroring of the female condition,[32] while maybe presenting a disappointing view of reality, also holds for the reader a certain power of objectivity and lucidity in relation to the cultural and social scene. Nevertheless Duras' texts from 1964 onwards, though less 'militant', increasingly represent the ruin of a social order, with the notable presence of those unknowable and apparently desireless female characters constructed at the focal point of a dismantled social structure. Furthermore, while the undisputed power of women too often remains in sexuality and reproduction, the Durasian female figure inflates this power in becoming enigma and in dragging with her, in this realm of absence and lack, a good few male characters.[33] To concentrate her argumentation, as does Selous, on the fact that the female figure occupies the passive position of object in relation to the male look, overlooks an important element of Duras' fiction. Whether the woman character is portrayed as active or as passive does not take anything away from her female power. The

---

[31]"Mais qu'est-ce qu'un vrai désir, puisque la répression, elle aussi, est désirée?" (Gilles Deleuze & Félix Guattari, *L'Anti-Oedipe* (Minuit, 1972) pp.138-139). Deleuze and Guattari support this view, that repressed individuals may desire their own repression, since "...les investissements inconscients se font d'après des positions de 'désir' et des usages de synthèse, très différents des intérêts du sujet qui désire, individuel ou collectif" (p.124).

[32]In this female condition women as objects of male desire are nevertheless powerful within the problematic of sexuality, but otherwise too often locked in the position of the Other of culture.

[33]One could also wonder at this point who is the male onlooker himself, in most cases a stranger, an outsider in relation to the social structure.

problematic of the Durasian text is not simply a question of female subjection to the male scopic drive, it is a question of power beyond rationality and knowledge; an aspect particularly evident in one of Duras' latest texts, *La Maladie de la Mort*, where the woman willingly allows herself to be watched by a man, but remains - even more so that Lol or the woman of *L'Amour* - the initiator, and occupies the position of knowledge.

Selous characteristically dismisses Duras' social and political position on the grounds that, while destroying a social order, in narratives like *L'Amour*, for instance, she does not offer an alternative. Selous resents particularly this chaos, naturalness being brought into Durasian narratives as an alternative to social order. But Selous' rational position does not (again) engage, in my view, with an important aspect of Duras' fiction. She admits being increasingly disturbed by the 'destroyed' characters of Duras' later novels - from *Détruire Dit-elle* onwards - which do not capture her imagination. I would argue that this lack of involvement in Duras' fictions marks the refused challenge on the part of Selous' own rationality. Gaps in Duras' later novels, holes in the chain of meaning, constitute a major defiance of rationality, and account for the frustration of many readers, of whom Selous is but an example. To read these 'blancs', as Selous does, exclusively as an opportunity for the reader to bring into play her/his psychic organisation, notably his/her fetishism, undermines a very specific element in Duras' fiction in my view; namely that these "blancs", which obviously constitute an invitation to the reader to be filled in with a plurality of meanings, occupy the place of the unconscious, of irrationality, and remain ultimately uninterpretable since, as recalls the narrator of *L'Homme Atlantique*, "c'est à votre incompréhension que je m'adresse toujours" (HA p.18). This view is very closely connected to my own position, which sustains that what is at work in Duras' narratives constitutes an alternative ideological order and ultimately a radical dismissal of rational assumptions.

SECTION II

THE PASSAGE FROM MADNESS TO UNREASON IN "THE CYCLE OF LOL.V STEIN"

"Even when silenced and excluded madness has value as a language and its content assumes meaning, on the basis of that which denounces and rejects it as madness."[1]

"L'homme de nos jours n'a de vérité que dans l'énigme du fou qu'il est et qu'il n'est pas." (HF p.548)

---

[1] Michel Foucault, *Mental Illness and Psychology*, transl. Alan Sheridan (Harper Colopton, 1976) p.125

Chapter 3

LE RAVISSEMENT DE LOL V.STEIN, OR MADNESS AS MENTAL ILLNESS

> "Freud n'a pas découvert l'identité perdue d'un sens; il
> a cerné la figure irruptive d'un signifiant qui n'est
> *absolument pas* comme les autres (...) Et par le fait
> même, la folie est apparue, non pas comme la ruse
> d'une signification cachée, mais comme une prodigieuse
> *réserve* de sens. Encore faut-il entendre comme il
> convient ce mot de 'réserve': beaucoup plus que d'une
> provision, il s'agit d'une figure qui retient et suspend le
> sens..." (HF p.579)

Le Ravissement de Lol V.Stein constitutes a turning-point in
Marguerite Duras' writing. "...with *Le Ravissement de Lol V.Stein*,
she has freed herself from the thematic and generic constraints"
remarks Michael Sheringham. She has also inaugurated "a fictional
world based on a body of material susceptible of different kinds of
treatment".[1] What Sheringham does not explore is the possible
reason for such a change in Duras' writing, which is primarily due

---

[1]Michael Sheringham, 'Knowledge and Repetition in *Le Ravissement de Lol
V.Stein*', in *The Nouveau Roman (Romance Studies* no.2 (1983)) p.125. Verena
Andermatt also draws attention to the characters' loss of human attributes in
Duras' later writing ('Rodomontages of *Le Ravissement de Lol V.Stein*' in *Locus,
Space, Landscape, Decor in Modern French Fiction* (Yale French Studies no.57
(1979)) p.23).

to a priority given in her fiction to this element which escapes signification, this "figure qui retient et suspend le sens", an alternative way of being often identified as madness or unreason.

It has been commonly recognized that *Le Ravissement de Lol V.Stein* has to do with madness:

> "Si on considère Lol V.Stein comme un personnage distinct, le diagnostic de folie larvée, virtuelle, puis, à la fin du roman, manifeste, ne peut pas ne pas être posé"[2]

But as Sheringham rightly mentions,

> "madness is of course a very slippery notion in the context of Marguerite Duras' texts (...) Duras suggested that it was only in the eyes of the other characters that Lol is mad: 'la maladie mentale... est vraiment nommée de l'extérieur...on ne peut pas dire que je traite d'une maladie dans *Lol V.Stein*'"[3]

However, Jacques Hold, like Peter Morgan in *Le Vice- consul*, sets out to explore Lol's 'madness', and again Duras mentions:

> "La folie de Lol V.Stein est comme une folie locale, de l'individu. La folie de la mendiante est une folie infiniment plus vaste, comme un territoire qui serait atteint"[4]

Duras rightly stresses here the way in which, in *Le Ravissement*, Lol's madness happens to be circumscribed by the society in which she lives and apprehended as an individual experience, while in *Le Vice-consul*, unreason and madness mostly become relevant in terms of the whole social structure: Indians versus whites.[5]

In this chapter I propose to examine how the story of Lol's madness, mediated by Jacques Hold's narrative, becomes that of a "prodigieuse réserve de sens", not only in the sense meant by Foucault in the opening quotation, whereby madness becomes

---

[2]Michèle Montrelay, 'Sur *Le Ravissement de Lol V.Stein*' in *L'Ombre et le Nom* (Minuit, Paris 1977) p.23

[3]Sheringham op.cit. p.139, quoting Marguerite Duras in *Cahiers Renaud-Barrault* no.91 (1976) pp.22-23

[4]Marguerite Duras in *Marguerite Duras à Montréal* (Spirale, Montréal 1981) (rencontre du 10 avril 1981) p.41

[5]cf. the study of *Le Vice-consul*, Chapter 4 below.

"réserve" or "retenue" of meaning, but also in the sense of "provision", a source of renewed meaning. Throughout this study, the approach chosen will be mostly thematic, with an evaluation, where appropriate, of some of the considerable critical discourse produced around *Le Ravissement de Lol V.Stein*. I shall therefore, consider, in the first instance, how Lol's madness takes on the meaning of 'mental illness' and indeed becomes, through Hold's narrative, the "figure qui retient et suspend le sens". I shall then examine how Lol's problematic can in fact be primarily explained in terms of a social impossibility. In the final part of the chapter we shall go beyond the conception expressed in most critical discourse and consider in what way Lol's madness becomes a powerful and positive reserve of meaning.

1 Lol's madness as 'retenue du sens'

In *Le Marin de Gibraltar*, a male first person narrator conducts the fiction. We are faced with a similar narrative instance in *Le Ravissement* where Jacques Hold, the narrator,[6] gradually enters the fiction as a protagonist.[7]

In the first instance it is worth considering how Lol's madness becomes exclusively a consequence of Hold's act of reason, by which Lol exists in a fictional world constructed by the narrator as an ideological reflection of the society in which she lives.[8] To examine such a claim, we need to consider the way in which, for a

---

[6]The first-person narrative is relatively common in Duras' fiction: already placed in *La Vie Tranquille* with the presence of a female narrator, later repeated in *L'Homme Atlantique*, *Emily-L* and *L'Homme Assis dans le Couloir* with a female first-person narrator who remains outside the fiction. Male first-person narrators are in fact rarer, present only in *Le Marin de Gibraltar*, *Le Ravissement*, and Peter Morgan's story of the beggar-woman in *Le Vice-consul*. Whether male or female, however, the narrator in Duras' texts often occupies a dual position within the fiction.

[7]Michael Sheringham rightly stresses the accumulation of Jacques Hold's functions within the fiction: "As the text proceeds he accumulates functions: first of all he is Tatiana's lover in the 'story', then he becomes Lol's accomplice in a sort of 'counterplot' made up of encounters (...) finally he is the narrator, subjective witness and Lol's legatee" (op.cit. p.129)

[8]Verena Andermatt, retracing the summary on the back cover of *Le Ravissement*, rightly points out about the use of the word 'story' that "Duras emphasizes the word 'story' indicating that the ambiguity in the text results from the narration: from what can - and cannot - be told" (op.cit. p.24)

third of the text, Jacques Hold's account of Lol's traumatic experience at the ball (and subsequent 'madness') relies on various relays of information and, as Alleins suggests, becomes "le chef d'oeuvre de la relation indirecte",[9] by which madness takes on the full meaning of mental illness.

The aetiology of an illness

> "Le fou sera celui qui est rangé du côté de la non-communication, de l'isolement, de 'l'autisme'"[10]

During the first part of the narrative (RLVS pp.11-74) Lol is doubly, or even triply, mediated: by Jacques Hold the narrator, by her best school friend Tatiana Karl, and by her husband Jean Bedford, or her mother, or even by the anonymous voice of public opinion.

Very few of these mediations are in fact the result of Hold's direct observation. Most of the information about Lol comes from Tatiana, who "ne croit pas au rôle prépondérant du bal dans la maladie de Lol V.Stein" and who, according to Jacques Hold, is 'deeply reassured' to notice the "survivance même pâlie de la folie de Lol" (RLVS p.65). "Condamnée par ses choix à être superficielle, elle croit, veut croire à une anomalie chez Lol antérieure à la nuit du bal".[11]

As the text unfolds, we can note Jacques Hold's increasing use of inference in relation to the story of Lol V. Stein. Not only does he increasingly rely on his own memory but sometimes, in a puzzling narrative shift, he fully identifies with Lol's position. The most striking example of this can be found in the following example: "Je me souviens, *l'homme* vient tandis qu'elle s'occupe de sa chevelure" (RLVS p.65). "L'Homme" refers to the protagonist Jacques and the hair mentioned belongs to Tatiana. The juxtaposition of the first-person pronoun in "je me souviens" and the distanciated "l'homme" used to refer to the narrator himself clearly indicates Jacques Hold's complete identification with Lol's perception of the two lovers in the hotel room. The reliance on

---

[9]Madeleine Alleins, *Marguerite Duras, Médium du Réel* (L'Age d'Homme 1984) p.114

[10]Guy Rosalato, 'Culpabilité et Sacrifice, Actes du Colloque de Milan 1974' in *Psychanalyse et Sémiotique* (10/18 1975) p.76

[11]Alleins op.cit. p.114

second-hand information and the increasing recourse to the narrator's self-identification with Lol's experience make of Hold's narrative an activity of conjecture, punctuated by the regular "je vois" and "j'invente" (RLVS pp.53,56,59,62 etc.) where "il faut inventer les chaînons qui (...) manquent dans l'histoire de Lol V.Stein" (RLVS p.37).

Such reliance on indirect accounts however remains quite justifiable in terms of Jacques Hold's external position[12] in relation to the narrative rather than, as Alleins sees it, in terms of "l'aspiration naturelle de l'amour assoiffé de connaissances". She continues:

> "Pour Marguerite Duras, étant donné les limitations de chacun, la vérité ne saurait résider toute entière dans telle ou telle saisie individuelle, mais dans le rapprochement, la mise en commun de diverses appréhensions. Le procédé qui consiste à additionner les avis des uns et des autres souligne la nécessaire complémentarité des êtres et d'une technique fait une métaphysique."[13]

To equate Jacques Hold's motivation with Duras' writing drive constitutes a regrettable conflation; consequently to imply a metaphysical concern at the heart of Hold's account is surely to exaggerate its significance. Hold's narrative at the start of *Le Ravissement* is sustained by his personal interest in Lol, as Alleins otherwise rightly mentions[14]. But his technique of using various testimonies is wholly due to his position as external narrator; in the first instance he has to rely on what people tell him, even if later his narrative enterprise leads him, as we shall see, to a different approach and self- realisation.

---

[12]"The first thing that needs to be stressed" asserts Michael Sheringham rightly, "is the extraneous position of the narrator and the belatedness of his entry into the first dimension, the public fiction" (op.cit. p.130)

[13]Alleins op.cit. p.114

[14]Though I broadly agree with Alleins' approach on *Le Ravissement de Lol V.Stein* - and I shall recall some of her perceptive points throughout this chapter -, it is regrettable that, in addition to a few instances of metalanguage, concepts such as truth and reality in relation to Duras' prose often tend to remain vague and potentially mystifying.

Straight from the start of Hold's narrative, Lol is presented through what closely resembles a case-study:

> "Lol V.Stein est née ici, à S.Tahla, et elle y a vécu une grande partie de sa jeunesse. Son père était professeur à l'Université. Elle a un frère plus agé qu'elle de neuf ans - je ne l'ai jamais vu - on dit qu'il vit à Paris. Ses parents sont morts." (RLVS pp.11-12)

But in fact I would agree with Tison-Braun that

> "la folie de Lol est affirmée plutôt qu'étudiée, puisque, la majeure partie du roman se déroule entre les deux crises décisives".[15]

The original trauma of the ball at T.Beach is indeed not directly reported and Lol's entrance into unreason corresponds to the end of the narrative.[16] Madness is primarily asserted in the narrative as mental illness and the logic of the story as a whole strongly relies on the recognizeable elements which constitute the aetiology of an illness, namely antecedents, trauma, symptoms, recovery, and the suspected relapse of Lol's condition. The table below (Table 1) summarises the different stages of Lol's illness as mentioned throughout Jacques Hold's narrative.

Table 1. *Summary of Lol's Illness*

1. Antecedents	*Lol's mental absence* "Au collège (...) il manquait déjà quelque chose à Lol pour être (...) là" (p.12) "elle était étrangement incomplète" (p.80) *Indifference and inability to suffer* "gloire de douceur mais aussi d'indifférence (...) jamais elle n'avait paru souffrir ou être peinée" (pp.12 & 80)

---

[15]Micheline Tison-Braun, *Marguerite Duras, Le Cycle de la Folie* (Rodopi, Amsterdam 1984) p.59

[16]This is a feature which reappears at the end of *Le Vice-consul* when Anne-Marie Stretter leaves the palace to lie down on the path. The passage to the outside, like that of Lol on the beach at the end of Hold's narrative, indicates the character's entrance into unreason.

contd.	*Problem of finding an identity* "Elle avait vécu sa jeunesse dans la sollicitation de ce qu'elle serait et qu'elle n'arrivait pas à devenir" (p.80)
2. Trauma	*The ball*: "la crise de Lol" (p.13) *Inability to suffer* (p.19) *Lol's shout* "Lol avait crié sans discontinuer des chose sensées (p.22) *She faints* when the lovers disappear (p.22)
3. Symptoms	a) *Symptoms following the trauma of the ball:* *Prostration*: enclosement in her bedroom (p.23) *Obsession*: "elle disait toujours les mêmes choses" (p.23) *Anger directed at her own name* "elle prononçait son nom avec colère: Lol V.Stein - c'est ainsi qu'elle se désignait" (p.23) *Waiting state* "elle se plaignit, plus explicitement, d'éprouver une fatigue insupportable à attendre de la sorte. Elle s'ennuyait, à crier" (p.23) *Silence*: "sa difficulté devant la recherche d'un seul mot paraissait insurmontable. Elle parut n'attendre plus rien" (p.24) b) *Other symptoms* *Aimless wandering* "elle n'allait pas dans une direction précise" (p.26) "elle avançait, mais ni plus ni moins que le vent qui s'engouffre là où il trouve du champ" (p.28) *Lol's indifference*: she cannot cry when her mother dies (p.33)
4. Recovery	*She resumes eating*, sleeping, and appreciates peoples' company (p.25) *She hears of* Michael Richardson and Anne-Marie Stretter's separation with composure "son calme fut jugé de bonne augure" (p.25) *She resumes going out* (p.25)

contd.	*Normalised behaviour*: married to J.Bedford for ten years, Lol becomes "virtualité irréprochable" (p.70) "De sa folie détruite, rasée, rien ne paraissait subsister" (p.77)
5. Relapse	a) *Latent symptoms*
	Her walks become a compulsive habit "Ces promenades lui deviennent très vite indispensables comme la ponctualité, l'ordre, le sommeil" (p.36)
	Loss of memory: she forgets the location of the house she lived in U.Bridge (p.152). Memory lapse in relation to S.Tahla: "en quelque point qu'elle s'y trouve, Lol y est comme une première fois" (p.43)
	Abandonment of her normalised order "Elle lui dit un jour que (...) cet ordre n'était peut-être pas celui qu'il fallait - elle ne dit pas pourquoi - il était possible qu'elle en change, un peu plus tard" (p.43)
	Lol's 'distraction maladive': Tatiana is convinced that Lol is still ill (p.144) "Pierre Beugner dit: - Lol V.Stein est encore malade, vous avez vu à table cette absence, comme c'était impressionnant, et c'est sans doute ca qui intéresse Jacques Hold" (p.156)
	Adulterated awareness of time "elle croyait qu'un temps était possible qui se remplit et se vide alternativement, puis qui est prêt encore, toujours, à servir (...) elle le croira toujours, jamais elle ne guérira" (p.159)
	Incoherence of speech: cf. unfinished sentences (pp.168,170, 175 etc.)
	b) *The final crisis*
	Hallucinations at the hotel at T.Beach: she imagines the police outside, people being beaten up. She does not recognize Jacques Hold. (p.187)
	Loss of sense of personal identity "elle se nomme de deux noms" (p.189) "il n'y a plus de différence entre elle et Tatiana" (p.189)

What seems to be at stake in Hold's narrative has mainly to do with the question: has Lol gone mad? If we give importance to the final crisis (RLVS pp.187-189), we can deduce with Sheringham that Lol has indeed gone mad,[17] though the narrative specifies that the next day she has regained her reason and thus questions the latest interpretation. Once more one cannot help noticing that the different stages of Lol's illness rely largely on an interpretation of the symptoms rather than on an objective account. Her inability to suffer or to cry at her mother's death constitutes a sign of abnormality only in relation to a socially normalised behaviour. The converse could be said of her newly-found punctuality and order during her recovery phase, regularity being highly valued in a logical societal system. As Jacques Hold remarks in the train going to T.Beach, Lol's madness is difficult to perceive: "son contentement respire profondément à mes côtés - Aucun signe de sa différence sous ma main, sous mes yeux" (RLVS p.168). Very few bare facts constitute irrefutable indications of illness as such; only perhaps the mental crisis following the episode of the ball, her loss of memory in S.Tahla and the hallucinations of the last crisis would probably 'objectively' support a diagnosis of mental illness.

Nevertheless Lol's existence throughout the elaboration of symptoms gathered in Hold's narrative takes on the full meaning of mental illness. It is worth noting again, though, that such a meaning corresponds to that of alienated madness, madness seen from the restrictive side of reason, and not apprehended in the positivity of unreason.

Lol as figure of the void

Lol's symptoms provide the narration with a fullness of signs which mostly serve to hide a void: that of a protagonist whose existence resists the epistemology of knowledge used by the narrator Jacques Hold. Much has been written about this aspect of *Le Ravissement de Lol V.Stein*,[18] but far too often without linking

---

[17]"...the book ends by leaving a gap between the moment of the narration and the end of the fiction, the reader is likely to fill this gap with the hypothesis that Lol does in fact go mad" (Sheringham op.cit. p.128)

[18]Among the most coherent texts treating Lol as a void, we find Beatrice Didier's 'Thèmes et Structures de L'Absence dans *Le Ravissement de Lol V.Stein*' in *Ecrire, Dit-elle* pp.63-83. We also find references to this aspect in Montrelay's *L'Ombre et le Nom* (Minuit, Paris 1977) and in Andermatt op.cit.

it to the wider problematic of the novel: that of Hold's logical approach in relation to the unrepresentability of madness or unreason itself. However it is only, as we propose to see, in the establishment of such a link that Lol's existence can ultimately find its relevance.

The narrator multiplies the relays of information to reconstitute Lol's past. Paradoxically we find ourselves faced, as Didier suggests, with "une thématique, extrêmement ramifiée, de l'absence sous toutes ses formes".[19] This thematic, however, bears witness to the fact that the character of Lol exists mostly as a construction of Hold's narrative act. The very choice of narrative instance could be viewed as an implicit move to present Lol as absence: the "je" of Jacques Hold could enter into a dialogue with a "tu", while Lol is in fact designated in the third person: "cette troisième personne que les grammairiens arabes, nous dit Benveniste, nomment très judicieusement l'absent".[20] Lol's name also provides Hold with a tempting invitation to elaborate on her as representation of the void. The loss of the 'a' in Lola's name takes away the voluptuousness often associated with appellations like Lola, Lolita etc., and presents an image of disincarnation.

> "The tracing of the three letters, the double L around the perfect shape of the o, the tracing of which conceals and contains its own void, imposes an enigmatic name which leads to endless speculation".

Andermatt also sees in the three letters of Lol's name

> "the schematic representation of the three figures of the story: Lol, Michael Richardson and Anne-Marie Stretter with Lol in the middle as zero, nothingness, a hole, an absence".[21]

Again it is worth noting that Lol is a representation of absence largely as a result of the narrative process. And in fact we shall see later in this chapter how her mode of absence and self-annihilation in relation to the other couple, Anne-Marie Stretter and Michael Richardson, does not quite equate a position

---

[19]Didier op.cit. p.71

[20]Roger Gentis, *N'être* (Flammarion, Paris 1977) p.138

[21]Andermatt op.cit. p.27

of nothingness. Instead of Andermatt's unproblematic view of Lol as a void, I would favour instead Lacan's pun,[22] whereby the two 'L's of Lol's name are seen as wings, and succinctly but effectively evoke the problematic of liberation which underlies her very absence.

As the narrative unfolds, however, Lol increasingly appears as an inscription of absence. The narrative instance, instead of anchoring the fiction, asserts Lol as a void through a rhetoric of doubt whereby she is the absent centre, "centre qui est à la fois partout et nulle part".[23]

Jacques Hold, trapped between the stereotyped ficticity of Tatiana's testimony and his own doubt, litters his narrative with multiple signifiers of the doubt:

- "Voici, tout au long, mêlés, à la fois, ce faux
  semblant que raconte Tatiana Karl et ce que j'invente sur la nuit du casino de T.Beach" (p.14)
- "(...) *il faut inventer* les chaînons qui me manquent
  dans l'histoire de Lol V.Stein" (p.37)
- "*J'aime à croire*, comme je l'aime, que si Lol est
  silencieuse dans la vie c'est qu'elle a cru, l'espace
  d'un éclair, que ce mot pouvait exister" (p.48)
- "Ce qui s'est passe entre eux, après le bal (...)
  je crois que Lol n'y pense jamais" (p.50)
- "Je vois ceci..." (p.55)
- "...j'invente, je vois..." (p.56)
- "Etait-elle ainsi Tatiana ce jour-là? Ou un peu ou
  tout à fait autrement? (...) *je crois voir ce qu'a
  dû voir* Lol V.Stein" (p.59)
- "*Je crois encore* que c'est la première fois qu'elle
  est là sans idée d'y être" (p.62)
- "*Je crois ceci...*" (p.71)   (*my emphasis*)

Alleins sees Jacques Hold's expression of the doubt - often expressed as "je vois ceci" (p.55), "je crois encore" (p.62), "je crois voir" (p.59) - as a sign of the narrator's integrity; he expresses his method honestly,

---

[22]Jacques Lacan, 'Hommage fait à Marguerite Duras, du *Ravissement de Lol V.Stein*' in *Marguerite Duras par Marguerite Duras* (Albatros, Paris 1975) pp.93-99
[23]Didier op.cit. p.72

"pour empêcher le lecteur de perdre sa liberté de jugement et la distance qu'il doit maintenir s'il veut réfléchir à ce qui lui est proposé".[24]

However, the reader's 'freedom' is also fictive, since the narrative does not give him/her any possibility of 'objective' interpretation. Absence, at work behind the mode of the doubt, stresses the fictitious aspect of a narrative enterprise caught in the "empty rhetoric of negation".[25]

As a result, Lol's character becomes a metaphor of the void, a figure of negation which supports Montrelay's view:

"On parle de 'n'importe quelle Lol V.Stein', de 'toute Lol V.Stein possible'. On se tient dans l'indéfini, ne cherchant plus à fixer les repères classiques d'une identité".[26]

Lol's life is centred around the triangular problematic of the episode of the ball whereby she has been abandoned by her lover in favour of Anne-Marie Stretter. After the ball, "elle vit dans un état de manque, de vide laissé par le défaut de l'amour"[27]. This explains the fact that critics like Didier have approached the episode of Hold's account as a "témoignage essentiellement négatif sur ce qui a été un 'trou', un vide, une expérience de la négativité".[28] I shall come back shortly and in greater detail to the significance of the episode of the ball in order to refute this latest assertion. I shall show that, contrary to Tatiana's (and many critics') version, the ball does not for Lol constitute an experience of negativity as such, but rather the discovery of a new modality of desire. Nevertheless, if one remains at the level of the enunciative instance, Lol's experience at the ball appears as an experience of the lack, though it is worth stressing again that because of the indirect nature of the various testimonies on which Hold's narrative rests in the first section of the fiction, we are not dealing with "un drame vécu" but with a fantasmatic representation of what happened to Lol.

---

[24]Alleins op.cit. p.115

[25]Sheringham op.cit. p.134

[26]Montrelay op.cit. p.12

[27]Montrelay op.cit. p.12

[28]Didier op.cit. p.64

The scene in the rye-field which re-enacts the structure of the ball, where Lol watches the window of the hotel room where Jacques Hold and Tatiana meet (RLVS pp.62-65) also pictures Lol's mental and physical existence in terms of the void.

> "L'idée de ce qu'elle fait ne la traverse pas. Je crois encore que c'est la première fois, qu'elle est là sans idée d'y être (...)
> (...) Les yeux rivés à la fenêtre éclairée, une femme entend le vide - se nourrir, dévorer ce spectacle inexistant, invisible, la lumière d'une chambre où d'autres sont" (RLVS pp.62-63)

Like Elisabeth in *Détruire, Dit-elle*, whose presence is also associated with illness following the traumatic episode of the loss of a child (DDE p.58), Lol contemplates the void. She watches the window, "une petite fenêtre rectangulaire, une scène étroite (...) où aucun personnage encore ne s'est montré" (RLVS p.63). The symbiosis with the void in Lol who "entend le vide" extends to her whole life:

> "On aurait dit (...) qu'elle était devenue un désert dans lequel une faculté nomade l'avait lancée dans la poursuite interminable de quoi? On ne savait pas" (RLVS p.24)

Her inner life remains an enigma: Lol does not volunteer any information, and Jacques Hold's lapidary writing and incomplete fragments reflect her cicumspection over the last ten years:

> "Ses avis étaient rares, ses récits, inexistants". (RLVS p.44)
> "Qu'avait-elle fait à ces heures-là pendant les deux années qui avaient précédé? Je le lui ai demandé. Elle n'a pas su bien me dire quoi. A ces mêmes heures ne s'occupait-elle à rien à U.Bridge? A rien. Mais encore? Elle ne savait dire comment, rien". (RLVS p.45)

She remains a vacant space open to various contradictory judgements. Later pictured in Hold's account as "gouffre et soeur" (RLVS p.166), she elaborates an existential void which threatens Hold and the people around her. She is "l'être de négation" presented through a negative syntax:

"(...) gloire de douceur mais aussi d'indifférence, découvrait-on très vite, *jamais* elle n'aurait paru souffrir ou être peinée, *jamais* on ne lui avait vu une larme de jeune fille" (RLVS p.12) (*my emphasis*)

The leitmotif of the "rien" constantly recurs in relation to Lol:

"*Rien* ne pouvait plus arriver à cette femme, pensa Tatiana" (p.16)
"*Rien* dans sa mise ne disait son état, sauf sa chevelure" (p.26)
"- J'habite très près d'ici, dit Jean Bedford. Si vous cherchez quelque chose, je peux vous renseigner.
Elle répondit avec netteté:
- *Rien*" (p.27)
"*Rien d'ailleurs dans les vêtements*, dans la conduite de Lol ne pouvait la signaler à une attention plus précise" (p.40)
"Quand il pleuvait, *elle ne s'occupait à rien*" (p.44)
"Lol dit:
- *Rien ne me gêne* dans l'histoire de ma jeunesse. Même si les choses devaient recommencer pour moi, elles *ne me gêneraient en rien*" (p.109)
"Par des voies contraires (...) ils sont arrivés au même résultat que Lol V.Stein, eux, à force de faire, de dire (...) et *elle, Lol, à force de rien*" (p.60)
"*Rien ne se passe en elle* qu'une reconnaissance formelle, toujours très pure, très calme, un peu amusée peut-être" (p.177)
"Sa main s'endort avec elle, posée sur le sable. Je joue avec son alliance. *Elle ne sait rien* (...)
J'enlève l'alliance, je la sens, elle n'a pas d'odeur je la remets. *Elle ne sait rien*" (p.182)

(*my emphasis*)

Most of the above quotations refer to the apprehension of Lol's existence through an external look, that of Jacques Hold or of Tatiana (cf. pp.16,44,60,177,182); but even when Lol's more direct asserted presence is referred to (e.g. p.109), it tends to occur in the negative mode. Indeed, as Montrelay suggests, "le rien du

Ravissement procède d'un bouleversement de perspective"[29] where
the character of Lol is not rendered via the plenitude of realist
writing but through the "retenue du sens" in which "le rien", "le
jamais" and even the redundancy of negative repetitions (e.g.
p.182) take on a gratuitous meaning which contributes to the
elaboration of Lol as metaphor of the void in the text.

Indeed even the inscription of the character of Lol as an
active and fuller presence refers to the void. The fixed order of her
house, which is presented as a sign of regained normality,
represents an "immobility which calls attention to its own
emptiness",[30] akin to her house which becomes in her absence "la
scène vide où se jouait le soliloque d'une passion absolue dont le
sens échappait" (RLVS p.34). And Lol's eagerness to describe her
last house in U.Bridge to her friend Tatiana represents once more
a manifestation of the void: "elle raconte en fait le dépeuplement
d'une demeure avec sa venue", conclut Jacques Hold (RLVS
p.82).

Similarly, Lol's walks in S.Tahla translate on the surface her
determination to become physically active: "elle sortit sans prétexte
régulièrement" (RLVS p.36); "elle allait partout, ne repassant pas
au même endroit" (RLVS p.40). But in fact, according to Jacques
Hold's version, her physical activity expresses only her alleged need
to exist as absence. "Une fois sortie de chez elle (...) la promenade
la captivait complètement, la délivrait de vouloir être ou faire"
(RLVS p.39). She is reassured to know that her walks remain
unnoticed (RLVS p.40). During these walks, "le vide d'une rue"
(RLVS p.40) influences her route. The characteristics of absence
inscribed in the anonymity of Lol's presence and in the invisibility
of her activity even extend to S.Tahla itself:

> "cet endroit du monde où on croit qu'elle a vécu sa
> douleur passée, cette prétendue douleur, s'efface peu à
> peu de sa mémoire dans sa matérialité" (RLVS p.43).

The town becomes "ville pure méconnaissable" where Lol
walks "dans le palais fastueux de l'oubli de S.Tahla" (RLVS p.43).
It is worth noting, however, that the ambiguity of the genitive case
in "oubli de S.Tahla" can be interpreted in two ways: in the

[29]Montrelay op.cit. p.12
[30]Andermatt op.cit. p.29

objective and the subjective sense. Is forgetfulness in relation to
S.Tahla lived by Lol as the metaphysical discovery of a palace, or
is S.Tahla a palace of forgetfulness where Lol is kept? The second
meaning is in fact more plausible since Jacques Hold mentions that
people pretend not to recognize her (RLVS p.41); hence a
conception of memory where the knowledge of the past and its
recollection happens to be split and when "le lieu retrouvé" does
not send any more signals to confirm the past. The inhabitants of
S.Tahla, in pretending by discretion to ignore Lol, transform her
town into absence.

Ultimately Lol's tangible existence can only be apprehended
through the plenitude of the meaning of mental illness; and yet
even here the fullness of Lol's symptoms constitutes in itself a
manifestation of absence. Let us recall that the absence of
suffering at the ball (RLVS p.19) or when her mother dies (RLVS
p.32) is interpreted as being at the root of her illness. The allusion
to Lol's silence, or even to her speech acts later in the narrative,
does point to the representation of the void. "Pour la première fois
mon nom prononcé ne nomme pas" (RLVS p.113), remarks
Jacques Hold about Lol. Her unfinished sentences are often
reported, and contribute to establishing the narrative as a syntactic
image of the void:

- "Ecoute Jean. Parfois il joue jusqu'à quatre heures du
  matin. Il nous a complètement oubliées.
- Tu écoutes toujours?
- Presque toujours. Surtout quand je. Tatiana attend. *Le
  reste de la phrase ne viendra pas.*" (p.93)
- "Dis-moi encore Lol.
- je ne suis pas allée sur la plage, *je*, dit Lol.Tatiana n'insiste
  pas" (p.152)
- "Vous voulez que je vous emmène à l'hôtel tout à l'heure
- Je ne crois pas. *J'ai cette envie. Plus. Ça ne continue pas.*"
  (p.168)
- "Quand vous regardez Tatiana sans la voir comme l'autre
  soir, il me semble que je reconnais quelqu'un d'oublié,
  Tatiana elle-même pendant le bal. Alors, j'ai un peu peur.
  *Peut-être qu'il ne faudrait plus que je vous voie ensemble
  sauf...*" (p.175) (*my emphasis*)

Lol's loss of memory represents the most obvious sign of her
absence, and tends to inscribe her in the narrative as

unmistakeably mentally ill - or at least to confirm Tatiana in her own belief in Lol's madness (RLVS p.146):

> "...elle dit que la mer n'est pas loin de la villa qu'elle habitait à U.Bridge. Tatiana a un sursaut: La mer est à deux heures de U.Bridge" (RLVS p.82).

And when Lol is asked about her house in U.Bridge, Hold reports:

> "...Lol ne répond pas tout de suite, tous la regardent, il passe quelque chose dans ses yeux comme un frisson (...) Elle répond qu'elle ignore avoir jamais habité. La phrase n'est pas terminée" (RLVS pp.145-146).

As the narrative progresses, Lol increasingly appears as an inscription of absence which justifies Didier's comments:

> "L'espace fondamental du roman est un vide. Un vide que rien ne doit combler, sous peine de faire perdre au texte son sens ou plutôt cette déconstruction du sens qui le construit".[31]

Indeed behind the difficulty of making sense of Lol's existence resides the very significance of Hold's narrative. Hold has approached Lol's character from the expected and reassuring side of logic and reason, and soon becomes trapped in the limitations of an epistemology based on knowledge and on the logic of causality and circumstance. The narrator's doubt and confusion contribute to the construction of a character apprehended as absence.

Nevertheless, Jacques Hold's investigation of Lol is more faithful to her as a character than is Peter Morgan's account of the beggar-woman's madness in *Le Vice-consul*, which, primarily represents a defence mechanism on the part of its male narrator. In *Le Ravissement* Hold's narrative paradoxically translates madness closer to its nature as defined by Foucault. Hold has constructed Lol as a figure of the void because it appears more suited to his object of investigation:

> "Aplanir le terrain, le défoncer, ouvrir des tombeaux où Lol fait la morte, me paraît plus juste", explains Hold

---

[31]Didier op.cit. p.74

"que de fabriquer des montagnes, d'édifier des obstacles, des accidents. Et je crois, connaissant cette femme, qu'elle aurait préféré que je remédie dans ce sens à la pénurie des faits de sa vie" (RLVS p.37).[32]

The narrative successfully establishes a field of virtuality which does not restrict meaning but operates fully through its negations, doubts and suspension of belief; meaning is kept open to accommodate the problematic of unreason. In fact, in Hold's account of Lol's character, 'madness' as such is absent and his narrative points to

"la forme vide d'où vient cette oeuvre c'est-à-dire le lieu d'où elle ne cesse d'être absente, où jamais on ne la trouvera parce qu'elle ne s'y est jamais trouvée".[33]

In this sense one can conclude that if madness is absence, Lol is the prototype of all the 'mad' absent women who occupy most of Duras' texts from *Le Ravissement* to *Emily-L*. One can also assert that if madness is emptiness and corresponds to this evacuation of reason and logical meaning, then not only is Lol a figure of the void as a result of Jacques Hold's narration, but the void also remains an inherent part of her fantasy, and through her, of Hold's realization of another order of desire.

Lol's mental illness as social impossibility

"... although the notion of mental illness made good *historical* sense (...) it made no *rational* sense. Mental illness might have been a useful concept in the

---

[32]As we shall see, and as the quotation also indicates, rather than being simply a figure of the void, Lol, apprehended from the outside as mad, constitutes an enigmatic figure which resists the operations of language which would make of her the object of discourse.

[33]Foucault continues: "Là en cette région pâle, sous cette cache essentielle, se dévoile l'incompatibilité gémellaire de l'oeuvre et la folie; c'est le point aveugle de la possibilité à chacune et de leur exclusion mutuelle (...) Il est temps de s'apercevoir que le langage de la littérature ne se définit pas par ce qu'il dit, ni non plus par les structures qui rendent signifiant. Mais qu'il y a un être et que c'est sur cet être qu'il faut l'interroger. Cet être quel est-il exactement? Quelque chose sans doute qui a affaire à l'auto-implication, au double et au vide qui se creuse en lui. En ce sens l'être de la littérature, tel qu'il se produit depuis Mallarmé et vient jusqu'à nous, gagne la région où se fait depuis Freud l'expérience de la folie" (HF p.581)

nineteenth century; today it is scientifically worthless and socially harmful"[34]

I would now like to concentrate more specifically on the fictional dimension of *Le Ravissement*, on what Sheringham defines as the level of subjective reality:

> "At the heart of *Le Ravissement* is a domain of inter-subjective experience which falls outside the usual coordinates of self and others and which seems antithetical to familiar constructions of love and sexuality".[35]

At the level of intersubjective experience Lol's madness also appears as a repressed reserve of meaning, and I would argue that this has mostly to do with a social impossibility. To sustain such a view, I shall consider how Jacques Hold's narration reflects the general impossibility of Lol's existence in her specific difference, and how, at the interrelational level, the trauma of the night at T.Beach functions as a manifestation of the impossibility of the actualisation of desire in a triangular relationship.

a)   The impossibility of Lol's existence in her difference

> "L'être humain se caractérise par un certain rapport à la vérité, mais il détient comme lui appartenant en propre, à la fois offerte et cachée, une vérité" (HF p.549)

Didier argues that Lol constitutes an absence of character.[36] This is true insofar that Lol can only remain a virtuality in her given social structure and therefore appears as absence in relation to Reason and in comparison with the rounded character of realist writing. However, when her 'symptoms' - silence, unfinished sentences, absentmindedness, loss of memory - are not interpreted as signs of illness, Lol's desire fully reveals itself in her approach

---

[34]Thomas Szasz, *The Myth of Mental Illness* (Paladin 1975) p.13

[35]Sheringham op.cit. p.132. Sheringham sees the fictional structure of *Le Ravissement* as repetition and variations on three basic sequences: the social scenes, the hotel scenes and the private scenes. Subjective reality would, as expected, be present in the last of these and is in fact seen by Sheringham as located between the realms of fiction and narration.

[36]Didier op.cit. p.75

towards Jacques[37] and in her implicit determination to be fused to Jacques and Tatiana's couple (RLVS P.103). Her determination is present to such an extent that Hold wonders: "Dans quel univers perdu, Lol V.Stein a-t-elle appris la volonté farouche, la méthode?" (RLVS p.71). Her erasure in the narrative does not imply that she does not exist strongly as a character, and her silent determination in fact has an effect on all the characters of *Le Ravissement*. The narrative instance itself is influenced by Lol's presence, and I have already commented on the switch of narrative point of view in "je me souviens l'homme vient tandis qu'elle s'occupe de sa chevelure" (RLVS p.64) in which the "je"/narrator unexpectedly becomes a distanced "il".

However, Lol is set to remain a virtuality in Hold's narrative since "pour son entourage, sa différence est folie".[38] Her difference is interpreted as lack:

> "Au collège (...) il manquait quelque chose à Lol, (...) elle était merveille de douceur et d'indifférence, elle changeait d'amies, elle ne luttait jamais contre l'ennui, jamais une larme de jeune fille" (RLVS p.80)

Tatiana's account continues:

> "elle avait vécu la jeunesse comme dans une sollicitation de ce qu'elle serait mais qu'elle n'arrivait pas à devenir" (RLVS p.80)

However this translates, at this point, not so much, as Alleins sees it, "le peu d'intérêt que Lol se portait à elle-même",[39] but rather her inability to exist in her difference - a difference which condemns her to remain absent - and the phase of latency of desire in which, like Anne-Marie Stretter in *Le Vice-consul*, she tends to remain.

---

[37]During Lol's visit to Tatiana, Jacques wonders why Lol has chosen him: "Je saurais pourquoi, de quelque façon que je doive m'y prendre, pourquoi, moi" (RLVS p.79) and he later concludes: "je devais la connaître parce qu'elle désirait que cela se produise" (RLVS pp.83-84)

[38]Alleins op.cit. p.123

[39]Alleins op.cit. p.114

b)   Lol's desire and the social impossibility of being three

The need to be three, defined by Sheringham as the "device of the third pole",[40] is among the most recurrent features of Duras' fiction from *Moderato Cantabile* to *Emily-L*. The triadic relationship is in fact already in place in *Le Marin de Gibraltar* with the male narrator and the American woman's search for the mythical figure of the sailor. Such a pattern is later confirmed and in *Détruire, Dit-elle,* for instance, Alissa, Thor and Stein manage to successfully actualise the problematic of Lol's fantasy at the ball of T.Beach. *L'Amour* constitutes the aesthetic realisation of the triadic pattern with the constant reference to the shifting movements on the beach of the traveller, the mad man and the woman. *L'Homme Assis dans le Couloir* presents a situation similar to the scene of Lol in the rye field in front of the hotel window: a female first-person narrator presides like a voyeur over the sexual activity of the other two characters. And *Les Yeux Bleus, Cheveux Noirs* can be seen as a reenactment of Lol's trauma, this time with a homosexual male character in the place of Lol: the fiction indeed opens with the departure, with a woman, of the young stranger whom the homosexual man loves. Later in the narrative, sexual fulfilment can only exist for the man through the memory of the young stranger or the memory of his female partner's lover. Indeed sexual desire in Marguerite Duras' fiction needs a third term in order to remain alive and active.

In *Le Ravissement de Lol V.Stein*, the need to be fused to the couple of Anne-Marie Stretter and Michael Richardson is declared in the narrative as being at the root of Lol's trauma. However it is not a simple question of being three, in the 'vaudevillesque' mode of bourgeois comedy; Lol's fantasy is more essentially transgressive. Of course it is undeniable, as Foucault states, that

> "Il n'y a pas une seule culture au monde où il soit permis de tout faire. Et on sait bien depuis longtemps que l'homme ne commence pas avec la liberté mais avec la limite et la ligne de l'infranchissable" (HF p.578)

One also knows that infidelity among couples and hidden triadic relationships are not unusual practices in Western societies. It is the specific modality of the actualisation of Lol's desire,

---

[40]Sheringham op.cit. p.126

however, which makes it impossible in the given social context. There is indeed, in *Le Ravissement*, to borrow Marini's expression, "l'engendrement d'autres scénarios imaginaires que ceux de la légitimité socio-culturelle".[41]

In spite of what the fiction suggests "in the reenactment of the trauma of the ball where Lol seems less interested in Tatiana than in Tatiana's lover",[42] what is ultimately at stake is Lol's relationship to the other woman. We shall explore this aspect further in our last chapter; let us mention here that Lol has not chosen Jacques because of any particular attraction (RLVS p.52) or of any resemblance to Michael Richardson, but because she saw "Tatiana nue sous ses cheveux noirs" passing in front of the hotel window: "elle ignore que c'est elle (=Tatiana) qu'elle a suivi à travers cet homme de S.Tahla" (RLVS p.53). I agree with Daniel Sibony's psychoanalytical interpretation that in Lol's madness lies a manifestation of "le mystère de l'entre-deux femmes".[43]

> "Dans l'impasse excédée du remplacement du corps (...) elle (Lol) se trompe sur l'appartenance de son corps (...) Ce n'est peut-être pas le sien, sans qu'il appartienne pour autant à l'autre (...) Elle vit son corps comme celui d'une autre"[44]

For Sibony the attraction towards the other woman has furthermore to do with a phallic tension, with "la course folle de la substitution impossible":[45]

> "Elle avait aimé son fiancé en attendant que l'Autre femme lui prouve qu'elle pouvait le reprendre; et l'autre femme le lui reprend, et l'arrache, elle, non pas au

---

[41]Marini, in *Ecrire Dit-elle* p.25

[42]Sheringham op.cit. p.128

[43]Daniel Sibony, *La Haine du Désir* (Bourgois, 1984) p.120

[44]ibid. p.119. Such a view is corroborated by Kristeva in *Soleil Noir*: "Elle est amoureuse du couple, de Tatiana surtout: elle voudra en prendre la place dans les mêmes bras, dans le même lit. Cette absorption de la passion de l'autre femme - Tatiana étant ici le substitut de la première rivale, Anne-Marie Stretter, et, en dernier ressort, de la mère - se fait aussi en sens inverse: Tatiana, jusqu'alors légère et ludique se met à souffrir" (op.cit. p.257)

[45]Sibony op.cit. p.124

corps aimé, mais à la certitude factice, fragile, de son propre corps"[46]

Indeed what is at stake in the substitution with the other woman, in Sibony's view, is primarily the possession of the phallus by which *Le Ravissement* becomes "une prise d'homme".[47]

At this point, however, I disagree with Sibony's interpretation, which falls under the same masculinist bias as the Freudian argumentation by which woman's identity remains possible only in relation to the phallus, or rather to its absence. This interpretation not only reinforces the assumptions of a male-orientated society where the phallus remains at the root of any possible meaning, but, more importantly here, does not represent fairly what is at work in the Durasian text. Sibony continues:

> "La haine qui 'viserait' 'les hommes' de la part des femmes (...) cette haine se révèle en fait 'à l'adresse' de l'Autre-femme et 'les hommes' n'y sont que latéralement concernés, en (petite) partie, en tant qu'au delà de cette partie pointe l'enjeu phallique entre une femme et la Femme".[48]

But the relation to the other woman has not to do, in Duras, with hatred and rivalry; on the contrary, as the story of the beggar-woman exemplifies in *Le Vice-consul*, it is a matter of peace and harmony in a dreamt return to the womb[49] has to do with an essential identification rather tham a mere substitution, where love would have a role to play in keeping the phallus in its place - be it the penis, the Law, or God - and make it remain "Dieu, ce truc" (A p.143), external to the individual's fulfilment. The need for identification with the other woman is to a great extent linked to

---

[46]ibid. p.121

[47]ibid. p.50

[48]ibid. p.50

[49]This aspect of the fantasy is also present in the topology of *L'Amour*, which reflects in spatial terms the configurations of Lol's desire. (cf. in particular of chapter 6 below on the spatialisation of Lol's madness).

the desired fusion to the mother,[50] with what Sibony otherwise rightly formulates:

> "le temps de la naissance articule - jointure injouable - l'enjeu enlisé et l'image invisible où l'une était (dans) l'autre, ou l'une s'étaie de l'autre, étayage de la même impasse narcissique".[51]

But rather than, as Sibony continues, being reduced to the status of object, as representative of "le pénis-envie", the man remains essential in Duras' fiction, though secondary in the interaction between the three protagonists.[52] The new scenario of love which occupies the centre of the narrative of Le Ravissement goes beyond the psychoanalytic and clinical explanation. It is rather situated at the level of another order of logic. I shall return to this matter and explore it further in the last chapter of the present book. As far as Le Ravissement is concerned, what can be interpreted here in the social setting of the fiction as a relapse of Lol's earlier illness with the return of her memory during her walks in S.Tahla and the journey to T.Beach constitutes instead the very condition of her access to liberation - a liberation which is symbolised at the end of the book by her presence on the beach, and which is later developed further in L'Amour. 'Liberation' is understood here in terms of Lol's inner problematic and actualisation of desire, and not as social liberation, which remains essentially impossible within the social setting of Le Ravissement.

Lol's trauma at the ball of T.Beach came from the fact that as a passive victim of her fiancé's ravishing by Anne- Marie Stretter, she was denied any possible control over her own positioning; a position then defined in terms of a fusion with the newly-formed couple of Anne-Marie Stretter and Michael Richardson. I would agree at this point with Alleins:

---

[50] I have indicated in chapter 1 ('La Mise en Scène de la Folie') that at the psychological level, it is the separation from the mother and the exclusion from the love scene which prove to be at the root of many female disturbances.

[51] Sibony op.cit. p.123

[52] The man has indeed lost his position of primacy in the love interaction, since the primordial requisite for love with him is rooted in the fusion with the other woman. The only possibility left for the male figure in Duras' fiction is to lose his identity and to identify with the state of the woman.

"Ainsi à la vue de l'homme aimé complètement absorbé par une autre, ce n'était pas sous le coup de la souffrance que son être avait explosé mais d'une révélation dont l'ampleur dépassait celle du sentiment".[53]

And indeed this revelation has to do with another mode of being, with a fusion to the other couple which is not so much linked, as Alleins suggests, to "un anéantissement de velours de sa propre personne", but mainly to a positive determination to be fused, otherwise successfully actualised in other Durasian texts such as *Détruire Dit-elle*.[54] I shall come back shortly to the fact that the erasure of self is only important so long as it frees the individual from the ego and allows a displacement of the terms of desire. What constituted Lol's "ravissement" or delight[55] in the "instant précis de T.Beach" was, with daybreak and the closure of the ball, interrupted and withdrawn from her without any possible appeal.

With Jacques and Tatiana, Lol chooses this time to be the active subject in what many critics have seen to be the reenactment

---

[53]Alleins op. cit. p.117

[54]What Lol is dreaming of is in fact unporblematically represented between Stain, Alissa and Thor:

"Max Thor tend la main et prend celle glacée d'Alissa, sa femme écartelée dans un regard bleu.
- Ne souffrez plus, Alissa dit Stein.
Stein se rapproche, il pose sa tête sur les jambes nues d'Alissa. Il les caresse, il les embrasse.
- Comme je te désire, dit Max Thor
- Comme il vous désire, dit Stein, comme il vous aime"

(DDE p.42). Triangulation occurs successfully in *Détruire Dit-elle* because of the reliable presence of a social space which allows desire to exist in another mode: the circulation of desire can occur so long as the characters remain within the hotel-sanatorium.

[55]Lol's 'ravishing' is indeed to be associated with the beginning of something else, as Sheringham suggests, rather than simply with "a cruel ravishing" (op.cit. p.127). It has, however, to do with a new positioning in relation to desire and love, with a fusion which includes and allows desire to flow, rather than with exclusion and conflict, as Sheringham argues. Similarly, in her interpretation according to which Lol's trauma would essentially come from an erasure of her position in relation to the other couple, Alleins ignores the sense of delight which, in my opinion, is a most powerful meaning of *Le Ravissement*.

of the drama of T.Beach. Such a situation is epitomised during the sequence of the improvised ball in Lol's lounge (RLVS pp.153-158).[56] Through a shifting of roles Lol secures for herself what had been Anne-Marie Stretter's position in T.Beach, and Jacques becomes the object of her desire. Jacques Hold writes:

> "L'approche de Lol n'existe pas. On ne peut pas se rapprocher ou s'éloigner d'elle. Il faut attendre qu'elle vienne vous chercher, qu'elle veuille". (RLVS p.105)

Through Jacques, fusion with Tatiana is made possible. She then recreates, as her "je vous ai choisi" (RLVS p.112) to Jacques confirms, the very conditions which escaped her in T.Beach; she takes the place she had not managed to secure there. Through her relationship with Jacques and her fusion to Tatiana, the free flow of her non-preferential desire can come into being. With such an actualisation, Lol emerges from her "irréprochable virtualité" (RLVS p.24) and asserts, with her idiosyncratic mode of being, a reality which does not correspond to the usual accepted references. Such an alternative constitutes primarily the expression of a social impossibility, a different communicative behaviour which has more to do with a language than with illness. And as such Lol's desire constitutes the greatest threat to the established order, by which "la déraison se recupère dans le silence de l'interdiction". (HF p.549)

2 Lol's madness as 'positive and powerful reserve of meaning'

Lol's state of being has been identified by Sheringham as the level of "intersubjective experience which falls outside the co-ordinates of self and other, and which seems antithetical to familiar constructions of love and sexuality". Sheringham sees this reality of Lol's fantasy and desire as "sandwiched" between "the realms of fiction and narration", "both of which are fully

---

[56]The analogy of situation contains a degradation process, however. The partners Lol and Jacques are less accomplished dancers than are Anne-Marie Stretter and Michael Richardson: "Tatiana suit des yeux notre pénible révolution autour du salon" (RLVS p.153) comments Jacques Hold. The fine geometrical pattern is corrupted by the intrusion of Lol's deceptive lies and of pain for Tatiana, the third term of the triangle. As Kristeva remarks, "Cette absorption de la passion de l'autre femme (...) se fait (...) en sens inverse. Tatiana jusqu'alors légère et ludique se met à souffrir" (*Soleil Noir: Dépression et Mélancolie* (NRF Gallimard, Paris 1987, p.257)

represented and both of which threaten to disqualify and obliterate the experience".[57] In spite of this danger of obliteration, it is nevertheless Lol's subjective reality and the type of intersubjectivity it produces between Lol and Jacques which influences Jacques Hold's narration and challenges the fictional dimension rightly and succinctly identified by Sheringham as the story of "the poor Lol going mad again".[58] In a move contrary to Kristeva's interpretation, according to which Lol is the representative of certain traits of female sexuality, "un être tout de tristesse" who shows "un épuisement des pulsions érotiques",[59] and in spite of her representation in Hold's narrative as the figure of the void, I now want to show that Lol in fact exists as active representative of a desire, the contagious effect of which on Jacques Hold's dual position in the fiction of narrator and protagonist becomes increasingly important as the narrative progresses.

Lol's problematic of desire

> "Puis un jour ce corps infirme remue dans le ventre de Dieu" (RLVS p.51)

In spite of what Alleins suggests, it is not so much a matter of the spiritual adventure that Lol experiences in *Le Ravissement*,[60] but rather a question of an alternative epistemology linked to another version of selfhood.

> "Les romans de Marguerite Duras, tous, racontent la recherche d'un moment perdu. Un événement s'est produit par hasard. Il a duré un instant. On ne sait pas quelle certitude définitive, depuis, demeure (...) Mais elle reste sans objet"[61]

The certainty linked to the emergence of this new epistemology does not need an object. I shall show in the last chapter that the specificity of a love object as such has disappeared. This

---

[57] Sheringham op.cit. p.132

[58] ibid. p.132

[59] Kristeva op.cit. (*Soleil Noir*) p.251

[60] Alleins op.cit. p.116. "*Le Ravissement* est écrit dans une perspective de transcendance" she continues (ibid.p.123).

[61] Montrelay op.cit. p.9

certainty, however, has to do with the loss of subjective limits in the movement of desire which can thus take place.

The problematic of self-erasure which is at the root of the epistemology suggested in *Le Ravissement* had already been announced in Duras' early fiction. The narrator of *Le Marin* abandons his professional and affective security to follow a woman in search of her own love fantasy. Alleins also argues that this new mode of being, and the effects produced on the individual by the formation of a new couple, were already in place in *Dix Heures et Demie du Soir en Eté* and *L'Après-Midi de Monsieur Andesmas*:

> "Si Monsieur Andesmas n'avait pas eu une conscience aussi aiguë de sa décrépitude, sans doute ne serait-il pas aussi vite arrivé à l'idée qu'il devait s'effacer. A la femme de Michel Arc, pour s'incliner devant une nécessité identique, il avait fallu une année".[62]

In *Le Ravisssement de Lol V.Stein*, the attraction for the end of the ball, "la fin du monde" mentioned by Jacques Hold, is linked for Lol to the stripping away of her ego, to reach "the point where it is no longer of any importance whether one says I or not".[63] However in T.Beach Lol does not manage to experience this "anéantissement de sa propre personne" (RLVS p.50), since, as Alleins mentions, Lol has never been able to witness the love scene between Michael Richardson and Anne-Marie Stretter.[64] But it is worth mentioning that the nature of self-erasure is not linked for Lol to a simple substitution by another woman, as Alleins implies.[65] It is rather connected to the movement of liberation

---

[62]Alleins op.cit. p.113

[63]Gilles Deleuze and Felix Guattari, 'Rhizome' in *On The Line* (Semiotext(e), 1983) p.1

[64]"Elle est restée privée du geste qui l'aurait totalement effacée: Michael Richardson, foudroyé par la volupté, perdant jusqu'à la possibilité de se souvenir qu'elle existait" (Alleins op.cit. p.116)

[65]"Emotion de se voir remplacée, effacée, conséquences à long-terme de cette soudaine, totale annulation..." (ibid. p.123). To see Lol as haunted by the predominance of an Other who would postulate her own annulation presupposes that Lol's mode of being is based on singularity and exclusion. This constitutes in my view a misreading of the text which goes against Duras' conception of love, as will be shown in the last chapter below. Indeed for Lol, the love relationship exists in a fusion to the other two terms of the triangle, and the tertiary relationship is what allows the free flow of desire.

from the fixity of the ego which allows the process of displacement of desire to take place. If there is for Lol "hésitation infinie et certaine de son propre corps",[66] it is not, as Sibony implies, a sign of morbidity per se, but rather the condition necessary for identification and fusion with the other two terms of the triangle. Similarly, in the re-enactment of the ball with Jacques and Tatiana, what matters for Lol is not so much the fixity of a subjective choice in relation to Jacques, but the displacement of desire made possible between Jacques, Tatiana and herself.[67] The problematic of ego-loss finds its apogee at the end of *Le Ravissement*. It is described by Jacques Hold as "le commencement sans fin de Lol" (RLVS p.184) where "Lol rêve d'un autre temps où la même chose qui va se produire se produirait différemment" (RLVS p.187).

Desire in *Le Ravissement* and in Duras' fiction in general is predominantly linked to a rhetoric of displacement, an aspect not adequately stressed in most critical studies which tend to give priority to isolated moments of the problematic of Durasian desire, such as the aspect of ego-loss referred to above. Lol's positioning in relation to Jacques and Tatiana is based on a type of relationship which allows the non-preferential flow of desire to come into being. There is indeed for Lol no preferential choice in her relationship to Jacques; Hold reports:

> "(...) inanité partagée par tous les hommes de S.Tahla aussi définissante de moi-même que le parcours de mon sang. Elle m'a cueilli, m'a pris au nid. Pour la première fois mon nom prononcé ne nomme pas (...) Son choix est exempt de toute préférence. Je suis l'homme de S.Tahla qu'elle a decidé de suivre" (RLVS pp.112-113).

Lol's marriage to Bedford fits in with this conception of desire:

---

[66]Sibony op.cit. p.135

[67]In that sense I would disagree with Sheringham, who sees in Jacques "the fantasized object of Lol's gaze in a scenario where Lol is imagined to be involving him in a sort of remake of the triangular situation of her 'ravissement'" (op.cit. p.130). The only, though essential, "remake" of the ball of T.Beach is the triangular structure repeated between Jacques, Tatiana and Lol. However, as the rest of the text shows, Jacques does not play the passive role of the "fantasized object", but gradually relativises his own problematic of knowledge and reason to enter into Lol's active process of desire. I shall return in greater detail to this matter.

"Lol fut mariée sans l'avoir voulu (...) sans avoir à plagier le crime qu'aurait été, aux yeux de quelques-uns, le remplacement par un être unique du partant de T.Beach" (RLVS p.31).

Her marriage is presented as a way of remaining faithful to Richardson, but I would argue that after Lol's 'ravishing' at the ball, the problematic of her desire has changed. The concept of fidelity in relation to her husband Jean Bedford has lost its relevance and she encourages him to betray her (RLVS p.33); exclusivity does not enter into her conception of love.

Lol is "sans port d'attache singulier" (RLVS p.54) and existence of a love relationship in her problematic does not exclude the third term. This explains why Lol begs Jacques, when he announces his decision to leave Tatiana, not to break away from her:

"- Je vais quitter Tatiana Karl
Elle se laisse glisser sur le sol, muette, *elle prend une pose d'une supplication infinie.*
- *Je vous en supplie, je vous en conjure: ne le faites pas.*
Je cours vers elle, je la relève. D'autres pourraient s'y tromper. Son visage n'exprime aucune douleur, mais de la confiance.
- quoi?
- Je vous en supplie
- Dites pourquoi? Elle dit
- Je ne veux pas"   (RLVS pp.117-118) (*my emphasis*)

Later Jacques Hold understands:

"*Elle* (=*Lol*) *aime, aime celui qui doit aimer Tatiana,* Personne. Personne n'aime Tatiana en moi. Je fais partie d'une perspective qu'elle est en train de construire avec une obstination impressionnante, je ne lutterai pas" (RLVS p.133)) (*my emphasis*)

To exclude Tatiana is to take a major risk in relation to Lol; Jacques realizes: "J'ai oublié Tatiana, ce crime, je l'ai commis" (RLVS p.157). Rather than referring to Tatiana's jealousy, the word "crime" alludes to the necessity of including the third term which paradoxically allows love to be stronger.[68] Jacques Hold mentions Tatiana's presence as "enlisée" in them (RLVS p.167), and notices the interchangeability of the two women in Lol's perspective when she names herself by the two names: "Il n'y a plus de différence entre elle et Tatiana, elle se nomme des deux noms"(RLVS p.89).[69]

Similarly, Jacques finds himself inhabited by the memory of "un mort inconnu":

> "(...) l'éternel Richardson, l'homme de T.Beach, on se mélangera à lui, pêle-mêle tout ça ne va faire qu'un, on ne va plus reconnaître qui de qui, ni avant, ni après, ni pendant, on va se perdre de vue, de nom..." (RLVS p.113).

Non-preferentiality in relation to the object of love presupposes a denial of subjectivity, already implied in the experience of ego-loss mentioned earlier. "Partout le sentiment, on glisse sur cette graisse" (RLVS p.159) proposes Hold's narrative as Lol's imagined response to Tatiana's suffering. However even Lol appears tempted by subjectivity. he mentions the feeling of happiness she experiences in her love for Jacques (RLVS p.169), and when Jacques admits that he cannot do without Tatiana, he notices that

> "Des larmes ont rempli ses yeux. Elle réprime une souffrance très grande dans laquelle elle ne sombre pas, qu'elle maintient au contraire, de toutes ses forces, au bord de son expression culminante qui serait celle du bonheur" (RLVS p.132).

But as the quotation observes, happiness in Lol's terms is the extreme expression of suffering and has more to do with the suffering of subjectivity. Pain is experienced as a reflection of preferential/restrictive desire and the overcoming of suffering in

---

[68]The actualisation of such a problematic is to be found in *Détruire Dit-elle*. The triangular relationship between Thor, Alissa and Stein secures in Alissa and Thor's couple a stronger bond. Similarly, Stein asserts that Thor's attraction for Elisabeth secures more tightly the link between Thor and Alissa (DDE pp.50-51).

[69]Duras confirms this during her interviews in Montréal: "Jacques Hold fait l'amour avec Lol V.Stein avec Tatiana. Lol V.Stein est témoin de cet amour que lui fait Jacques Hold avec Tatiana" (*Marguerite Duras à Montréal* p.19)

Lol shows the absence of subjective limits. Pain is "un garde-fou, une limite dont Lol est démunie";[70] she escapes the trap of her own identity and remains in that zone of objectivity in which, beyond the insufficiency of feelings and the realm of sensitivity, individual love remains ultimately impossible. Hence Lol's ambiguous declaration to Jacques:

> "Je ne vous aime pas cependant je vous aime" (RLVS p.169)
> "Je me sens bien sans vous depuis que je vous connais. C'est peut-être dans ces moments-là (...) que je suis le mieux, celle que je dois" (RLVS p.170).

We shall analyse further in the last chapter how the impossibility of personal love,[71] constantly to be found at the heart of Duras' production, justifies the motto of *Les Petits Chevaux de Tarquinia*: "Aucun amour au monde ne peut tenir lieu de l'amour, il n'y a rien à faire" (PCT p.168).

Beyond the limits of the individual, Lol's existence reaches the level of the universal whereby she finds herself "dans une équivalence certaine avec les autres femmes" (RLVS p.54) and where love becomes a perspective rather than a feeling. "Je ne sais pas si l'amour est un sentiment", the female narrator of *Emily-L* confirms, "parfois je crois qu'aimer c'est voir" (EL p.139). Possession of the other therefore remains impossible in Lol's terms, as Jacques experiences during his journey to T.Beach with her:

> "Et durant le voyage toute la journée cette situation est restée inchangée, elle a été à côté de moi séparée de moi, gouffre et soeur. Puisque je sais - ai-je jamais su à ce point? - qu'elle m'est inconnaissable..." (RLVS p.166).

Later Jacques Hold's narrative records the disappearance of the singularity of love in favour of the universal dimension:

---

[70]Montrelay op.cit. (*L'Ombre et le Nom*) p.13

[71]The same problematic of presence-absence is echoed by Alissa in *Détruire Dit-elle*: "c'est quand tu es là que je peux t'oublier" she declares to M.Thor (DDE p.45).

"D'autres déroulements auraient pu se produire, d'autres révolutions, entre d'autres gens à notre place, avec d'autres noms, des autres durées auraient pu avoir lieu, plus longues ou plus courtes (...) d'autres nuits longues, d'amour sans fin, que sais-je?" (RLVS p.184).

As the narrative unfolds, Lol's existence takes on a very different meaning from that of the aetiology of an illness retraced by the narrator Jacques Hold. Another epistemology slowly emerges which fundamentally questions accepted modes of understanding. Lol's search for the establishment of a triangular relationship - a strong taboo in a society based on the supremacy and the exclusivity of the couple - and for a dynamic of triangulation rooted in the complementary features of ego-loss and non-preferentiality, becomes the basis for a powerful renewal of meaning. The effect of this on Jacques Hold becomes increasingly noticeable at both the fictional and the narrative level.

"Lol devient transformante pour qui, par amour, fait l'effort de la connaître" writes Alleins,[72] and indeed Jacques Hold is led to question himself in relation to Lol: "Qu'est-ce que j'ignore de moi-même à ce point et qu'elle me met en demeure de connaître" (RLVS p.105). This question "fait tache d'huile, de Lol aux personnages, des personnages au 'narrateur' et enfin au lecteur" asserts Didier.[73] And Jacques Hold takes the difficult position of both narrator and protagonist; Sheringham comments:

"As a protagonist, Jacques can take his place in a circuit of desire; but as a narrator (...) Jacques Hold remains throughout in the grip of discourse and hence of knowledge".[74]

But the influence of knowledge on Jacques Hold the narrator is not as clear-cut as Sheringham tends to suggest. Nor is the rhetoric of negation only an effect of the "contradictory drives of knowledge and desire" in him. We have seen in the first part of this chapter that it is rather the result of Hold's understanding of Lol's problematic of unreason. If one takes the evolution of the narration into account, one notices indeed that a process of

---

[72]Alleins op.cit. p.118
[73]Didier op.cit. p.67
[74]Sheringham op.cit. p.134

questioning and doubt takes over, until Hold experiences another order of selfhood which fundamentally undermines the mastery of his discourse: "Nous sommes dans ses mains. Pourquoi? Comment? Je ne sais rien" (RLVS p.90), we read about Lol. I shall now examine how the process of desire initiated by Lol takes over Jacques Hold.

Effect of Lol's mode of being on the protagonist Jacques

> "Des chemins s'ouvrent. Sa bouche s'ouvre sur la mienne. Sa main ouverte posée sur mon bras préfigure un avenir multiforme et unique, main rayonnante et unie aux phalanges courbées (...) qui ont, pour moi, la nouveauté d'une fleur" (RLVS p.113)

Jacques Hold

> "writes in order to register and ideally to contain or exorcise disquiet, unease brought about by a conflict between systems of understanding, between epistemologies".[75]

He also wants to account for "l'écrasante réalité de cette femme" in his life (RLVS p.14). Like the guardian with the female protagonist of *Emily-L* (EL p.124), he ends up acquiring the deepest understanding of Lol. Just as Hold's position of empathy had made of Lol's existence the representation of a void in the first third of the text, it is increasingly in relation to his position of protagonist as subject of desire that he pursues his narrative: "Je connais Lol de la seule façon que je puisse, d'amour" (RLVS p.46).

As a result, Jacques Hold understands that the meaning of Lol's madness is mostly the sign of another epistemology, that of the emptying of meaning whereby "ne rien savoir de Lol était la connaître déjà" (RLVS p.81). Because he approaches Lol through his love, he perceives the meaning of the ball for her, that of a triangulation with the two lovers:

> "Je connais Lol.V.Stein de la seule façon que je puisse, d'amour. C'est en raison de cette connaissance que je suis arrivé à croire ceci: dans les multiples aspects du

[75]Sheringham op.cit. p.133

bal de T.Beach, c'est la fin qui retient Lol" (RLVS p.46).

He perceives with Lol "l'inconnu sur lequel s'ouvre cet instant" (RLVS p.47), a new relationship which cannot be named, because it has no equivalence, no possible meaning in the society in which Lol lives:

> "Lol ne va pas loin dans l'inconnu sur lequel s'ouvre cet instant (...) elle n'a aucune idée sur cet inconnu. Mais ce qu'elle croit, c'est qu'elle devait y pénétrer, que c'était ce qu'il lui fallait faire, que ç'aurait été pour toujours, pour sa tête et pour son corps, leur plus grande douleur et leur plus grande joie confondues jusque dans leur définition devenue unique mais innommable faute d'un mot (...) si Lol est silencieuse dans la vie c'est qu'elle a cru, l'espace d'un éclair, que ce mot pouvait exister. Faute de son existence elle se tait. Ç'aurait été un mot-absence, un mot trou, creusé en son centre d'un trou, de ce trou où tous les autres mots auraient été enterrés (...) Immense, sans fin, un gong vide, il aurait retenu ceux qui voulaient partir, il les aurait convaincus de l'impossible" (RLVS pp.47-48)

This new concept, which is unknown to reason and which therefore remains unformulable, would nevertheless have retained the lovers at the ball of T.Beach, "les aurait convaincus de l'impossible"; an impossible defined in terms of another positioning in relation to love and desire. However, in the social structure in which the experience of the ball takes place, this alternative libidinal conception can only become an experience of enclosure and separation in "le bal muré" (RLVS p.49).

Jacques not only enters Lol's perception to understand her experience of T.Beach; he also allows himself to be influenced by her presence. The reference to Lol's presence in the rye field during the sequence when she and Jacques are alone mainly emphasises Jacques' reaction to Lol's discourse:

> "Votre chambre s'est éclairée et j'ai vu Tatiana qui passait dans la lumière. Elle était nue sous ses cheveux noirs. (...) Cette phrase est encore la dernière qui a été prononcée. J'entends "nue sous ses cheveux noirs, nue, nue, cheveux noirs". Les deux derniers mots surtout

sonnent avec une égale et étrange intensité. Il est vrai
que Tatiana était ainsi que Lol vient de la décrire, nue
sous ses cheveux noirs. Elle était ainsi dans la chambre
fermée, pour son amant. L'intensité de la phrase
augmente tout à coup, l'air a claqué autour d'elle, la
phrase éclate, elle crève le sens. Je l'entends avec une
force assourdissante et je ne la comprends pas, je ne
comprends même plus qu'elle ne veut rien dire" (RLVS
pp.115-116)

Sheringham remarks:

"Lol's words force Jacques to interpolate her gaze into
the field of his relationship with Tatiana (...) The
episode in the hotel room is bleached of its affective
and psychological colouring and becomes part of
something far less defined, far more abstract and yet no
less powerful - and no less real for being in a sense no
more than a product of the imagination"[76]

Indeed Jacques has decidedly abandoned the "entity mode" of
understanding through which Lol tended to be defined as mad,[77]
and has let himself be touched by Lol's own perception. What
Sheringham qualifies as "less defined, far more abstract and yet no
less powerful" has to do with this 'otherness' which cannot be
apprehended by the reason of the society in which both Lol and
Jacques live. The episode of the hotel room, which as Sheringham
mentions becomes "no less real for being a product of the
imagination", mostly manifests Jacques' understanding of Lol's
perceptions, of this alternative positioning by which love and desire
are primarily linked to a dynamic rather than to the reassuring
unicity of love and feeling.

"Cet homme ouvert et mourant à la volupté entrevoit auprès
de Lol une façon plus définitive de perdre pied" writes Alleins.[78]
I would argue that "perdre pied" is not itself a search, albeit

---

[76]Sheringham op.cit. p.132

[77]The mode of conceptualisation of Lol's behaviour used by Tatiana and Lol's
social circle rests indeed on "entity thinking", whereby, as Szasz would put it,
"substantives: living things, mental illnesses and so forth" are privileged to the
detriment of a process theory of personal conduct. (cf. op.cit. p.17)

[78]Alleins op.cit. p.118

unconscious, for the protagonist Jacques Hold, but rather the effect of his increased proximity with Lol. Such proximity is most obvious in the sequence where Lol announces that she has found happiness (RLVS pp.148-152). The mysterious complicity thus established between Lol and Jacques arouses suspicions:

> "Tatiana soupire, soupire longuement, se plaint, se plaint, au bord des larmes.
> - Mais ce bonheur, ce bonheur, dis-moi, ah! dis-moi un peu.
> Je dis:
> - Lol V.Stein l'avait sans doute en elle, déjà, lorsqu'elle l'a rencontré.
> Avec la même lenteur qu'un moment avant Tatiana s'est retournée vers moi. Je pâlis. Le rideau vient de s'ouvrir sur le tourment de Tatiana Karl. Mais curieusement, sa suspicion ne porte pas immédiatement sur Lol.
> - Comment savez-vous ces choses-là sur Lol?" (RLVS pp.150-151)

Tatiana's suspicion indeed arises from Jacques' explicit understanding of Lol's most intimate reactions - as his intervention in the conversation shows. The fiction offers later in the same sequence the parallelism of two images as confirmation of the fundamental rhythm shared by Lol and Jacques, even when one of them is irritated with the other. When Lol explains that the image of the sea reflected in a mirror on the wall has motivated her journey to T.Beach the very same day, Jacques is suddenly assailed by the image of the rye field:

> "L'image du champ de seigle me revient, brutale, je me demande jusqu'à la torture, je me demande à quoi m'attendre encore de Lol. A quoi? Je suis, je serais donc dupe par sa folie même? Qu'a-t-elle été chercher au bord de la mer, où je ne suis pas, quelle pâture? loin de moi" (RLVS p.152)

After the moment of irritation in front of the unpredictability of Lol's madness, Jacques is suddenly taken over by a sense of jealousy when he feels excluded from one of Lol's mental representations:

"Lol rêve d'un autre temps où la même chose qui va se produire se produirait différemment (...) ce rêve me contamine" (RLVS p.187).

The effect of contamination is particularly striking in some instances of parallelism between both Lol's and Jacques' behaviour or inner experience. After accompanying Lol in her rediscovery of the place where the ball took place in T.Beach, Jacques copies her mode of being and falls asleep on the beach (RLVS p.182). In another sequence, he tries to order the objects of his room " en accord avec la vision qu'elle en aurait eue elle" (RLVS p.172). His failure disappoints him deeply. Lol in turn recalls a similar experience when she tried in vain to find a place for her body, and the suffering which ensued. At the end of the narrative, Jacques, who has been increasingly influenced by Lol's perspective, can even note: "J'ai commencé à me souvenir de son souvenir" (RLVS p.180).

Lol's contamination of the character Jacques Hold is most evident in relation to the conception of non-preferentiality and inclusion which can be found at the root of her problematic of desire. Alleins posits that when Lol begs Jacques not to leave Tatiana,

"Jacques Hold ressent un vacillement général, qui pourrait être celui de la raison dont sont sapées les bases sur quoi elle édifiait un comportement".[79]

Indeed Jacques' frightened reason had pressed him to escape Lol's dictatorial will:

"Je suis dans la nuit de T.Beach. C'est fait. Là, on ne donne rien à Lol V.Stein. Elle prend. J'ai encore envie de fuir" (RLVS p.112).

Lol's power is such, though, that Jacques' choice has already been made.

"Qu'elle m'emporte, qu'il en aille enfin différemment de l'aventure désormais, qu'elle me broie avec le reste, je

---

[79]ibid. p.120

serais servile, que l'espoir soit d'être broyé avec le reste, d'être servile" (RLVS p.106).[80]

However, a subjectivity most often associated with the exclusivity of a love relationship is not easy to renounce, even if Jacques was already partially freed from its limitations before meeting Lol. When Lol meets him and Tatiana for the first time, Jacques Hold notes:

> "Leur allure ne la trompe pas, elle. Ils ne s'aiment pas (...) D'autres liens les tiennent dans une emprise qui n'est pas celle du sentiment, ni celle du bonheur, il s'agit d'autre chose qui ne prodigue ni peine ni joie. Ils ne sont ni heureux ni malheureux. Leur union est faite d'insensibilité, d'une manière qui est générale et qu'ils appréhendent momentanément, toute préférence en est bannie (...) Par des voies contraires ils sont arrivés au même résultat que Lol V.Stein, eux, à force de faire, de dire, d'essayer, de se tromper (...) et elle, Lol, à force de rien" (RLVS p.60).

Nevertheless it is only at the end of the narrative that Jacques Hold realizes that he can include Tatiana, or any other woman, in his relation with Lol:

> "Tatiana est là, comme une autre, Tatiana par exemple, enlisée en nous, celle d'hier et celle de demain, quelle qu'elle soit" (RLVS p.167).

To share Lol's epistemology of desire is, however, not devoid of existential risks. The image of "les murs lisses" arises when she asks Jacques to include Tatiana in their relationship. With the feeling of claustrophobia which recalls the alienation of the ball experienced by Lol[81] in T.Beach, Jacques shares the feeling of

---

[80]The power of sexual attraction is as usual associated in Duras with violence and domination: "Qu'elle me broie avec le reste, je serai servile" writes Jacques Hold. The submission to the other's violence recalls the lovers' sadomasochistic problematic of *L'Homme Assis dans le Couloir*, and to a lesser extent *La Maladie de la Mort* and *Les Yeux Bleus, Cheveux Noirs*. Such aspects point to the impossibility of harmony within the love relationship. I shall come back to this essential feature of Duras' writing in Chapter 7 below.

[81]Didier indeed suggests that enclosure, with errancy, constitute the main elements of Lol's existence: "enfermement dans la salle de casino, dans la

separation from society, and finds himself with her "de l'autre côté du fleuve" (RLVS p.42). Later in the narration, he records:

> "Autour de nous, les murs: j'essaie de remonter, je m'accroche, je retombe, je recommence, peut-être, peut-être, mais ma raison reste égale, impavide et je tombe" (RLVS p.169)

This experience of separation affects not only Jacques and Lol; if we believe Marguerite Duras, it tends metaphorically to extend to the readers of the book:

> "*Le Ravissement de Lol V.Stein* est un livre à part. Un livre seul. Qui opère à lui seul une séparation entre certains lecteurs: ceux qui ont adhéré à la folie de Lol V.Stein et les autres lecteurs du livre" (VM p.32).

The characters' feeling of enclosure and passion linked to the limitation of a dominant social structure will subsequently disappear from Duras' fiction. It is only with *L'Amour*, where we can assume that Jacques has followed Lol in her unreason to become the madman who haunts the beach while Michael Richardson reappears as the traveller, that we find a closeness of relationship between the woman and the traveller[82] reminiscent of the captain and his wife: "Si seuls au monde ils étaient, ils ne savaient plus rien de la solitude" (EL p.91). Indeed Jacques Hold, who is one of the few male characters in Duras' writing who accepts to be transformed by the female's mode of being, can be compared to the captain of *Emily-L*, who gradually "cherche un sens à sa vie en raison de celle de cette femme" (EL p.100).

---

chambre, dans la folie; mais l'espace est finalement le même, ni ouvert, ni fermé, puisque la folie est à la fois errance et enfermement (...) je prononce le mot de 'folie' faute de mieux, mais je sais bien que dans cette absence généralisée, le mot qui pourrait désigner l'état de Lol, lui aussi, est absent, que folie n'est qu'une approximation qui fausse considérablement les choses" (op. cit. p.73). Didier rightly stresses the inadequacy of the term 'madness', since enclosement is largely the result of the impossibility of Lol's existing in her difference in a dominant social structure.

[82]The identity of the protagonists is established during their final journey in *L'Amour*: it is said that the woman fell ill after the ball, that she married a musician (A p.113). The traveller affirms that he is Michael Richardson after his visit to the casino: "On voit aussi la porte par laquelle nous sommes sortis séparés" (A p.134).

Jacques' apprehension of Lol may be evoked in terms similar to those used in *Emily-L*: the captain looks at his wife:

> "il la regarde longuement comme on ferait d'un paysage bouleversant et insaisissable: celui du vide de la mer" (EL p.94).

Confrontation of the narrator Jacques Hold with Lol's epistemology

Let us recall that what Jacques Hold pursues in his narrative act is primarily an account of Lol's influence in relation to himself, rather than an elucidation of what has happened to Lol as such. He consequently tends to abandon, to borrow Sheringham's terms, "the narrator's position as subject of knowledge" and to acquire "the protagonist's position as subject of desire".[83]

> "La transformation de Jacques Hold nous montre, étalé dans le temps, grillage en opérations successives, ce qui, chez Lol, s'est produit sous le coup de l'illumination. Ce roman nous rend témoins d'un démantèlement libérateur qui agit sur tous les plans".[84]

Such liberating deconstruction is perhaps more evident at the narrative level in the doubt and the undermining of knowledge which increasingly pervades Jacques Hold's discourse. "In so far as he is a narrator, Jacques Hold remains in the grip of discourse and knowledge".[85] This is true in so far that Jacques Hold indeed cannot completely escape the order of discourse in which he has situated himself; knowledge is nevertheless considerably undermined in his discourse, and we shall see that the narrator's position is at one point practically relinquished under the influence of Lol's mode of being.

We have already mentioned in the first part of this chapter that Jacques Hold relies on Tatiana for the basic information he gathers about Lol. At the same time, he increasingly doubts the validity of her testimony: "Je ne crois plus à rien de ce que dit Tatiana, je ne suis convaincu de rien" (RLVS p.14). He also questions the validity of his own discourse, and, as has already been shown earlier, foregrounds the textual mechanism with

---

[83]Sheringham op.cit. p.134

[84]Alleins op.cit. p.119

[85]Sheringham op.cit. p.134

numerous declarations of doubt. He furthermore questions the status of his narrative with explicit references to his play with fiction: "j'invente" he declares repeatedly (RLVS pp.56,154...).

> "Voici, tout au long, mêlés, à la fois, ce faux semblant que raconte Tatiana Karl et *ce que j'invente* sur la nuit du casino de T.Beach" (RLVS p.14). (*my emphasis*)

He denounces further the deceptiveness of his enterprise: "je mens" he asserts (RLVS p.121); "en ce moment, moi seul de tous ces faussaires, je sais: je ne sais rien" (RLVS p.81). The ambiguity of the text indeed results from what can and cannot be told. Jacques Hold realizes that Lol's reality cannot be explained in words, unless it is precisely via the "mot-absence" mentioned earlier.[86] He suspects that it is in this "mot-absence" that resides the nature of Lol's silence:

> "(...) si Lol est silencieuse dans la vie c'est qu'elle a cru, l'espace d'un éclair, que ce mot pouvait exister. Faute de son existence, elle se tait" (RLVS p.48).

Jacques himself, because of his position of empathy in relation to Lol, experiences the fatal lack of language:

> "Je voudrais faire, dire, dire un long mugissement fait de tous mots fondus et revenus au même magma, intelligible à Lol V.Stein. Je me tais" (RLVS p.130)

In Hold's narrative enterprise, the primacy of word over discourse exists as a challenge to the logical order of discourse, and questions his own position of knowledge: "...ce mot qui n'existe pas, pourtant est là: il vous attend au tournant du langage, il vous défie" (RLVS p.48). The "mot- absence" constitutes the 'unsaid', the signifier of another logic which subsists when presence has

---

[86]I disagree at this point with Sheringham's interpretation: he sees the reference to the "mot- absence" as a manoeuvre on the part of Jacques Hold, by which Lol's experience "loses its distinctiveness and becomes to some extent assimilated to Jacques' experience of trying to apprehend it" (op.cit. p.136). Such a view is tempting since it does take into account the fact that *Le Ravissement* is indeed a result of Jacques Hold's enterprise of writing; but to reduce Lol's experience to a textual strategy does not address the operation of contamination at work in the text. Lol's impact on Jacques is variously manifested through the parallelisms of behaviour between the two characters, the changes in Jacques' subjectivity, and the shared experience of enclosement and separation.

become impossible. Such a signifier exists as an 'elsewhere'; it is nonetheless in the text as "gong vide" (RLVS p.48), and as such becomes, as Marini rightly points out, a source of renewed meaning:

> "Isoler le mot du discours qui le limite ou l'étreint, l'entendre et le faire résonner avec des connotations subjectives et intersubjectives multiples, ouvre la voie à d'autres ensembles discursifs que ces morts qui nous gangrènent. Le mot, loin d'être un point fixe du sens auquel se raccrocher dans la débacle, devient un lieu vivant d'incertitude du sens: mis en relation plus directe avec l'expérience, il permet alors de trouver des modes à la fois divers et jamais définitifs de vivre et de dire sa vie inséparablement".[87]

Indeed if Lol's language existed, it would have a disturbing similarity with the "parole transgressive" defined by Foucault.

> "(...) langage structurellement ésotérique. C'est à dire qu'il ne communique pas, en la cachant, une signification interdite, il s'installe d'entrée de jeu dans un repli essentiel de la parole. Repli qui la creuse de l'intérieur et peut-être jusqu'à l'infini. Peu importe alors ce qui se dit dans un pareil langage et les significations qui y sont délivrées. C'est cette libération obscure et centrale de la parole au coeur d'elle-même, sa fuite incontrôlable vers un foyer toujours sans lumière, qu'aucune culture ne peut accepter immédiatement. Non pas dans son sens, non pas dans sa matière verbale, mais dans son *jeu*, une telle parole est transgressive" (HF p.578).

The undermining of knowledge in Jacques Hold's position constitutes the most obvious effect of this "parole transgressive" or signifier of unreason. And Hold admits: "Manquant ce mot, il gâche tous les autres, les contamine" (RLVS p.48). Similarly the portrayal of Lol as absence and negativity leads Hold to the extreme relativisation of his own epistemology. He discovers that "ne rien savoir de Lol était la connaître déjà" (RLVS p.81).

---

[87]Marini op.cit. (*Ecrire Dit-elle*) p.24

> "l'absence de parole rejoint l'absence de connaissance, cette ignorance qui circule dans tout le roman et qui frappe successivement tous les personnages (...) Reste à découvrir par un étrange renversement que cette non-connaissance est la seule connaissance possible. Paradoxe et retournement de la négativité".[88]

In his struggle with writing, the apprentice writer Jacques Hold is gradually dispossessed of his own certainty and of his mastery over language. Fiction remains lies or artifice, and Lol as 'character' or 'case study' escapes the author, whether the latter is fictive or not. This recalls the fact that reading is a 'game' and that truth, this "mot-absence", is only a vanishing-point.

The 'abandonment' of Jacques Hold's position of knowledge can be detected in the operation of negation of logical meaning which pervades his narrative both at the lexical and the syntactic level. The relativisation of knowledge is for instance reflected in the reiterative vagueness of several lexical items which appear loaded with an essential meaning, the most obvious example of which is a reference to the "mot- absence" variously interpreted during this chapter. We have also already stressed the importance of the "rien". We also find various references to the "quelque chose" whose function mainly suggests that the 'aura' of what is lived goes far beyond the analytical purpose of the narrator:

> "Alors, comme moi, de mon côté, je crois me souvenir aussi de *quelque chose*, je continue..." (RLVS p.87)
> "D'autres liens les tiennent dans une emprise qui n'est pas celle du sentiment, ni celle du bonheur, il s'agit d'*autre chose* qui ne prodigue ni peine, ni joie" (RLVS p.60). (*my emphasis*)

Sometimes the baroque redundancy of a past participle and of an adjectival form used together implodes the strict logical meaning contained in the substantive:

> "Elle est *débordée* par l'aboutissement, *même inaccompli*, de son désir" (RLVS p.131). (*my emphasis*)

---

[88]Didier op.cit. p.67

The importance of Lol's desire takes over any logical description. The reference to an "ailleurs" has a similar function:

> "...elle devait trouver, dans la monotonie de la pluie, cet *ailleurs*, uniforme, fade et sublime..." (RLVS p.44)
> "j'ai été longtemps à le (= Lol's body) mettre *ailleurs* que là où il aurait dû être. Maintenant je crois que je me rapproche de *là* où il serait heureux" (RLVS p.173). (*my emphasis*)

The ambiguity of the adverbial expression takes on a metaphorical power which alternatively suggests Lol's experience of 'insanity' and the idealised translation of desire. The "ailleurs" of p.44 may perhaps be interpreted as the fantasy of a morbid mind, but most often the "ailleurs" spares the narrator a more abstract formulation and suggests an ideal, as strongly anchored in the concrete world as in space:

> "Lol rêve d'un autre temps où la même chose qui va se produire se produirait différemment. Autrement. Mille fois. Partout. *Ailleurs*" (RLVS p.187). (*my emphasis*)

The position of "ailleurs" in the above example, at the end of a series of other signifiers, opens meaning onto the myth. Sometimes the metaphor of the "ailleurs" takes on, through its geographical evocation, the strength of an ancient truth. It suggests the primitive 'elsewhere' of the human psyche, beyond the character's individual case:

> "Lol a un accent que je ne lui connaissais pas encore, plaintif et aigu. La bête séparée de la forêt dort, elle rêve de l'équateur de la naissance, dans un frémissement, son rêve solaire pleure" (RLVS p.117).

As the "ailleurs" exemplifies, we find in Jacques Hold's narrative a vocabulary of enigmatic intensity which challenges the logical representations of knowlege and which suggests that a primordial meaning is at work behind the anecdotal line. Such is also the impact of the repeated references to the 'crime':

> "J'ai oublié Tatiana Karl, *ce crime*, je l'ai commis" (RLVS p.157)

> "J'ai dansé avec la femme de U.Bridge, bien,et je lui ai parlé, *j'ai commis ce crime aussi*, avec soulagement, je l'ai commis" (RLVS p.158).
>
> (*my emphasis*)

The word "crime" can be variously interpreted as a sign of Tatiana's jealousy or as a threat to Lol's desire. The expression "pour toujours" takes on a similar function and gives gravity to what otherwise would appear to be a pitiful "intrigue à trois":

> "J'ai éprouvé, cependant que je m'attendais à tout, une émotion très violente dont je n'ai pas su tout de suite la vraie nature entre (...) la tentation de crier gare, de secourir, de repousser pour toujours ou de me perdre *pour toujours*, pour toute Lol V.Stein, d'amour" (RLVS p.120). (*my emphasis*)

The lexical variants of the word "fin", loaded with subjective intensity, again bring conceptual vagueness to the narrative, and thus punctuate the textual progression towards its end:

> "De nouveau, sagement, Lol danse, me suit. Quand Tatiana ne voit pas je l'écarte un peu pour voir ses yeux. Je les vois: une transparence me regarde (...) La transparence m'a traversé, je la vois encore, buée maintenant, elle est allée vers autre chose de plus vague, *sans fin*. Elle ira vers autre chose que je ne connaîtrai jamais, *sans fin*.
> - Lol Valérie Stein, éh?
> - Ah oui.
> Je lui ai fait mal, je l'ai senti a un 'ah' chaud dans mon cou
> - Il faudra en finir, quand?" (RLVS p.155).
>
> (*my emphasis*)

In this sequence, where Jacques dances with Lol under Tatiana's attentive gaze, Lol's answer to his question "il faudra en finir, quand?" occurs at the end of a long imaginary conversation between Tatiana and Pierre Beugner: she says "si on savait quand" (RLVS 157). Such an answer does not, however, dismiss the ambiguity of the original question. Is Jacques' request meant as a way of getting rid of the deceptive lies in relation to Tatiana or Jean Bedford, or is it a matter of giving reality to their love? Or perhaps Jacques Hold refers here to the end of Lol's dependency in relation to the ball. The narrator keeps on playing with the concept of end/"fin", and unexpectedly refers to it again in another passage: "Dans quelques heures ou dans quelques jours, quand la fin viendra-t-elle?" (RLVS p.170).

In the sequence which evokes the reference to other durations and which, as already mentioned, points to the negation of the individualist conception of the couple, we can read:

> "Lol mange, elle se nourrit.
> Je nie *la fin* qui va venir probablement nous séparer, sa facilité, sa simplicité désolante, car du moment que je la nie, celle-là, j'accepte l'autre, celle *qui est à inventer, que je ne connais pas, que personne encore n'a inventée*: la fin sans fin, le commencement sans fin de Lol V.Stein.
> A la voir manger, j'oublie" (RLVS p.184).
>
> (*my emphasis*)

The succession of relative clauses, through the various allusions they contain, give to the word "fin" an enigmatic resonance which opens up meaning to interpretation. The vagueness of the formulation constitutes a call to the imaginary: "j'accepte l'autre, celle qui est à inventer...". The lexicality used indeed indicates an attitude of messianic waiting. The passage ends with two paradoxical propositions which translate the undefinability of the object of Jacques' hope: "la fin sans fin, le commencement sans fin de Lol V.Stein". The reinforcement of the paradox by the synonymy established via the juxtaposition of terms forces one to abandon the conception of logical succession and to accept the challenge of opposite meanings.

As the text progresses, the rhythm of the narrative alters. The mechanisms which indicate the presence of the imaginary increasingly challenge the sense of a recognizable reality: the text "s'affole" in its narrative nature as does a compass needle at the approach of a pole. The sequence of the dance with Lol and of the dialogue which accompanies it offers a syntactic example of this phenomenon:

> "Lol me répond:
> - si on savait quand.
> J'ai oublié Tatiana, ce crime, je l'ai commis.
> J'étais dans le train, je l'avais près de moi, pour des

> heures, nous roulions déjà vers T.Beach.
> - Pourquoi faire ce voyage maintenant?
> - C'est l'été. C'est le moment.
> Comme je ne lui réponds pas, elle m'explique
> - Et puis, il faut aller vite, Tatiana s'est mise à vous.
> Elle s'arrête. Lol désirait-elle que ceci que j'invente se
> passe entre Pierre Beugner et Tatiana?
> - Vous le vouliez?
> - Oui. Mais vous deviez aussi. Elle ne devait rien savoir"
> (RLVS p.157)

In this sequence, the logical progression of the narrative is suddenly interrupted by Jacques' declaration: "J'ai oublié Tatiana Karl..." which implies his meditation about the danger he inflicts on Lol's representation of a triangular relationship. The following clauses contradict the temporal logic of the passage: "j'étais dans le train, je l'avais près de moi...". Does Jacques dream or anticipate a future in the past? Does he remember a complacently imagined past? The continuation of the dialogue adds yet more hesitation in relation to temporal continuity: "Pourquoi faire ce voyage?". The subsequent use of the narrative present: "je ne lui réponds pas, elle m'explique" brings the reader back to the progression of the scene, but the imperfects which follow make us hesitate again. The flexibility in the rapid changes of point of view from the narrator to the character Jacques, the constant reminders of the absence of relevance of the hypotheses brought up in the text to account for the characters' behaviour, the syntactic changes in mode of expression and tense, all express Jacques Hold's weakened mastery of knowledge and discourse. The enigmatic atmosphere thus created suggests that the narrative has lost some of its reality-status and has acquired the texture of a dream.

In one last passage, which has already been mentioned above, I wish to show how the illogic of Jacques Hold's discourse confronts the power of the metaphor and reveals his choice of epistemology.

> "Autour de nous, les murs: j'essaie de remonter, je
> m'accroche, je retombe, je recommence, peut-être,
> peut-être, mais ma raison reste égale, impavide et je
> tombe" (RLVS p.169).

The narrative here notes Jacques' efforts to climb up along the walls, his failure to do so and his renewed attempt. So far the textual development remains logical, but ambiguity sets in with the "peut-être, peut-être, ma raison reste égale". The order of the clauses establishes a relation of succession between the lucidity of reason and the fall. Rather than concluding that the sanity of Jacques' reason condemns him to remain prisoner of the enclosed world of Lol's madness and of her love, we have to take into account the relevance of the metaphor. The word "impavide" used to qualify the lucidity of Jacques' reason is essential and suggests on the contrary that the absence of fear in relation to Lol's 'madness' and to his love relationship link him irremediably to her fate. Rather than endorsing a denial of knowledge as such, the ambiguity of the narrative stresses Jacques Hold's deliberate choice of epistemology. He chooses to join Lol in the field of unreason.

> "...toutes les femmes de mes livres, quel que soit leur âge, découlent de Lol V.Stein. C'est à dire, d'un certain oubli d'elles-mêmes" (VM p.32)

Finally, and as a conclusion to this chapter, I would like briefly to question the validity of certain critical approaches with respect to *Le Ravissement de Lol V.Stein*.

In spite of Lol's epistemological power - noticeable both within and outside the fiction of *Le Ravissement*, with her influence on Jacques Hold and also on other protagonists in Duras' prose -, there is paradoxically no liberation of unreason, as such, in *Le Ravissement de Lol V.Stein*. The ball of T.Beach and its re-enactment with Jacques and Tatiana remain experiences of enclosement whereby Jacques comes to share Lol's predicament. Such a situation stems on both occasions from the impossibility of the inclusion of a third term.[89] Contrary to the experience of Mary Barnes, Lol remains enclosed in the midst of a society which represses differences of subjecthood and views them primarily as pathological symptoms.

---

[89]Tatiana indeed remains outside the problematic of Lol's desire. The narrative ascertains the fact that Lol and Jacques decide not to inform Tatiana of their meetings.
"Bien qu'il n'ait rien été convenu à ce sujet, il décide de mentir à Tatiana. Lol s'arrête.
- Tatiana ne comprendrait pas, dit-elle" (RLVS p.135)

The pathologising interpretation of Lol's experience is a tempting option, since *L'Amour* can indeed be read as a representation of her mental illness in its ultimate state.[90] The scenario of *La Femme du Gange* indeed confirms the hypothesis of Lol's definite relapse into madness (FG p.137); this is why several critics view 'the cycle of Lol V.Stein' as "le cycle de la folie".[91]

To limit the texts of the cycle of Lol V.Stein to the experience of madness is however to ignore that the main attributes of Lol's unreason remain potent in most of Duras' subsequent female characters after 1964, and central to all Durasian texts up to her latest fiction. Madness[92] as mental illness constitutes a convenient exemplification of the alternative mode of desire at work in Duras' production.

Certain critics have gone further in the interpretation of Lol's experience viewed as mental illness. Sibony, Kristeva, and even Makward and Montrelay[93] have apprehended Lol's character as a clinical manifestation of hysteria : "...l'ubiquité de l'obsessionnel prend racine dans l'hystérie, dans cette course folle de la substitution impossible"[94], asserts Sibony. He is supported by Makward: "le comportement typique de l'hystérie serait une forme de 'béance' psychique, une disponibilité totale à l'identification à l'autre".[95] Marguerite Duras herself, in a paradoxical utterance which contradicts an earlier statement, seems to endorse such a view:[96]

---

[90]The narrative of *L'Amour* describes what has happened to the character who is likely to be Lol: "elle n'a jamais guéri". She now lives in S.Thala prison (A pp.78-79).

[91]Tison-Brown, op.cit. (Marguerite Duras) p.57

[92]Madness also admittedly functions, as Tison-Brown suggests, as an antidote for Marguerite Duras herself: "l'essentiel de l'oeuvre est la création de l'univers autonome - onirique et léthéen - de la folie, dont la présence hallucinante semble exorciser une vieille hantise de l'auteur: 'se libérer de la crainte de la folie" op.cit. p.59

[93]cf. Sibony, *La Haine du Désir*; Kristeva, *Soleil Noir*; Makward, 'Structures du Silence du Délire', in *Poétique* no.35, 1978 ; Montrelay, *L'Ombre et le Nom*.

[94]Sibony op.cit. p.119

[95]Makward op.cit. p.316

[96]Leslie Hill rightly signals the critical caution needed when dealing with Marguerite Duras' own statements: "It is important (...)to distinguish between some of the terms of Duras' self-commentary and her own fictional or cinematographic texts. More pertinently, an effort must be made to read the

"Lol V.Stein n'est plus nulle part (...) elle est déjà comme Anne-Marie Stretter, elle est déjà atteinte définitivement. Elle ne parle plus, elle vit avec des fous, des malades mentaux, sur la plage"[97]

Apart from the problematic nature of the concept of hysteria itself, both in 'real' terms[98] and in its application to literature, such an approach to Lol's behaviour remains predictably inscribed in a historical position originating from Freud. In the Freudian perspective, the psychological patterns of female behaviour reflected primarily a constructed idea of femininity, with undue stress placed on womens' intuition as contrasted with mens' rationality.[99] It is essential of course to relativise the relevance of such a psychoanalytic approach;[100] as Juliet Mitchell, after Freud,[101] recalls:

"The same mechanisms operate in psychotic, neurotic and normal states (in different degrees and ways of

---

former as an after-hours extension of the latter and not as a privileged theoretical (or, as it more often is, anti-theoretical) discourse which might provide an adequate translation of what is at stake in Duras' fiction and films". ('Marguerite Duras and the Limits of Fiction' in *Paragraph* vol.12 no.1 (March 1989) p.2)

[97] in *Marguerite Duras à Montréal* p.40

[98] Szasz remarks that at the time of Freud and of early psychoanalysis 'hysteria' was regarded as a type of counterfeit illness, albeit a special one where the patient did not know what (s)he was 'simulating'. But the concept of simulation is in itself interesting: "This poses a logical dilemma - the dilemma of the existence of an alleged entity called 'mental illness' which, even when deliberately counterfeited, is still 'mental illness'" (op.cit. p.27).

[99] One of Freud's first major published works was a series of studies on hysteria, and "...although Freud staked his reputation on his support of Charcot's revolutionary idea of male hysteria, most hysterics were women (...) His last result was the conclusion that the 'feminine' (being a woman in the psychological sense) was in part a hysterical formation" (Juliet Mitchell, *Psychoanalysis and Feminism* (Penguin 1975) p.48).

[100] "...l'hystérie, liée au refoulement de la sexualité, était la maladie ethnique de la bourgeoisie à la fin du 19e siècle; c'était la manière convenable d'être anormal" (Jaccard op.cit. p.73). Mitchell notes that "sexual mores are different, women have gained a degree of emancipation, hysteria is no longer the most prevalent manifestation of neurosis among middle-class women" (op.cit. p.9).

[101] Freud indeed stresses: "Every normal person, in fact is only normal on the average, his ego approximates to that of the psychotic in some part or other, and to a greater or lesser extent" (*Analysis Terminable and Interminable* (S.E.vol. XXIII 1937) p.235)

course). Normal life, like the other two conditions, is a compromise with reality"[102]

The satisfaction of being able to apply a label does not in itself explain anything about the nature of the observed behaviour, but is in turn more revealing about the society which applies the label. When Lol's existence is viewed in itself, it has more to do with a new position of desire and with a major challenge to social expectations. Indeed if hysteria constitutes the most tempting (and admittedly perhaps the most suitable) diagnosis for Lol, and with her for all Duras' absent women, it is mainly because that state constitutes a condition "where desire is far more prevalent than the act".[103] Furthermore, to stress the importance of social formations in relation to those of the unconscious does not, as Mitchell implies, necessarily mean a negation of the unconscious:

> "Feminist criticisms of Freud claim that he was denying what really happened and that the women he analysed were simply responding to really oppressive conditions. But there is no such thing as a simple response to reality. External reality has to be 'acquired'. To deny that there is anything other than external reality gets us back to the same proposition: it is the denial of the unconscious"[104]

Mitchell tends to assume that there is only one acceptable understanding of the unconscious: that defined by Freud. The female unconscious pictured in Duras' texts however has far more to do with that "mouvement vital", a point of disjunction where the subject "(...) n'est pas lui-même au centre (...) mais sur le bord, sans identité fixe, toujours décentré, *conclu* des états par lesquels il passe."[105] (*original emphasis*)

We shall have cause to come back to this observation at several points and especially in the final conclusion of this work. As a result of unconscious formations centred wholly around the

---

[102]Mitchell op.cit. p.12

[103]ibid. p.9

[104]ibid. p.12

[105]Deleuze and Guattari op.cit. (*Anti-Oedipe*) p.27

pursuit of desire rather than on repression,[106] Lol's existence becomes relevant primarily in terms of a radical social transgression where the presence of a third term and therefore the necessity of a different social structure, becomes essential.

---

[106]The Freudian psychoanalytic model, based largely on oedipal repression, indeed tends to silence too much the transgressive impact of Lol's experience.

Chapter 4

MADNESS IN THE *VICE-CONSUL* OR THE INVASION OF THE WORLD OF REASON BY UNREASON

With the study of *Le Vice-consul* we abandon the concept of madness taken at the personal level as mental illness - as was the case in *Le Ravissement de Lol V.Stein* -, in order to apprehend madness, or rather unreason, in its relation to the whole social structure represented in the narrative. As Ninette Bailey suggests,[1] the narrative of *Le Vice-consul* seems to simultaneously propose several individual anecdotes: a love story (that of a titular character), the account of a criminal deed and that of the travels of a Cambodian woman banished by her family. However, beyond the anecdotal level, or rather through it, we soon realize that one important interest of the text lies in its social dimension. The narrative of *Le Vice-consul* articulates a social reality, closely connected to the political situation represented in the novel, of the Europeans, lost, 'exiled' in a huge foreign continent. Through this conflictual position, the text articulates the constant interplay between two contrasting social structures: the Western world versus the Indian reality.[2]

---

[1]Ninette Bailey, 'Discours Social: Lecture Sociocritique du Vice-Consul', in *Literature and Society*, University of Birmingham 1980

[2]It is important to note that *Le Vice-consul* constitutes an exception in Duras' production. Sociality does not exist as such in the Duras text and most Durasian narratives, from *L'Après-midi de M.Andesmas* onwards, do not elaborate on the social aspect. *L'Amour* constitutes the ultimate example of a social dimension

The Indians, assembled outside the Embassy, constitute for the whites a constant, inescapable presence; they also represent a silent, passive, almost occult threat, infallibly present, in the shadows of the trees, ordered in circles (VC p.164), or spread along the river bank (VC p.150). Their number, inconceivable for an occidental mind, carries in its very indifferentiation the threat of its inhumanity. The only way the natives can be apprehended is therefore through abstraction as "la horde dolente" or "le nid de fourmis". This reality of India tends to be counteracted in the whites by an escapist defensive mood which sees in India a realm of pure convention or imagination, "il y a mes Indes, les vôtres, celles-ci, celles-là..." (VC p.157). Nevertheless India as a whole remains a world of indifference, "un gouffre d'indifférence dans lequel tout est noyé..." which escapes the whites' apprehension both in physical and in mental terms and in which, through this very fact, occidental reason is already at stake. Reason is confronted with an opponent which defies all Western understanding, be it in terms of number, space, or the permanence of the threat.

1 The outside threat as symbol of Unreason

Central to the Indians' presence are the significations of contagion and morbidity embodied in the image of leprosy:

> "Et voici les pèlerins au loin, déjà et encore, les lépreux qui surgissent de la lèpre, hilares, dans leur sempiternelle agonie" (VC p.167)
> Elle est là...à l'ombre d'un buisson creux... Tout à côté de son corps endormi il y a ceux des lépreux.
> Les lépreux se réveillent." (VC p.29)
> ...Il dépasse les arbres à l'ombre desquels les lépreux hilares attendent." (VC p.34)

Through these quotations several phenomena can be discerned. At a general level, we can observe that with leprosy the

---

reduced to its bare minimum with only a few references to disconnected or indistinguishable noises in S.Thala as isolated reminders of a social world. If the narrative of *Le Vice-consul* constitutes an exception at this level, I would suggest that it is mostly because its social dimension finds its greatest relevance in relation to madness and unreason and in the problematic interaction between reason and its opposite.

whites are confronted with an ancestral fear experienced in the Middle Ages and described by Foucault in these terms: "la lèpre a fait apparaître des plages stériles, hantées par la mort, inhabitables qui appartiennent à l'inhumain" (HF p.13). At a more literal level the lepers are evoked waiting (VC p.164), lying down, but they also constitute an animated mass: "les lépreux surgissent" (VC p.167), "se réveillent" (VC p.29), "les lépreux hilares attendent". It then starts to become clear that the threat posed by the lepers is not so much linked to their presence as to their movement. "La réduction des indigènes à une réalité immobile permet d'éliminer ou au moins de réduire la menace.".[3] As Homi Bhabha points out, the European imaginary functions with the stereotype of fixity, which makes its entrance

> "...in the ideological construction of otherness. Fixity...is a paradoxical mode of communication: it connotes rigidity and an unchanging order as well as disorder, degeneracy and daemonic repetition".[4]

The stereotypical fixed vision of the natives does not work any more for the whites of *Le Vice-consul*. In spite of the whites' static mode of apprehension of the Indian reality through the episodic recourse to exoticism, the Indians can no longer be taken as a fixed reality, they are not entirely "knowable and visible" but are felt to be in constant movement. The mesmerising threat of the beggar-woman's peregrination, for instance, resides both in its endless animation and in the obscure power of its unknowable motivation, the power of the lack, of unreason, which remains beyond grasp and allows the "traumatic impact of the return of the oppressed"[5] symbolised in the literal animation of leprosy itself, "la lèpre amoncelée se sépare, bouge, se répand" (VC p.166).

Through their movement, the lepers therefore emulate and reinforce the fear of contagion, a collective fear expressed by the public voice: "savez-vous que les lépreux éclatent sous les coups comme des sacs de poussière" (VC p.114). Indeed dust is allied to the presence of the Indian, - let us recall the evocation of the

---

[3] Jacques Leenhardt, *Lecture Politique du Roman: La Jalousie d'Alain Robbe-Grillet* (Minuit Paris 1973) p.113

[4] Homi Bhabha, 'The Other Question', in *Screen* vol.24 no.6 Nov/Dec 1983

[5] ibid. p.6

servants' movement: "Après le passage, l'odeur reste, de cotonnade et de poussière" (VC p.47) - dust which, like the Indians, cannot be grasped and covers everything with its permanent and insidious presence, even Anne-Marie Stretter's bicycle. This latter image functions metaphorically as a precursory sign of Anne-Marie Stretter's contagion.

What is ultimately at stake is the threat not only of contagious illness, but more generally of madness itself. The lepers' waiting remains enigmatic for the Europeans and symbolises the impossibility of the Other, which repeatedly resists signification. The mention of the "hilarious lepers" (VC pp.34,167) decidedly allies leprosy to madness, a madness which besides is variously and literally mentioned in other instances such as the reference to the lepers as "les fous de Calcutta" (VC pp.105,149). What is at work is a fight between reason and unreason, again strikingly exemplified by the multitude of lepers:

> "Ce qu'on voit avant tout c'est l'enceinte première le long du Gange. Ils sont en rangs ou en cercles, sous les arbres, de loin en loin. Parfois ils disent quelques paroles, Charles Rossett croit les voir de mieux en mieux et que sa vision augmente chaque jour en intensité. Il croit voir maintenant de quoi ils sont faits, d'une matière friable et une lymphe claire circule dans leurs corps. Armées d'hommes en son sans plus de forces, hommes de son à cervelles de son, indolores. Charles Rossett repart.
> Il prend une avenue perpendiculaire au Gange pour éviter les arroseuses qui arrivent lentement du fond du boulevard." (VC p.165)

Unreason is metaphorically represented by this army of dehumanised spectres, an unlocalised danger to which reason can only oppose the mechanical army of the watering machines in a sort of disincarnated fight. This kind of science-fictional confrontation constitutes repeated attempts not only to sweep away the dust of Calcutta, but that of these "hommes de son à cervelles de son", who remain the carriers of contagion. The fear of contagion furthermore provokes madness among the whites; a woman tells the vice-consul:

"la femme d'un secrétaire, chez nous, au consulat d'Espagne, elle devenait folle, elle croyait qu'elle avait attrapé la lèpre, il a fallu la renvoyer, impossible de lui enlever cette idée de la tête" (VC p.112)

In front of a Reason already weakened, the myth of Unreason attacks the whites. Leprosy, which feeds a collective fear among Europeans, can produce madness, but this fear is in itself a sign of non-reason, an irrational symptom, since in fact very few Europeans become mad (VC p.114). What the fear also signifies, however, is the power of the myth of the Indian in the European imaginary by which white reason is placed in a position of impossible confrontation with the imagined danger. The adversary perceived in terms of collective abstraction and permanent threat indeed defies any possible occidental and logical understanding.[6]

Indians are invariably associated in *Le Vice-consul* with deprivation, poverty, ill-health, and lack in general. It is true to say that in a Western culture like that depicted in *Le Vice-consul*, which also functions stereotypically with natives as Other, the anxiety associated with lack and difference constitutes a major threat for the white imaginary.

In *Le Vice-consul*, however, it is not, as in other colonialist literature, so much the position of the whites as ideological subjects in a foreign land which is at stake. It is rather their survival at an almost primary physical level that is threatened. Behind the threat given in terms of illness/physical depravation and encapsulated in the image of leprosy lurks the power of unreason/madness. As such the problematic of *Le Vice-consul* differs from that of most colonial novels and points to a more

---

[6]It is worth noting at this point that fear associated with the multiplicity of Asiatic presence is not unique to the problematic of *Le Vice-consul*, and its significance therefore cannot be restricted to a colonial reading. We are indeed also dealing with a characteristic of the Durasian unconscious. In *Emily-L*, for instance, the female narrator hallucinates another Asiatic presence: "(les Coréens)...Il s'agit d'une même présence indéfiniment multipliée (...) Ces gens paraissent n'avoir qu'un seul et même visage, c'est pourquoi ils sont effrayants" (EL p.11). The link established with fear and unreason is clearly stated: "C'est en moi, secrété par moi. Ça vit d'une vie paradoxale, géniale et cellulaire à la fois. C'est là sans langage pour se dire. C'est une cruauté nue, muette, de moi à moi, logée dans ma tête, dans le cachot mental. Etanche. Avec des percées vers la raison. La vraisemblance, la clarté." (EL p.51)

fundamental operation which attacks the foundations of Western logic, Reason.

As a result, the practice of keeping at a distance exists among the white community of Calcutta in *Le Vice-Consul* as an attempt to negate the threat of what is felt as a danger. Isolated in the foreign land which surrounds them, the European minority cannot, as a means of protection and recuperation of reason, concretely effect the exclusion of the undesirable elements, the natives: in a 'normally' constituted occidental society, Reason would dominate and the structure of confinement would swiftly move into place.[7] But, the Ambassador recalls, the society of the whites in Calcutta is an 'abnormal' one[8] which carries the mark of its own degradation, of its impotence against the external forces of Unreason.

'Exclusion', in its degraded form of non-inclusion, appears in *Le Vice-Consul* to be restricted to the strict observance of separation of places - the whites for instance never visit the Blue Moon, the cabaret situated in Indian territory -, and is also concretely reinforced by the erection of gates around the white residences, themselves surrounded by their gardens.

Yet despite the defence mechanisms set up by the whites around the Embassy or the Prince of Wales to protect their material as well as mental integrity (gates, guards, fences etc.), impermeability between the two worlds cannot be sustained.[9] The mechanism of exclusion fails completely when it allows one outsider to enter without apparent discrimination. Michael Richard's major intrusion, the day when he first met Anne-Marie Stretter by clandestinely penetrating the Embassy, could have been fatal to the group of whites. He recalls how, attracted by Anne-Marie Stretter's music, he easily passed the gates

---

[7]Foucault points out that since the classical age, madness and unreason have been recognized by society as Other, foreign, excluded, and "(...) a été liée à cette terre de l'internement, et au geste qui la lui désignait comme son lieu naturel" (HF p.59)

[8]"les lois qui régissent une société normale, ici, n'ont pas cours" (VC p.135)

[9]This is not *a priori* surprising since impermeability between the two worlds, or total separation of races and cultures in a colonialist context, tends to constitute a (not, of course, exclusively) white fantasy, a protective mechanism inscribed in the history of the white race from the moment when Reason came to assert or safeguard itself as supreme value.

unchallenged: "...un soir, je suis entré dans le parc, les sentinelles m'ont laissé passer, tout était ouvert, je suis entré dans cette pièce où nous étions hier soir" (VC p.187). After such a precedent, it is no wonder that the vice-consul, who, as we shall now see, represents a major and concrete threat of contagion for the white community, should also have to be admitted into the heart of this "...Inde blanche" (VC p.121).

2 The vice-consul as major threat of Unreason

The character of the Vice-consul indeed represents, for the whites, the major threat of Unreason: a menace which cannot be eluded or diffused by the recourse to fictionalisation as was the case for the beggar-woman.[10] With the arrival of the vice-consul, the white group is confronted with unmediated madness. Our main purpose in this part of the chapter will be to explore the ways in which this confrontation takes place in the text.

To cast light upon the impact and the significance of the vice-consul's trangressive presence among the whites, I shall successively consider two contrasting lines of enquiry: first, that which corresponds to the whites' position with the diagnosis of madness applied to the vice-consul, and secondly that according to which the vice-consul asserts himself as a positive figure of transgression. From these two opposing positions, I shall finally show that the vice-consul, like Peter Morgan's fictionalised beggar-woman, becomes a 'figure' of exclusion in the social setting of the Embassy.

In spite of the ambiguity of the term, the word 'figure' appears particularly relevant to the character of the vice-consul and to the theme of madness which concerns us here. If we look at the word 'figure', we find the following:

1. forme extérieure d'un corps
2. illustration, image
3. faire figure: jouer un personnage important
4. personnalité marquante

---

[10]Indeed it could be demonstrated that in Peter Morgan's written account, the beggar-woman's story is depicted as exile, the result of a social curse, and that his account constitutes the most successful device used by the whites to counteract their anguish.

> 5. représentation par le langage
> (vocabulaire ou style)
> a) figures de mots
> b) figures de constructions
> c) figures de rhétorique
>
> (*Le Petit Robert de la Langue Française* 1970 p.704)

We shall endeavour to show in this examination of the vice-consul's madness that the character of Jean-Marc de H-- does not exist in the narrative in its own right, but that he primarily constitutes an image (defn.2), an empty shape or the mirror reflection of a group, always apprehended from the outside (defn.1) via an ideological and moral interpretation, be it public opinion, a circumstantiated file, or the enigma of his gestures and behaviour. The vice-consul as a result becomes pure representation, metaphor of madness (defn.5c) (rhetorical figures), though at the level of his own existence rather than that of language. We shall also see that the vice-consul has a personal impact which remains central (defn.3), as his titular position indicates, and that he is indeed imbued with the chief threat of contagion for the whites.

Throughout this study and whenever appropriate, a comparison with the situation of the fictionalised beggar-woman will also be established to bring to light the specificity of the vice-consul's 'madness'.

The Vice-consul as figure of ambiguity

From the moment of his arrival among the whites, the vice-consul carries the seal of his marginality and becomes for the whites a figure of ambiguity. The whites appear victims of their own mode of thinking when the vice-consul is, on humanitarian grounds, brought into the heart of their community. Anne-Marie Stretter has invited him to the reception since, as the Ambassador recalls,

> "...Nous luttons, ma femme et moi, autant que le protocole le permet contre les exclusions, si justifiées qu'elles puissent paraître" (VC p.44).

The invitation appears justified since in spite of his suspicious past the vice-consul seems indeed to have settled down in Calcutta.

However, despite his apparent regained normality, the vice-consul appears to embody the split between Reason and Unreason; duality constitutes his mode of existence.

Indeed while his appearance can seem familiar and reassuring: "il est grand...il porte le smoking avec aisance" (VC p.123), his physical presence makes his peers feel ill at ease, as if another personality was lurking in the dark; "Aspect trompeur de la silhouette et du visage aux traits réguliers" (VC p.123). The uneasiness stems mainly from his voice and from the expression of his eyes, "la voix d'un autre" (VC p.131) and "le regard d'un autre" (VC p.132). His voice for instance contrasts sharply with his appearance; "une voix ingrate, comme greffée"..."A voir les gens on leur prête des voix qu'ils n'ont pas toujours, c'est son cas" (VC p.131), comments Anne-Marie Stretter. His voice thus alternates between a neutral intonation, "...une voix blanche? On ne sait pas s'il vous questionne ou s'il vous répond" (VC p.112), and a strange whistling (VC pp.75,167) which can also function as metonymy for the whole character, "Près de Charles Rossett la voix sifflante..." (VC p.137); or else the voice can strangely lack resonance:

> "La voix du vice-consul, quand il parle à Anne-Marie Stretter pour la première fois, est distinguée, mais bizarrement privée de timbre, un rien trop aiguë comme s'il se retenait de hurler" (VC p.124).

In addition to possessing this strange voice, the vice-consul also alternatively adopts a fixed, dead gaze, "...cet homme au regard mort...Le regard est fixe" (VC p.119) or a penetrating glance, "un regard difficile à supporter" (VC p.140) which frightens people: "il y a dans son regard une pénétration effrayante. Charles Rossett s'aperçoit qu'il éprouve une légère peur" (VC p.169). Moreover the character's giggle, "il ricane" (VC p.169), and the falseness of the laughter, "le vice-consul rit comme dans un film doublé, faux, faux" (VC p.118),[11] add to the oddity of the

---

[11]Incongruous laughter, incidentally, is not specific to the characters of *Le Vice-Consul* since it often recurs in the Durasian text. Like tears, it mostly constitutes an unexpected occurrence or an ambiguous manifestation, be it that of Elisabeth in *Détruire Dit-elle* (pp.84,87,135) or the same false "il ricane" of B.Alione in the same text, or else the duality of laughter and fear in the captain's wife of *Emily-L* (p.97), or again the complicit but short-lived laughter of *Les Yeux Bleus, Cheveux Noirs* surrounded by constant references to tears. As mentioned

vice-consul's weird expression and explain why people avoid him, "personne ici ne le voit" (VC p.42), or ignore him: "les gens s'écartent instinctivement...c'est un homme qui fait peur" (VC p.103). Even the Ambassador, renowned for his humanitarian presence, hesitates to put his hand on the vice-consul's shoulder and seems to be embarrassed by the latter's gaze (VC p.117).

The strangeness of the vice-consul's physical presence appears to be further reinforced by the sign of an enigmatic sexuality, already directly alluded to in his administrative file: "seul fait marquant, l'absence, apparemment, de liaisons féminines" (VC p.40): "abstinence terrifiante" specifies the public voice (VC p.123). Rossett seems to witness it in the Embassy gardens one day, when the vice-consul approaches Anne-Marie Stretter's bicycle:

> "Le Vice-consul quitte l'allée et s'approche de la bicyclette.
> Il fait quelque chose. A cette distance, il est difficile de savoir exactement quoi. Il a l'air de la regarder, de la toucher, il se penche sur elle longuement, il se redresse, la regarde encore" (VC p.49).

Through this act the vice-consul is posited as the deviant. As could also be shown of the beggar-woman of Morgan's fiction, he bears the stamp of culpability. The words "obscur" and "abominable" express a moral judgement which puts the vice-consul, on the side of moral transgression.[12] And indeed sexual deviancy constitutes a moral crime against the rules of a society which excludes difference to promote normality.

Antecedents of the Vice-consul's Unreason

The arrival of the vice-consul in Calcutta hides an "obscure crime" committed in Lahore, where he shot at random at the lepers piled up in the Shalimar Gardens, outside his residence.

---

above (cf. Chapter 2 p.53) laughter for the Durasian character expresses an alternative mode of being which swiftly alternates with pain and fear, and has more to do with an "impossibilité d'être" in a social context.

[12] I would agree with Marcelle Marini that the term 'solitary' used to qualify his actions is an indirect allusion to masturbation: "...il s'agit d'une masturbation, où se dévoile un corps mimant en sa jouissance la scène sexuelle sous les yeux d'un témoin bouleversé qui se dérobe à une partie de ce qu'il voit...jouissance solitaire où se répète en son corps l'alternance: phallique/châtré, tandis que la bicyclette fétiche représente le corps feminin..." (TF pp.150-151).

"C'est à ce point repoussant Lahore qu'on ne voit rien qui puisse lui être comparé" (VC p.104). Indeed Lahore exists for the Europeans as the tangible proof, albeit remote and distant in the past, of the vice-consul's madness.

With the 'crime' of Lahore, the motivations of which escape the logic of Reason, the vice-consul has concretely penetrated the realm of mental imbalance, of abnormality, and it is the gesture of moral transgression itself which seems to be condemned by the Europeans, "il a fait le pire, mais comment le dire?" (VC p.94), rather than the actual significance of his action: "est-ce tuer que de tuer des lépreux ou des chiens?" (VC p.94). The vice-consul's mad gesture places him on the side of the beggar-woman, on the side of Unreason, of social abnormality since, like her, he has breached the morals of the group. Even in Calcutta, where the vice-consul seems to have regained reason, symptoms reminiscent of the beggar-woman's increasing deprivation of language can be observed in him. In spite of his privileged position by comparison with that of the beggar-woman, a certain uneasiness, "un bafouillage" (VC p.122), in the use of the logical language of Logos betrays his unreason: "Parfois le vice-consul parle très longtemps, de façon inintelligible" (VC p.75).[13]

The hypothesis of congenital morbidity

Nevertheless the vice-consul's 'pathology' appears different from the beggar-woman's imagined unreason, at least if one takes fully into account the recorded information gathered on the vice-consul by the whites. It seems that there is a much more individual basis to the vice-consul's imbalance. Unreason does not appear as the result of a chastisement, of social interdiction, as was depicted in the story of the Cambodian woman banished by her mother, but is itself the primary cause of the mad behaviour which leads to the moral transgression of killing. A logical explanation is favoured by the Ambassador, who prefers to find in the vice-consul's childhood, rather than in the situation of Lahore itself, the cause of the vice-consul's imbalance: "je préfère qu'on en reste aux conjectures habituelles, qu'on cherche dans l'enfance" (VC p.42). The

[13]The incoherence of language as a pointer to madness does indeed occur in other Durasian texts. The incongruity of the "détruire dit-elle" of Alissa, in the text of the same name, appears enough to justify Stein's conclusion about her: "Vous ne m'aviez pas dit qu'Alissa était folle?" (DDE p.36)

hypothesis of congenital morbidity put forward by the group, which recognizes a personal basis for the vice-consul's imbalance, indeed seems based on several forewarnings in the character's past. A delicate state of health in childhood could easily have been at the root of his future state of nervousness, possibly reinforced by a solitary destiny and inclination; as his aunt recalls in a letter sent to the Ambassador, "Très vite il nous a tenues loin de lui, sa mère et moi, et de la moindre confidence bien entendu" (VC p.41). Later in his adolescence some sign of imbalance appears: he is expelled from school for bad behaviour, "il n'est pas précisé laquelle" (VC p.40), the biographical report states enigmatically. His disappearance from Paris remains similarly unexplained, "on ne sait pas pourquoi ni où il va" (VC p.40), while the only clear indication of 'abnormality' in his adult life, "le seul fait marquant", appears to be the absence of women; there are also of course the suspected fits in his Paris house: "C'était il y a moins longtemps, des fracas d'objets qui devaient être des miroirs se produisaient..." (VC p.35). This nervous vulnerability (by comparison with the rest of the Europeans) suggests how the vice-consul, placed in the anguishing mental structure of Lahore, could have become more receptive to the spectacle of suffering: "ses nerfs ont lâché..." (VC p.41) interpret the whites to explain his gesture.

The hypothesis of mental imbalance entertained by the whites to explain the vice-consul's mode of being also constitutes a major temptation for the whites, in order to contain Unreason within the realm of Reason itself. Mental illness nevertheless represents the last recourse for neutralising the vice-consul's threatening unbalance, since even that explanation carries a threat for the Europeans: the vice-consul recalls the possibility of unreason through the recollection of his once-mad behaviour and the ambiguity of his presence. His is a menace more powerful than contagion of unreason; reminiscent of the outside danger, it could spread from one individual to the next, the vice-consul being a member of the white community.

The whites' relativisation of the scenario of mental illness

It could be shown that the whites, when put into an anguishing situation, always resort to the erection of various defence mechanisms: to admit that one member of their group could be affected by madness would be to acknowledge their own vulnerability.[14] In order to meet the vice-consul's threatening psychological impact they minimise, in a very ambivalent move, the hypothesis of mental illness as such, by a strategy of normalisation of the vice-consul's behaviour. This is an enterprise already begun in Europe, if one believes the report on the vice-consul's file where his 'average' adolescent performance seems to be given as a guarantee of normality: "ses notes sont moyennes" (VC p.40) and is later confirmed as a quite average experience: "En somme rien que de très normal, à part cette absence de femmes, et encore, est-ce sûr?" (VC p.41). The final expression of doubt mitigates any allusion to abnormality, and even the vice-consul's disturbing behaviour of shooting at the lepers appears to have been recuperated at Lahore and annexed to reason; "c'est un farceur, un maniaque du revolver" (VC p.41). The former unbalanced behaviour in Lahore is described by the Ambassador as a simple irregularity (VC p.42), as at worst a sign of nervousness, and, in an attempt to make him look familiar, the whites itemise the vice-consul's expressions according to a regulating code; for instance the unbearable gaze suggests, to Charles Rossett, his need to be loved: "on dirait qu'il attend de la douceur et peut-être de l'amour" (VC p.168). His laugh and his discourse on Anne-Marie Stretter are interpreted as signs of inebriation: "il est soûl, pense Rossett" (VC p.120). In fact his laughing reactions, interpreted as forced or false, can, if not attributed to drunkenness, only be a result of fear. The Spanish consul's wife indeed feels relieved when the vice-consul enquires further about leprosy: "elle se rassure, croit avoir découvert enfin quelque sentiment familier chez le vice-consul: la peur" (VC p.113). To be afraid of leprosy is, in the context of Calcutta, an expected reaction, a sign of normality.

It therefore seems clear that this normalising enterprise constitutes a defence mechanism adopted by the whites. The diagnosis of mental illness, too threatening for the Europeans vis a vis the vice-consul's imbalance, is denied in an attempt to recuperate him and to minimise his abnormal behaviour. Such a regulating mechanism seems to serve only the main group, since the vice-consul occupies a marginal place, the place of exclusion:

---

[14]At a more superficial level, the vice-consul of course also represents for the white community a subject of conversation, in that his personality is an enigma to be 'solved'.

"Les intimes ne lui disent pas ce 'Joignez-vous à nous' qui mettrait fin à l'ostracisme, car 'ils ne le souhaitent pas', flairant qu'il n'est pas vraiment l'un des leurs" recalls Marini (TF p.147).[15]

In fact, what is refused in the vice-consul appears to be the alterity of his mode of existence, his very difference, the fact that he seemingly lives in agreement with his emotional drives and expresses them in fits of anger for instance, or in rebelling against the social mould, or even through his deviant sexuality. What cannot be accepted is primarily the coexistence of what is felt in the collective unconscious as Unreason with a surrounding system based on logic, on normative Reason; hence the ambiguous process by which the vice-consul comes to be partially recuperated into the European group and simultaneously kept at a distance on the marginal limit of the white circle.

3 The Vice-consul as positive figure of transgression

Contrary to the beggar-woman, the vice-consul appears not so much as a victim, but soon asserts himself as a positive presence, a figure of transgression. He rarely occupies the place of submission but more often confronts the situation, and ultimately provokes the whites into accepting him. Unreason soon appears to be the result of a choice which entails a different logic and consequently the denunciation of a status quo: the vice-consul seems to have abandoned Paris, moved by the motivation to verify what he already knew of India.

In coming to Lahore, he has functioned according to another mode of logic, an apprehension of reality which still informs him in Calcutta. The vice-consul suggests another type of understanding based on lived experience, where to understand becomes to visualise rather than to explain, to feel rather than to think: "il lui fallait voir Lahore pour être sûr de Lahore" (VC p.137). This sense of physical apprehension moreover recalls the Durasian mode of being hinted at in the character-narrator of *Le Marin de*

---

[15]We have already noted that people tend to avoid the vice-consul, but he is also made responsible for the position of ostracism he occupies: "Certains croient qu'il pourrait, s'il le voulait, les rejoindre mais qu'il ne le désire pas et que cette distance entre un homme et un autre homme, c'est lui, le vice-consul de Lahore, qui veut la garder telle qu'elle a été ce soir, ici, irréductible" (VC p.131)

Gibraltar, theorised in *L'Homme Atlantique*, properly developed in the character of Lol V.Stein and later to be found extensively in most subsequent Duras narratives from *L'Amour* to *Emily-L*.

Knowledge and thought have been evacuated in favour of a more physical stand which informs the vice-consul's apprehension of reality and indeed constitutes, as it does for most of the absent women of Duras' narratives, an important characteristic of someone who functions in the mode of Unreason. This mode is at first difficult to grasp even for Anne-Marie Stretter, who finds it hard to perceive, at the vice-consul's demand, the 'unavoidable' side of Lahore (VC p.127). In a tone which strongly recalls that of *L'Homme Atlantique*, the vice-consul suggests various visualisations: "essayez dans la lumière...aidez-vous de l'idée qu'on est un clown..." (VC p.127). Anne-Marie Stretter, who herself, as we shall see, is on the side of Unreason, still needs a long time to visually apprehend this contradiction in the terms proposed by the vice-consul: to 'perceive' the 'unavoidable' side of Lahore.

This initiation into the perception of Unreason reveals in the vice-consul a strong, assertive sense of being, very remote indeed from the beggar-woman's state of victimisation. The meaning attached by the vice-consul to the perception of Lahore contains a quest for redemption[16] and ultimately also a denunciation of the accepted white status quo. Indeed when faced with the unhealthy mental structure of Lahore in which a handful of wealthy Europeans live side by side with a totally deprived population, the vice-consul's sensitive perception helps him to face the situation rather than escape and take refuge in the usual European bad conscience.[17] What is refused through the criminal gesture of Lahore appears mainly to be the hypocrisy of a given situation. The significance of his gesture corresponds to an angry refusal of the Indian world of suffering and poverty which he already suspected in France. Lahore, says the vice-consul to Anne-Marie Stretter, was a form of hope, hope that this world may not exist after all:

---

[16]This sense of redemption also strongly announces the nature of the characters' unreason in *L'Amour*, which culminates with the anamnesis of the last pages.

[17]The aunt's explanation is shown to be right: "La conduite insensée de mon neveu à Lahore ne témoigne-t-elle pas en fin de compte que quelque secret état de l'âme, de quelque chose qui nous échappe, mais qui n'en est peut-être pas pour autant tout à fait indigne" (VC pp.42-43)

"quand il a été confirmé dans ce qu'il croyait qu'était Lahore avant de la voir il a appelé la mort sur Lahore...et parfois, la mort lui paraissait sans doute trop, une croyance abjecte, une erreur encore, alors il appelait sur Lahore le feu, la mer, des calamités matérielles, logiques, d'un monde exploré" (VC pp.137-139).

Such a redeeming attitude, in which the vice-consul refuses to co-operate with the accepted collective hypocrisy of Lahore, is later reasserted in Calcutta,[18] but at the same time the vice-consul reclaims full acceptance within the group of whites. Such a demand suggests a need for inclusion, a situation in which Unreason would be recognized in its full positivity. Such an insistence can be read, at the psychoanalytic level, as a strong need for fusion with the symbolic mother.[19] The Embassy and its group of whites indeed constitute a symbol of the metropolis, of the motherland, and the Vice-consul's main manifestation of madness in Calcutta seems linked to the refusal which he experiences: he is excluded, kept outside this metaphorically original place. The vice-consul in fact shows considerable distance and lucidity in regard to the effect he has on people: "Lahore fait peur. Je parle faux, vous entendez ma voix? Remarquez, je ne déplore rien. Tout est parfait." (VC p.138). In front of a perfect world epitomised in the final "tout est parfait", the vice-consul's "je parle faux" sets up in a few words the antinomy of individuality versus collectivity. As these words also reveal, the vice-consul does not intend to betray either the past or even his present predicament and, in a tight adherence to his own self, he repeatedly resists the process of normalisation carried out

---

[18]This had incidentally been prefigured at the boarding- school of Montfort. The vice-consul reveals the reason for his expulsion from the school in his conversation with the manager of the White Circle: "Le bonheur gai à Montfort consistait à détruire Montfort...Ils étaient nombreux à le vouloir. Sur la méthode à employer pour ce genre d'entreprise, le vice-consul dit qu'il n'en connaît pas de meilleure que celle de Montfort. Boules puantes d'abord à tous les repas, puis en études, puis en classe, puis au parloir, puis au dortoir, puis, puis..." (VC p.84)

[19]It does, however, appear that the need to regain a place close to the mother does not in itself constitute the root of the vice-consul's madness, as could be shown to be the case for the fictionalised beggar-woman.

by the whites to account for his past actions.[20] Most importantly, he declines to give any attenuating false excuse: "J'ajoute n'avoir pas agi à Lahore dans l'ivresse comme certains ont pu le prétendre" (VC p.39).

This refusal of normalisation constitutes an assertion of Unreason and a denial of exclusion based on his difference of being:- the very exclusion which constitutes the problematic at the heart of the uncomfortable situation of the whites in India. Through his past action and the stand of his personal position, the vice-consul recalls by extension the unacceptability of the Europeans' social position, and refuses or denounces their unbearable status quo. Because of the threat he represents, it therefore soon becomes obvious that, in spite of his active endeavours to be accepted, the vice-consul asserts himself as the man of rupture within the group.

4 The Vice-consul as figure of exclusion

The vice-consul is subjected in Calcutta to a certain form of exclusion: a dual ambiguous movement of exclusion, by which, as we have seen, the whites attempt on the one hand to assimilate him by minimising or normalising his 'exaggerated' behaviour and actions in order to lessen their own anxiety, and on the other hand to reject him or to reject his attitude, even paradoxically, in its more normalised form; to fall in love with Anne-Marie Stretter, for instance, after all the fate of any male European in the Embassy, appears to be denied as a possibility for the vice-consul.

Although exclusion at this stage is still not very clear, it is when the vice-consul happens to be perceived as an insistent figure of transgression, and when his unreason ultimately asserts itself, that he becomes the definite actualisation of madness among the whites.

---

[20]The vice-consul's own written declaration about what happened at Lahore simply acknowledges the facts gathered against him and, instead of providing excuses, simply asserts his inability to account reasonably for his actions: "...je me borne ici à constater l'impossibilité où je suis de rendre compte de façon compréhensible de ce qui s'est passé à Lahore" (VC p.39).

The Vice-consul as actualisation of madness

The fit of madness which seizes the vice-consul at the Embassy reception (VC pp.145-147), "la crise de folie", perfectly epitomises both the demand for inclusion on the part of the vice-consul and the mechanism of exclusion which sets itself up when madness so boldly asserts itself. An examination of the interplay of the various elements present in this episode sums up what has already been shown of the specificity of the vice-consul's unreason, both from his own point of view and from that of the whites. The analysis of this sudden manifestation of unreason which marks him as the madman, the man in rupture with the group, will also summarize the attitude of the occidental man in relation to the one who has dared to transgress established order to bluntly assert that which is sensed as a lack of reason.

Towards the end of the reception given by Anne-Marie Stretter, while the last drinks are poured at the already half-empty tables, the vice-consul, who has just left Anne- Marie Stretter at the end of their dance, suddenly becomes the blind prey of his pulsions and the actualisation of madness itself.

1   "Anne-Marie Stretter passe devant le buffet sans s'arrêter, elle se dirige vers l'autre salon. Elle vient d'y entrer lorsque le vice-consul de Lahore pousse son premier cri. Quelques uns comprennent:
5   Gardez-moi!
              On dit: il est ivre mort.
              Le vice-consul va vers Peter Morgan et Charles Rossett.
              - Je reste ce soir ici, avec vous! crie-t-il.
              Ils font les morts.
10   L'ambassadeur prend congé. dans le salon octogonal trois hommes soûls dorment dans des fauteuils. On sert à boire une dernière fois. Mais déjà les tables sont à moitié vides.
              - Vous devriez rentrer, dit Charles Rossett.
15   Peter Morgan attrape des sandwiches dans les plateaux qu'on enlève, demande qu'on en laisse, dit qu'il a faim.
              - Vous devriez rentrer, dit également Peter Morgan.
              Le vice-consul de Lahore traverse, croit-on, une crise d'arrogance.

20   - Pourquoi?
         Ils ne le regardent pas, ils ne lui répondent pas.
         Alors il crie encore:
         - Je veux rester avec vous, laissez-moi rester avec vous
         une fois.
25   Il les toise. On dira plus tard: Il nous toisait.
         On dira: Il y avait de l'écume collée à la commissure de ses
         lèvres. Nous n'étions plus que quelques-uns, on ne voyait que
         lui, il y avait un profond silence quand il a crié. C'est la
         colère, partout où il est allé il a dû se signaler par des colères
30   subites, des frénésies comme celles-là...On pense: Cet homme,
         c'est la colère et la voici, nous la voyons.
         Charles Rossett n'oubliera jamais: le lieu se vide,
         s'agrandit. Des lumières ont été éteintes. On enlève les
         plateaux. On a peur. L'heure du vice-consul est arrivée. Il
35   crie.
         - Soyez calme, dit Charles Rossett, je vous en supplie.
         - Je reste! hurle le vice-consul.
         Charles Rossett le prend par le revers de son smoking.
         - Vous êtes impossible, décidément.
40   Le vice-consul supplie.
         - Une fois. Un soir. Une seule fois, gardez- moi auprès
         de vous.
         - Ce n'est pas possible, dit Peter Morgan, excusez-nous,
         le personnage que vous êtes ne nous intéresse que lorsque
45   vous êtes absent.
         Le vice-consul se met à sangloter sans un mot.
         On entend: Quel malheur, mon Dieu.
         Et puis c'est le silence une deuxième fois.
         Anne-Marie Stretter paraît à la porte du salon. Derrière elle
50   il y a Michael Richard. Le vice-consul tremble de tous ses
         membres, il va vers elle en courant. Elle ne bouge pas. Le
         jeune Peter Morgan rattrape le vice-consul qui ne sanglote
         plus et le mène vers la porte du salon octogonal. Le
         vice-consul se laisse faire. On dirait qu'il attendait cela. On
55   voit Peter Morgan qui lui fait traverser le parc, on voit les
         sentinelles ouvrir les portes, le vice-consul qui passe, les
         portes qui se referment. On entend encore des cris. Et ces
         cris cessent. Alors Anne-Marie Stretter dit à Charles Rossett:
         Venez avec nous maintenant. Charles Rossett cloué sur place

60   la regarde. On entend:
      Ne riait-il pas tout en pleurant?
          Charles Rossett suit Anne-Marie Stretter."

                                              (VC pp.145-147)

This episode takes on all the sudden aspects of a violent
mental crisis, with a sudden disorientation of senses. The
symptomatology of the vice-consul's mental manifestations recalls
violent episodes of mental disturbance (lines 26-27, 50-51). In this
episode, wrapped in biblical overtones which allude mainly to its
premeditation, "l'heure du vice-consul est arrivée" (line 34), the
vice-consul confronts the group with the rupture of his Unreason.
He becomes Foucault's pure pathos. "il est la catastrophe" asserts
Anne-Marie Stretter, or he is a "lyrical explosion", a manifestation
usually obliterated behind the objective terms of mental illness.[21]
The group is confronted with the excess of his being, with the
explosion of his madness, with this "capacité de déchirement, de
souffrance, de vertige et d'émotion";[22] hence the vice-consul's
threatening impact which, as we propose to see in more detail
later, almost instantly sets up the structure of exclusion.

    In spite of its violent, unexpected manifestation, the
vice-consul's vigorous expression of unreason appears again to stem
from a premeditated demand for a recognized transgressive
existence. It is in this sense that the enigmatic biblical phrase
"l'heure du vice-consul est arrivée" takes on its full significance.
What appears to be a punctual episode, a sudden uncontrolled loss
of reason, had in fact already been envisaged by the vice-consul
and by Anne-Marie Stretter as a provocative demand for inclusion
among the whites. In a typically Durasian manner,[23] this demand
happens to correspond to the restaging of a previous occurrence,
in which the vice-consul strongly refused the normalising process
customary to the whites.

---

[21]Michel Foucault, preface to 1st edition of *L'Histoire de la Folie*, referred to in
Felman op.cit p.52

[22]Felman op.cit. p.52

[23]The Durasian reader is indeed accustomed to this endless restaging of events
or sequences in Duras' texts. Compared, for instance, with *Le Ravissement de Lol
V.Stein*, where the reduplication of the episode of the Ball structures the
story-line, or with the fictional circularity of *L'Amour*, repetitive devices are
nevertheless relatively rare in *Le Vice-consul*.

The vice-consul had previously refused to fit into the integrative mould of the white man afraid of leprosy, the symbol of death and unreason. His assertion to the Spanish consul's wife: "la lèpre je la désire au lieu d'en avoir peur" (VC p.131) appears to be ignored: "Il paraît que vous avez peur de la lèpre?" inquires the wife. Such a refusal of his problematic provokes an uncontrollable episode which prefigures his subsequent fit of madness at the Embassy reception:

> Le vice-consul pousse une basse exclamation de colère, il pâlit, il jette son verre qui se brise. Il y a un silence. Il rugit tout bas:
> - Je savais qu'on ferait un sort à une chose que je n'ai pas dite, comme c'est terrible...
> - Mais vous êtes fou...ça n'est pas déshonorant d'avoir peur de la lèpre...
> - C'est un mensonge. (VC p.139)

Anger then suddenly gives way to joy when the vice-consul realizes later that the false explanation stems from Anne-Marie Stretter's protective intervention. The latter's complicity appears established.

This incident leads the way to his subsequent premeditated defiance of the group. Encouraged by Anne-Marie Stretter's now admitted complicity, "je suis avec vous complètement comme avec personne d'autre, ici ce soir, aux Indes" (VC p.144), the vice-consul announces: "Je vais faire comme s'il était possible de rester avec vous ce soir ici" (VC p.144).

The fit of madness which defines him as the madman, the man in rupture with the group, therefore seems to reveal in the vice-consul a provocative and coldly premeditated demand for inclusion which again supports Foucault's thesis according to which one can discern a lot of reason in unreason. Once again, as this instance shows, the main characteristic of the vice-consul's acute manifestation of Unreason stems from anger: "cet homme c'est la colère...", anger at the hypocrisy of a situation, be it in Lahore or Calcutta, where at a personal level he denounces the pretence of his false inclusion among the whites, and insists on full recognition.

The Vice-consul as figure of false exclusion

With this demand, the vice-consul represents a major disruptive element in an ordered society, and his unacceptable request for real and complete integration manifests a refusal of the common social consensus based on marginal acceptance: "Il crie...gardez-moi..." (VC 146)

During this episode of madness, various explanations are suggested, again successively favoured by the White Reason in a now familiar attempt at masking reality and the real nature of the vice-consul's outburst. The repeated and insistent confrontation with the group - he shouts, shrieks, begs, sobs, etc. - precipitates the only possible recourse of complete exclusion for a Reason trapped in its own limitations. Peter Morgan expresses the wish of a group driven to the brink of its own impossibility: "Excusez-nous le personnage que vous êtes ne nous intéresse que lorsque vous êtes absent" (VC p.146 line 43-45). In a dramatic atmosphere of catastrophe, "quel malheur, mon Dieu" (line 47), the vice-consul suddenly becomes an excluded figure; Peter Morgan leads him outside: "on voit les sentinelles ouvrir les portes, le vice-consul qui passe, les portes qui se referment" (lines 54-57).[24]

Thus so long as the vice-consul adopts the whites' problematic, which consists of bearing the situation rather than confronting it, his inclusion inside the gates remains possible; but with his insistent request, the break from the group is unavoidable and the vice-consul becomes marked as the figure of exclusion.

Thus the vice-consul, in spite of his more positive and assertive mode of existence, finally repeats or duplicates the fate of the beggar-woman. At the end of the Embassy reception the vice-consul's situation is indeed, if only for one evening, assimilated to the beggar-woman's physical predicament. The vice-consul joins the same geographical place of exclusion, the place of madness and contagion, outside the safety of the gates: "titubant il commence à marcher le long du Gange entre les lépreux" (VC p.150), a place where he belongs; he later admits to Rossett in a hardly metaphorical way: "je sais, je suis une plaie" (VC p.168). Since "la

---

[24]The fact that it is precisely Peter Morgan, author of the account of the beggar-woman's fictionalised madness, who delivers the vice-consul's sentence of exclusion, reinforces our thesis, according to which in spite of his apparently real desire to approach and fuse himself with madness through the figure of the Cambodian woman, Morgan cannot really be taken seriously. His fear of madness and inbuilt instant mechanism of exclusion demonstrate that his literary effort corresponds primarily to a mythical apprehension of reality, the function of which is to reinforce the whites' defence mechanisms.

plaie" figuratively means 'the scourge', this can be read as a direct allusion to leprosy itself, and as suggesting the assimilation of the vice-consul to leprosy and to the threat of unreason which the latter symbolises.

The vice-consul does not, however, settle for very long as the figure of exclusion; soon, when his outburst of unreason seems to be over, he reintegrates himself into the marginality of the group. His place remains with the director of the European Circle adjacent to the Embassy palace, a similar outcast, "un ivrogne" recalls Rossett,[25] while his definitive exclusion away from Calcutta is envisaged; "où l'affecter?" (VC p.43) wonders the Ambassador. In fact this semi-reinsertion appears to be the result of an interaction between two concomitant structures of exclusion: Indians/whites on the one hand, and whites/vice-consul on the other. The chief structure of exclusion, Indians/whites, reinjects the vice-consul into the whites' circle. The structure of exclusion cannot be totally applied to the vice-consul in the colonial context of Calcutta because of his white origin; at most he can be sent away or transferred to another post. One is indulgent towards Jean-Marc de H. since the other external threat, that of the Indians, prevails; indeed as long as the main defence mechanisms aimed at negating the Indians are firmly set in place, the vice-consul can be tolerated closer to the group. Soon after the reception evening and the vice-consul's famous outburst, the whites again produce many explanations to minimise the episode of Unreason, be it drunkenness (VC p.152), comedy (VC p.160) or a simulation to seek attention (VC p.169). The vice-consul himself, wavering in his demand for recognition, declares to Rossett in a movement of regained reason: "J'ai perdu la tête, je me suis cru tout permis, je suis d'une maladresse impardonnable" (VC p.168)..."j'ai fait gaffe sur gaffe, hier au soir, ...comment rattraper cela?" (VC p.171). He soon utters a servile demand for rehabilitation: "je ne tiens pas le coup, il faut m'aider" (VC p.172), which justifies the European hypothesis of morbidity, and identifies him with the figure of passive victim.

The vice-consul ultimately appears as a false figure of exclusion, trapped between two antithetical poles, between the

---

[25]He has become, in a mode reminiscent of the lepers in 16th century Europe, that "figure insistante et redoutable" which has to be driven off. (cf. HF p.6)

desired recognition of his Unreason and the fear of exclusion, between his asserted difference and the need to be assimilated to the group. This clearly shows that his rupture with the group is not/cannot be complete in spite of his increased exclusion following the reception evening; hence it is that the vice-consul can fulfil his true function in this asepticized world of the Embassy and become a figure of contagion.

5 The vice-consul as figure of contagion

We have already shown that the vice-consul's lack of reason exists in response to an obstinate desire to face an external if withheld reality, to adhere to "le réel c'est à dire l'impossible".[26] Unreason for the vice-consul, however, exists more as a refusal than as an aspiration.

India constitutes the unifying place necessary to the vice-consul to sustain his state of Unreason. Through India the gap between interiority and exteriority, between the delirious belligerence of his internal being and his environment, can be narrowed so as to reach the essence of Unreason, which at the same time exists as "l'ivresse du sensible, la fascination de l'immédiat, et la douloureuse ironie où s'annonce la solitude du délire" (HF p.371). Only India can provide him with the suitable scope for Unreason; the extremity of its suffering added to that of its climate, this "fantastique saison", this "énorme été" (VC p.74) can give some relief to one who lives his emotional drives and can reconcile what too often remains as a split with the outside. Summer heat constitutes a recurrent feature in most of Duras' narratives. The unbearable heat of India, like that of the Italian summer of *Les Petits Chevaux de Tarquinia* or *Le Marin de Gibraltar*, while putting the characters in an extreme situation, leads them to abandon any reasonable position. To partake of this state of extremity appears to be the vice-consul's wish: "de l'enchevêtrement, de la confusion de toutes les douleurs, on dirait qu'il réclame sa part" (VC p.140).

However, despite what happens at the reception evening and his more general impact on the European group, the vice-consul cannot sustain a permanent state of Unreason. Let us recall his only (brief) experience of total exclusion, and his subsequent need

---

[26]Felman op.cit. p.74

to be partially recuperated by the group, to exist in a compromising marginality. Too full of himself, still too possessed by his own problematic, that of refusal, the vice-consul cannot let himself slip into a state of absence, that of the evacuation of Reason. He is unable to be fully carried by a detached movement of desire, since such desire only proves for him to be the locus of a major lack:

> "je me suis efforcé d'aimer à plusieurs reprises...je n'ai jamais été hors de l'effort d'aimer...Faute d'aimer, j'ai cherché à m'aimer, mais je n'y suis pas parvenu" (VC p.77).

Contrary to the female characters, from Lol to Emily, who embody the Durasian mode of being, the vice-consul, as we have observed, approaches Unreason more as a refusal than as an aspiration. His represents a first stage, albeit a necessary one, of the Durasian existence: that of refusal.[27] He has not reached the stage of indifference and lack of identity which otherwise typifies Duras' (female) characters. It is mainly because he cannot reach the state of Unreason which he suspects in Anne-Marie Stretter that his attraction towards her becomes so powerful and liberating: "Je suis sorti de cet effort (d'aimer)...depuis quelques semaines" (VC p.77). In her presence, he can even experience instantly the rise of feelings, the emptying pregnancy of desire:

> "le jour de mon arrivée, j'ai vu une femme traverser le parc de l'Ambassade. Elle se dirigeait vers les tennis déserts...je me suis aperçu qu'ils étaient déserts après son départ. Il s'était produit un déchirement de l'air, sa jupe contre les arbres. Et ses yeux m'avaient regardé" (VC pp.79-80).

This liberation remains, however, chiefly linked to the incidence of Anne-Marie Stretter's presence, inevitably bound to end with the vice-consul's expected departure for Bombay: "Je m'y vois, indéfiniment photographié sur une chaise longue au bord de la mer d'Oman" (VC p.212).

---

[27]In this sense the vice-consul belongs among Duras' earlier characters, for example the narrator of *Le Marin de Gibraltar* or the old woman of *Les Petits Chevaux de Tarquinia* who stubbornly refuses to sign a form to acknowledge her son's death.

At the end of this chapter we can finally assert that the vice-consul proves only to be a catalyst, a carrier of contagion. He exists mainly as the "man of passage" who threatens to spread the contagion of his madness and to unleash the obscure forces of Unreason. Having arrived from Lahore, and awaiting transfer to Bombay, the vice-consul perfectly epitomises the story of the passage of madness, a real and concrete threat of contagion in this white world, protected on all sides by sophisticated mental mechanisms. With his passage from the outside, from Lahore, metaphorical location of madness, to the inside of the palace, the vice-consul contaminates his environment by reactivating in Anne-Marie Stretter, queen of white Calcutta and the very symbol of imperialism, her latent state of Unreason. No longer isolated behind the safety of the Embassy gates, her dormant state of Unreason retaliates. The vice-consul therefore appears as a major agent of Unreason, hence the justification for his titular position; his contagion pervades the white nucleus of the Embassy centred around Anne-Marie Stretter.

As long as the vice-consul remains in his marginal position, the threat hovers over the whites without attacking their problematic in Calcutta, their ideological apparatus based on occidental reason and power being too deeply seated and unmovable. However, as in the action of Robbe-Grillet's *La Jalousie* and *L'Année Dernière à Marienbad*,[28] the vice-consul represents the newcomer who has penetrated a comparatively global structure of enclosure. We find indeed the same enclosed locus, the Embassy in which, as we shall show later, obsolete values and dead people prevail. The problematic which allows the vice-consul to become the active figure of contagion remains, however, very specific. In contrast to what happens in *La Jalousie* or in *L'Année Dernière à Marienbad*, in which what is at stake for the newcomer is the attempt to free another human being from the old world which detains (him) as a prisoner,[29] let us recall that

---

[28]"...Il est remarquable que *L'Année Dernière à Marienbad* se présente comme une reprise rigoureuse de la structure de l'action de *La Jalousie*. Celle-ci pourrait également se résumer: l'univers de *La Jalousie* est constitué par une structure close (la maison) où règnent des valeurs et des gens morts." (Jacques Leenhardt op. cit. p.28)

[29]"Il s'agit de transformer un être afin qu'il s'échappe de la prison où un monde trop vieux le retient." (ibid. p.28)

the presence of the vice-consul serves to reactivate the morbidity already present in the characters of this enclosed world, even if ultimately, after the vice-consul's removal to a safer distance, the episode of madness can be apprehended simply as an unsettling crisis in the seemingly eternal continuity of the secret world of the Embassy.

Chapter 5

ANNE-MARIE STRETTER'S STATE OF UNREASON

In this chapter, which could be viewed as an appendix to the analysis of the vice-consul's state of madness, I propose to examine the nature of Anne-Marie Stretter's unreason. Paradoxically, if we consider the importance of the character at the level of Durasian production[1] or, more relevantly here, in terms of the nature of Anne-Marie Stretter's marginality, we can only conduct the analysis of Anne-Marie Stretter's unreason indirectly, through the examination of the vice-consul's narrative function as carrier of contagion.

Indeed very little can be and ultimately is said about unreason and madness in *Le Vice-consul*, the fictional content of which remains within the linearity of reason, even if the major enterprise of the narrative ultimately aims at demonstrating the gradual erosion of reason by unreason. This is why the two characters of Anne-Marie Stretter and the beggar-woman outside the gates, who respectively end up embodying these dimensions of

---

[1]Marguerite Duras has repeatedly stressed the importance of the character of Anne-Marie Stretter: "C'est un des personnages dominants de mon enfance" (*Marguerite Duras à Montréal* p.133). "Elle est plus mon désir" asserts Duras to Michelle Porte, "que ce que je croyais être mon désir, elle répond plus que je ne questionne, si vous voulez" (quoted in 'Les Indes Impossibles', ibid. p.131)

An impressive amount of work has been produced about this character, including Marini's chapters in *Territoires du Féminin* ('Je-écris-elle'; pp.122-136), and Péraldi's 'Les Indes Impossibles' and Gagné's 'L'Ombilic des Indes', both in *Marguerite Duras à Montréal*.

unreason and madness, remain very cryptic, but nevertheless highly influential. They are viewed primarily from the outside as enigmatic, threatening presences. The narrative of *Le Vice-Consul* indeed stops where Anne-Marie Stretter's unreason starts. The text abandons her when she fully enters this new dimension, unable to elaborate further on what cannot be apprehended from the side of reason and proving therefore that the impact of the text resides rather in the confrontation between reason and unreason.

In a movement which fully respects both the problematic of the narrative of *Le Vice-consul* and my enterprise in the examination of madness in relation to society, I shall thus consider Anne-Marie Stretter's unreason in relation to her passage to this new state of being. Through this movement, we shall find ourselves in a position to ascribe to unreason a major shift of meaning, marked by a complete swing from the negative to the positive pole. In that process unreason will be linked to what Deleuze and Guattari qualify as "desiring-production" in their book *Anti-Oedipus*, in which desire is not viewed as goal-directed in its idealistic (dialectical, nihilistic) conception which causes one to look upon it primarily as a lack, but is rather apprehended as a production of reality.[2]

To conduct this study of the character of Anne-Marie Stretter in its relation to the shift which takes place in her, in the passage from a position of reason to that of unreason, I shall follow a broadly chronological approach situated in close connection with the text. I shall therefore be led into examining in detail certain key sequences of the text: for example Anne-Marie Stretter's interaction with the vice-consul at the reception evening (VC pp.112-128) or the final sequence which exemplifies her move towards unreason (VC pp.185-200).

---

[2]Deleuze and Guattari, op. cit. p.33. These authors signal that this conception goes against that of classical psychoanalysis, insofar as the latter supports the traditional logic of desire, by which desire is conceived of as production of fantasies, of an imaginary world which functions as a double for reality, the real object that desire lacks being related to an extrinsic social production. But, Deleuze and Guattari argue: "Il n'y a pas d'une part une production sociale de réalité, et d'autre part une production désirante de fantasme" (p.36). This presentation of desire supported by needs, where desire is regarded as what produces the fantasy and is produced by detaching itself from the object, intensifies the lack by making it absolute until it reaches "une insuffisance incurable de l'être."

Through Anne-Marie Stretter's passage to unreason, we shall see how, from being a full, positive character in the society of Calcutta, she gradually becomes trapped within her own accommodating function and is increasingly led to expose herself to the vice-consul's force of contagion. In this confrontation it will become apparent that her own latent state of unreason becomes reactivated until she finally locates herself in the realm of unreason itself.

1 Anne-Marie Stretter and the antinomy of 'être' and 'paraître'

Anne-Marie Stretter as representative of occidental logic

The contagion of unreason from the vice-consul to Anne-Marie Stretter happens insidiously. Indeed, through her contact with the vice-consul, this woman, who as we shall see used to live in the most perfect stereotype, "la reine de Calcutta" (TF p.195), gradually becomes rejected by her own unreason.

Before the vice-consul's arrival, Anne-Marie Stretter had appeared beyond reproach, "irréprochable" (VC p.100) in her representational function, or, as Marcelle Marini puts it, she could be seen as "une femme bien insérée dans la société, entourée d'un cercle exclusivement masculin" (TF p.102). Taken away from a local administrator by her husband seventeen years previously, she had become, in Calcutta, the major representation of the white colonialist presence.

Her role is indeed central in the European community of Calcutta, while her power appears multiform. Well established in 'society', she is the embodiment of the occidental presence. The bourgeois background of her previous existence moreover provides a guarantee for the fulfilment of her present function. Was she not at one time, as "un espoir de la musique occidentale" (VC p.186), educated in and initiated to the art of music in Venice, having learnt to play the piano from the age of seven; "J'en ai fait partout, longtemps, un peu tout le temps..." (VC p.111).[3] At the time of her

---

[3]Wealthy or comfortable middle-class backgrounds constantly recur throughout Duras' production, and this feature has been attacked by the anti-Durasian critic as a sign of her political and ideological ambiguity. This, however, shows a misunderstanding of Duras' fiction. In fact the function of wealthy backgrounds is to secrete boredom and idleness, and as such resembles that of holiday time, which is to be found in texts such as *Les Petits Chevaux de Tarquinia*. Wealth and

encounter with the vice-consul, however, she lives in Calcutta with her husband and her two daughters (VC p.94). She leads, in Calcutta, a very punctual and regular existence: "...tennis, promenades, parfois le Cercle européen le soir" (VC p.96); perfect mother and almost perfect wife, since the relationship to her husband, imbued with bourgeois morality, implicitly allows for the coexistence of her lovers: "On dit que ses amants sont anglais, inconnus du milieu des ambassades. On dit que l'ambassadeur sait" (VC p. 96). She also represents a kind of "image d'Epinal", immediately perceived by Rossett at the initial welcoming reception: "il y a un divan recouvert d'une cretonne rose sur lequel elle est assise...droite, sa robe est blanche, elle est pâle sous le hâle de Calcutta, comme tous les Blancs" (VC p.106). Fixed in her stereotyped function of representation, her whole physical being appears affected; with her stultified eyes "trop clairs...découpés comme ceux des statues" (VC p.92), she takes on the rigidity of a theatre figure.

However, beyond the rigidity of her conventional role she has acquired a well-deserved reputation in her world. Public opinion considers her the key figure in the white community at the Embassy. Her presence in Calcutta remains active - "elle est...occupée, cette femme-là de Calcutta" (VC p.96) - and her personal power undeniably exists at many complementary levels both ouside and inside the Embassy palace, be it through her foreign but charitable presence, through her potentially morally problematic power of seduction or through the conciliatory function which makes her a representative of occidental logic.

All these aspects make her particularly present to her surroundings. For example she performs perfectly her charitable task. Every day she gives orders to relieve the suffering of those who die of hunger outside the gates of the Embassy. The public voice, full of admiration, does not hesitate to assert: "c'est la femme la meilleure de Calcutta" (VC p.127). Her charisma then spreads beyond her charitable function. She is also renowned in her immediate surroundings for her exceptional welcoming

---

leisure, the effect of which is often reinforced by the summer heat, help promote, in the idle, heat-exhausted characters, the emergence of an inner state of being: that of Unreason.

qualities. Is she not, according to the vice-consul, one of those women,

> "celles qui ont l'air de dormir dans les eaux de la bonté sans discrimination...celles vers qui vont toutes les vagues de toutes les douleurs, ces femmes accueillantes" (VC p.120);

qualities which are particularly actualised during the reception evenings which she organizes at the palace for the whites' entertainment, or alternatively obvious in such generous gestures as the invitation to the reception, sent without hesitation to such an outcast as the vice-consul.

The antinomy of 'être' and 'paraître'

Her influence amid the white group, however, results primarily not from this particular trait of personality as such, but rather from the twofold dominance she exerts over her immediate surroundings, from the antinomy which she embodies between 'être' and 'paraître'.

Anne-Marie Stretter is indeed a kaleidoscopic character who on the one hand possesses an undeniable power of seduction which mainly affects her male audience, and who on the other hand represents a normalising power in the European society of Calcutta. Seduction nevertheless is the more immediate impression instantly generated in any newcomer[4] like Rossett: "Un seul regard et les portes de la blanche Calcutta doucement cèdent" (VC p.107). To refer to the vice-consul's words, she undoubtedly appears beautiful, attractive (VC pp.170,171) to her male counterparts, all the more so since beyond her pure physical attraction resides a wider personal seductive power. Her means of seduction are varied, from the more external musical charm which may attract passers-by from the street whenever she plays the piano,[5] to the most confidential tone she does not fail to adopt

---

[4]"A Calcutta, lieu unique de la fiction, l'ensemble des personnages masculins gravitent autour d'Anne-Marie Stretter, elle qui est au (le) coeur du Saint-Synode" remarks Marini (TF p.98).

[5]Let us recall that Michael Richard was drawn into the palace and consequently remained in Calcutta because of her: "Avant de connaître Anne-Marie, dit Michael Richard, je l'entendais jouer à Calcutta, le soir, sur le boulevard; ça m'intriguait beaucoup, je ne savais pas qui elle était, j'étais venu en touriste à

whenever she converses with any newcomer, inviting him instantly to penetrate further into her private sphere: "Elle a une façon comme confidentielle de parler du climat de Calcutta" (VC p.122).[6] Furthermore her constant availability, her lack of discrimination among her male partners, which may help to explain why she seems indifferent at times, add to her tantalizing charm. "C'est une femme qui n'a pas de...préférences, c'est cela...l'important" (VC p.171), indeed she is one of these women "qui rendent fou d'espoir" (VC p.120) summarises the vice-consul.

The availability of Anne-Marie Stretter is in tune with most of Duras' other female characters, from the woman of *L'Amour* to the captain's wife in *Emily-L*, and strongly recalls Lol's mode of desire after the ball at T.Beach. The word "fou" can also here be taken literally: it alludes to the radical impact which Duras' women recurrently have on men; be it Anna's influence on the narrator of *Le Marin de Gibraltar* or that of the woman in *L'Amour* on the traveller, or again Lol's influence on Jacques Hold. Durasian female figures do indeed frequently lead their male partners to a state of unreason which derives, as already variously mentioned, from desire and a gradual loss of identity.

Beyond this seductive power, Anne-Marie Stretter performs a normalizing function within her own group. She indeed occupies a referential position and, just as she shaped her husband's

---

Calcutta, je me souviens, je ne tenais pas du tout le coup...je voulais repartir dès le premier jour et...c'est elle, cette musique que j'entendais qui fait que je suis resté - que...j'ai pu rester à Calcutta" (VC p.187).

[6] Marcelle Marini reads further into the text and sees a premeditative element in Anne-Marie Stretter's seduction.

"Celle qui fait son choix, écrit ou dit: 'Venez', garde fixé à elle ses élus à l'intérieur de 'son boudoir élégant' quand elle n'emmène pas à son gré une nouvelle conquête dans sa villa des Iles: à elle on ne résiste jamais. Partout, toujours, dans le désir vécu de façons si diverses qui constituent les facettes d'Anne-Marie Stretter, s'inscrit la figure unique de la femme, qui réduit les hommes à être (se faire) les objets de son désir à elle" (TF p.99).

This claim, which could be supported by Rossett's unease vis a vis Anne-Marie Stretter when he feels pressurised into accepting her invitation to the Islands, stresses too strongly, in my view, the manipulative aspect of Anne-Marie Stretter's seduction; Marini misjudges here the nature of Anne-Marie Stretter's power of attraction, which exists, as for most other Durasian female figures, beyond the character's conscious or unconscious volition. As we have already shown with Lol, Duras' women characters attract men through their alternative mode of being, which is based on lack of preferential desire.

existence by, for instance, discouraging him from writing fictions (VC p.136), she now exerts a powerful influence upon the whites. Such power stems from the position of knowledge which she occupies: a multi-faceted knowledge which alternately embraces all degrees of understanding, from the simplest know-how, mentioned above in the performance of her conventional duties, to more factual knowledge and also, eventually, to the deeper intelligence of any given situation. She is for instance the only person able to provide concrete information about the beggar-woman who so mesmerises Peter Morgan and his peers; as Marini mentions:

> "le chant de la femme, Anne-Marie Stretter seule peut l'identifier, en dire l'origine - 'Savannakhet' -elle seule en (re)connaît la langue; l'unique événement qui permette de 'la retrouver dans le passé', en sa singularité, c'est 'la vente d'une enfant' à laquelle Anne-Marie Stretter 'a assisté il y a dix-sept ans'" (TF p.119).

Indeed Anne-Marie Stretter becomes endowed for the whites with a privileged knowledge about this living enigma, "appelée à être la médiatrice de cette figure inconnue, la traductrice en leur langage de cette musique pour eux incompréhensible" (TF pp.119-120).

Similarly, she becomes the only person able to mediate between the vice-consul and the group. Although Anne-Marie Stretter at first observes a reserve towards the vice-consul (VC p.37), she soon appears to be the only one who understands him, who dares to approach him, to converse with him at length: "Non seulement elle danse (...) mais elle va même lui parler" (VC p.121) observes the public voice admiringly. She also seems capable of explaining the vice-consul's behaviour to the others: not only can she ascertain facts about him for Michael Richard (since she has access to his file (VC p.159)) but she is also able to grasp the vice-consul's enigma; he is not desperate, but rather "un homme mort", "une catastrophe" (VC p.129).[7] Endowed with knowledge

---

[7] The use of the term 'catastrophe' can be explained through Anne-Marie Stretter's cultural awareness of the impossibility of accounting for the vice-consul's gesture in psychological terms. He is the 'catastrophe' for a world which cannot assimilate him and justify what has happened at Lahore. In a society glued to the literality of events, where to kill lepers appears worse than

and wisdom, she tries to appease the uneasiness around her and, with calm composure, advises everyone to forget about him: "Ça ne servirait à rien que nous en parlions...Il n'est pas nécessaire de chercher davantage" (VC p.129). With the disarray in which the vice-consul's fit of madness has left the whites, Anne-Marie Stretter's regulating influence becomes stronger. She reassures Rossett about the vice-consul: "laissez-le, je vous assure...Il n'a besoin de rien" (VC p.155). She provides answers to Morgan's anxious questions: "Que va-t-il faire vers les tennis? - Il va au hasard, il cherche au hasard" (VC p.154). She even volunteers to normalize further the vice-consul's behaviour in an attempt to set at rest the minds around her:

> "Elle parle en souriant.
> - C'est vrai qu'il a cru nécessaire d'en passer par la
>   comédie, lui plus qu'un autre je crois.
> - La comédie de?
> - la colère par exemple"   (VC p.160)

Anne-Marie Stretter appears therefore as a multi-faceted character who, at the level of her personal existence, exerts a considerable power of seduction while remaining faithful to her normalizing representational function. A dichotomy between 'être' and 'paraître' exists in Anne-Marie Stretter since, like Lol during her return to S.Thala, she has not yet fully entered the state of unreason. Paradoxically, if we consider the real nature of her character, she becomes the upholder of reason. Her composure and understanding of situations fit her position as guarantor of the order of a society in which, as she herself recalls, one only pronounces acceptable words to prevent the existence of others (VC p.124).

2 Anne-Marie Stretter's initiation to the vice-consul's unreason

I now propose to examine how, beyond the anodine initial exchange between Anne-Marie Stretter and the vice-consul, and the banal stereotyped conversation which appears to take place, an

---

to let them die of leprosy, the vice-consul's action seems devoid of any possible meaning. When Anne-Marie Stretter does not personally look for moral or psychological reasons to explain the vice-consul's action, and soon in fact adheres to his vision, she appears, in her proposed interpretation, fully aware of her own world's limitations in comprehending the vice-consul's existence.

intuitive understanding sets itself in place which leads to Anne-Marie Stretter's initiation to the vice-consul's unreason and eventually to a relation of intimacy which soon becomes an implied complicity between the two characters (VC pp.122-128).

At first Anne-Marie Stretter adopts the customary leading approach with the vice-consul (VC p.122), and the usual seductive manner in talking about the weather, the heat, while the vice-consul remains silent or stumbles through his words, uncomfortable in the stereotyped conversation to which he is subjected (VC p.123). However, they very soon relinquish the usual codes of communication. Anne-Marie Stretter herself initiates the change in her second sentence and attempts to go beyond the accepted speech of social discourse in order suddenly to express more:

> "A Pékin c'était pareil, tout le monde parlait...on n'entendait que des avis, tout ce qu'on disait était, comment vous dire, le mot le plus juste pour dire ça..." (VC p.123).

They soon both find themselves confronted by the failure of language, unable to find the adequate signifier, since, as Anne-Marie Stretter explains, "...le premier mot qui paraîtrait convenable, ici aussi, empêcherait les autres de vous venir" (VC p.124); later the vice-consul admits in turn:

> "...j'ai l'impression que si j'essayais de vous dire ce que j'aimerais arriver à vous dire, tout s'en irait en poussière... - il tremble - les mots pour vous dire, à vous, les mots...de moi...pour vous dire à vous, ils n'existent pas" (VC p.125).

But Anne-Marie Stretter abandons coded conversation; she does not follow up her initial response and does not even search for the missing word (VC p.124). Soon, when the vice-consul starts talking, she seems indifferent and hardly looks at him to encourage him to continue: "Elle ne demande pas, ne reprend pas, n'invite pas à continuer" (VC p.125).

Such a passage recalls the apsychological interactions common in Duras' narratives from *L'Amour* onwards. We have already mentioned that incoherence of language constitutes a hint of madness in the Durasian text; the fact that language fails both Anne-Marie Stretter and the vice-consul directly recalls J.Hold's narrative attempt to find "le mot trou", an impossible signifier which would translate Lol's state of unreason. For the Durasian being who enters unreason, language, the instrument of Logos, loses its relevance and is increasingly replaced in her latest fictions by its absence or by other physical occurrences:

> "Il ne parle pas de sa vie. Il ne lui est jamais venu à l'idée qu'on pouvait le faire. Les mots ne sont pas là, ni la phrase pour y mettre les mots. Pour eux dire ce qu'il leur arrive il y a le silence, ou bien le rire ou quelquefois, par exemple, avec elles, pleurer" (YB pp.64-65)

However, in spite of their inability to 'communicate' verbally, Anne-Marie Stretter and the vice-consul instinctively find an understanding. "Je crois avoir compris, ne cherchez pas" (VC p.124) says the latter reassuringly, and Anne-Marie Stretter admits to him that evening: "Je sais qui vous êtes...Nous n'avons pas besoin de nous connaître davantage" (VC p.143). As half-conscious lies and imprecisions appear decoded - Anne-Marie Stretter admits to the vice-consul that the European woman sent back to Spain was in fact never contaminated by leprosy (VC p.125) -, and as trust settles, - "on remarque dans leurs yeux à tous deux une expression commune" (VC p.127)-, the vice-consul confides "Je voudrais être entendu de vous, de vous ce soir" (VC p.126).

Anne-Marie Stretter becomes gradually initiated to the vice-consul's unreason and, as she had already transgressed the fear of contagion in going to the Blue Moon, the cabaret in Indian territory, she accepts to go beyond the limit between reason and unreason: "Mais essayez quand même, je vous en supplie, d'apercevoir Lahore" (VC p.127) begs the vice-consul. Anne-Marie Stretter obediently submits herself to this initiation to unreason: "C'est très difficile de l'apercevoir tout à fait...ce que je vois seulement c'est une possibilité dans le sommeil..." (VC p.127). Uncertain at first, she stops thinking in order to manage to perceive this unavoidable side of Lahore. Soon she starts to tremble: "elle tremble elle aussi, maintenant" and finally acknowledges: "J'aperçois le côté inévitable de Lahore, dit-elle. Je l'apercevais déjà hier mais je ne le savais pas" (VC p.128).

Anne-Marie Stretter, the established representative of European reason in Calcutta, thus suddenly appears closely connected with the vice-consul's side of unreason. She hopes still to remain at a safe distance, in the security of her helpful, normalizing and protective function. Protected by her social commitments, "...elle est occupée,...elle se doit de rester là pour dire bonsoir" (VC p.142), she tries to oppose the vice-consul's insistence when he approaches her to request a dance for a second time:

> "...il s'incline, elle ne comprend pas, il reste ainsi, incliné, les invités le considèrent, narquois, effrayés. Il relève la tête, la regarde, ne voit rien, qu'elle, elle seule, ne voit pas l'expression navrée de l'ambassadeur. Elle fait la grimace, elle sourit, elle dit:
> - si j'accepte je n'en finirai plus, et je n'ai plus envie de danser...
> Il dit
> - J'insiste.
> Elle s'excuse autour d'elle, le suit. Ils dansent"
>
> (VC p.142)

While she had hoped that implied complicity between them would be the only consequence of their deeper understanding, she gradually comes to the fearful realisation that the pervasive influence of the vice-consul's unreason cannot be avoided:

> "Le vice-consul vient de dire quelque chose à Anne-Marie Stretter, une chose qui la fait reculer. Il l'attire vers lui. Elle se dégage. Jusqu'où ira-t-il? L'ambassadeur aussi le surveille. Il ne recommence plus. Mais elle veut fuir, on dirait. Elle est désemparée, et peut-être a-t-elle peur?" (VC p.143)

She soon appears to feel uncomfortably trapped within the net of unreason and, while still acknowledging the intimate and complicit link with the vice-consul, she insists on her separation from him as an ultimate defence mechanism: "Nous n'avons pas besoin de nous connaître davantage" (VC p.143). Even if she implicitly admits the triviality of her life, she attempts to defend it: "je prends la vie légèrement", and in a non-commital manner justifies the freedom of meaning: "...Tout le monde a raison, pour moi, tout le monde a complètement, profondément raison" (VC p.143), thus holding onto her position at the edge of the two worlds of reason and unreason, denying for a little longer the alarming implications of her encounter with the vice-consul. But his perceptiveness overcomes her: "N'essayez pas de vous reprendre. Ça ne sert plus à rien." (VC p.143). She cannot resist his power of persuasion, and to the "vous êtes avec moi" proclaimed by the vice-consul, she echoes: "je suis avec vous"; soon she utters the ultimate admission of complete intimacy: "Je suis avec vous ici complètement, comme avec personne d'autre" (VC p.144). The prospect shared between them of his coming exclusion even becomes a promise of intimacy: "je vais faire comme s'il était possible de rester avec vous ce soir ici" decides the vice-consul, and later they confirm:

> "Pourquoi faisons-nous ça?
> Pour que quelque chose ait eu lieu.
> Entre vous et moi?
> Oui entre nous.
> Dans la rue, criez fort.
> Oui" (VC p.144)

However if secrecy and agreed complicity sever the link between them, Anne-Marie Stretter, aware of the foreseeable rules of exclusion, can still hope to escape the vice-consul's presence.

Soon after the vice-consul's episode of madness, she appears to manage the preservation of her status quo and remain faithful to her world. She lucidly recognizes the danger posed by the vice-consul's presence and bluntly refuses Rossett's request for a meeting with the vice-consul (VC p.192). She asserts with determination, "Il doit vivre comme il est là...et nous devons continuer de même de notre côté" (VC p.194).

But in spite of her repeated attempts to resist the movement initiated in her through her contact with the vice- consul, the passage from reason to unreason is already at work. Even if Anne-Marie Stretter insists on forgetting the vice-consul and on maintaining a safe distance, it is already too late; a change is looming in her which soon begins to revive the formerly latent state of unreason present within her.

3 The enigma of Anne-Marie Stretter

A dubious past

Her composure and irreproachable reputation as "la femme la meilleure de Calcutta" (VC p.127) notwithstanding, unreason was already dormant in Anne-Marie Stretter before her encounter with the vice-consul. Beyond the apparent normality of her public existence at the palace, various signs of estrangement had already been detected by people around her: "Que dissimule cette ombre qui accompagne la lumière dans laquelle apparaît toujours Anne-Marie Stretter?" (VC p.109),[8] wonders Rossett.

When she goes for walks with her daughters on the Chandernagor road, "parfois elle tombe dans un abattement profond" (VC p.109), the pervasive influence of which paradoxically seems to relax those who notice it: "certains ont parlé de cela dont on ignore la nature mais qui repose celui qui le voit, repose on ne sait pas au juste de quoi" (VC p.109). In spite of her generosity, she does at times appear very hard: "Regardez comme elle a l'air dur parfois, parfois on dirait que sa beauté change...y a-t-il de la férocité dans son regard?" ou au contraire - de la douceur? (VC p.125).

The enigma of her persona is further reinforced by several distant but disturbing facts from her past pointing to a previous history of mental disturbance. Did she not mysteriously disappear after one year in Calcutta, following a failed suicide attempt?

> "Que s'est-il passé à la fin de la première année de son séjour? Cette disparition que personne ne s'expliquait? Une ambulance au petit jour a été vue devant la Résidence. Tentative de suicide? Ce séjour ensuite dans les montagnes du Népal est resté inexpliqué" (VC p.110)

Had she also not found it increasingly difficult to adapt to Savannakhet seventeen years before? "On parlait, paraît-il, de la renvoyer en France, elle ne s'habituait pas" (VC p.99). And why was she kept there when her husband found her, guarded by armed men?

> "...A Calcutta on ne sait pas encore aujourd'hui si elle était reléguée au fond de la honte ou de la douleur à Savannakhet lorsqu'il l'a trouvée. Non, on n'a jamais su" (VC p.99).

---

[8]The shadow assimilates her to the Indian crowd, and also, as Marini suggests, to the beggar-woman: "La forme radieuse d'Anne-Marie ne peut se voir que sur ce fond d'obscurité dont elle se détache sans se séparer, ce fantôme noir qui l'auréole, la mendiante son dehors angoissant" (TF p.99)

What crime has she committed which would justify the blame which still hovers in peoples' minds? "Rien ne se voit, c'est ce que j'appelle irréprochable à Calcutta" (VC p.100).

Anne-Marie Stretter remains therefore this "eau qui dort" (VC p.110); indeed the seemingly full presence of her public existence appears to be sustained by occasional but intriguing physical absences. As for Lol in *Le Ravissement de Lol V.Stein*, the text elaborates on the lack in order to build the puzzling character of Anne-Marie Stretter and many questions remain unanswered. Even in her present life at the palace, "Personne ne sait très bien à quoi elle occupe son temps..." (VC p.93). Why this reading, enclosed at home, suspicious reading the content of which remains unrevealed: "Lecture de plaisir - plaisir caché - livres interdits qui parlent du plaisir, livres inconnus" (TF p.130) suggests Marini; why these car journeys with her daughters on the Chandernagor road (VC p.95), or the repeated excursions to the Blue Moon? Why also this 'physical lack', this thinness, impending sign of unreason; and does not the vice-consul share this worrying feature: "comme il reste maigre, le vice-consul"...(VC p.98). Anne-Marie Stretter's thinness contrasts with her privileged status, as if it remained as a sequel of her former mental disturbance: "Cette maigreur à son retour fait peur. Pas d'autres différences? Elle reste maigre, c'est tout" (VC p.110); a worrying thinness which increases with age (VC p.92) and which recalls too much the beggar-woman, and also Anne-Marie Stretter's belonging to another world, the world of the needy, of madness.

An inaccessible presence

Her mode of presence itself seems riddled with absence. This woman, who invites so much attention and desire among her peers, in fact remains inaccessible. It is impossible to have any personal involvement with Anne-Marie Stretter (VC p.169) since, as the vice-consul puts it, "c'est une femme qui n'a pas de préférences" (VC p.171); hence the discordant pain experienced by Rossett at the moment of his greatest intimacy with her:

> "...il l'embrasse, ils restent enlacés, et voilà que dans le baiser....il entre une douleur discordante, la brûlure d'une relation nouvelle entrevue mais déjà forclose" (VC p.189).

In fact, as the beggar-woman can be read as the stereotype of India, so Anne-Marie Stretter exists as the stereotype of all women, plural figure given to anyone who wishes it; the prostitute,[9] stresses Marini. Such a conclusion would be confirmed by the fact that, if one believes Marguerite Duras herself, Anne-Marie Stretter 'is' the female character involved in the erotic, almost pornographic, activity of *L'Homme Assis dans le Couloir*.[10] Rossett, after J.Hold in *Le Ravissement de Lol V.Stein*, confusedly understands it when he realizes that in his experience with her, it is as if "...il l'eût aimé déjà en d'autres femmes, en un autre temps, d'un amour...duquel?" (VC p.190). As for Lol and for most other Durasian female characters, such a state of being results from Anne-Marie Stretter's inability to live an exclusive relationship. Madeleine Alleins puts it in these terms:

> "Les gémissements de l'humanité blessée, niée, étouffée sont trop présents en elle pour qu'elle puisse s'attacher à la fugacité de ses mouvements personnels, aux préférences passagères du sentiment. Elle se prête à ses

---

[9]The figure of the prostitute, as opposed to that of the mother, both embodied in the character of Anne-Marie Stretter, is a very tempting representation for many of Duras' female figures. The prostitute is the antithesis of 'la femme sérieuse' referred to in *Le Marin de Gibraltar* and represented in Duras' earlier fictions like *Les Petits Chevaux de Tarquinia*. "Celles-là sont les pires de toutes...ce ne sont pas des femmes" (MG p.62). Such women also believe in happiness "dans le travail et la dignité" (MG p.85). As a contrast, Duras' 'absent' women are increasingly given, especially in her later fictions, to the non-preferentiality of desire, and such characters even accept contracts of prostitution in *Les Yeux Bleus, Cheveux Noirs* and *La Maladie de la Mort*. However, the term 'prostitute', as used by Marini in relation to Anne-Marie Stretter, contains too strong an internalisation of moral and social codes. Even when the female characters are socially defined as prostitutes, the label tends to correspond to an external reading which takes into account only one aspect of the inner coherence of the Durasian character. The lack of social discrimination of these women is, as we have examined with Lol V.Stein, linked to a coherent mode of being which challenges the social codes of conduct in love interactions. In my last chapter, entitled 'The Unreason of Love', the possible reasons for such a shift of emphasis from the faithful woman to the figure of the prostitute will be examined.

[10]Francoise Py, in 'La Constellation India Song' (*L'Arc*, Le Jas 1985), mentions that "si de l'aveu même de Marguerite Duras, cette nouvelle a été rédigée pour la première fois à l'époque où elle écrit le texte de *Hiroshima*, sa première parution a lieu dans *L'Arc* en 1962. On y trouve des indications surprenantes: l'héroïne de ce conte à tonalités pornographiques est en effet Anne-Marie Stretter dont c'est la première apparition dans l'oeuvre." (p.73)

ℬ   amis, à ses amants. Son mari, sans être complaisant le sait, l'accès de cette femme est libre. Elle est une place traversée. Immergée dans une compassion générale, elle ne peut plus s'arrêter à une relation exclusive."[11]

In spite of her European origin and consequent roots in the concept of individuality, Anne-Marie Stretter can be assimilated to the undifferentiated, to the mode of presence of the Indians outside:

> "...des millions d'individus sont à ce point niés dans leurs besoins essentiels, qu'ils n'ont plus la possibilité de se saisir en tant que personnes humaines".[12]

However, this feature of undifferentiation does not exist in Anne-Marie Stretter as a direct and immediate result of her extreme compassion for human suffering, as a humanitarian cultural feature, - as Alleins' text implies at that point - but rather as a consequence of her distant encounter with India, which, as for the vice-consul, allowed for the emergence of what was already there in her: existence through the mode of absence. Such a feature of existential absence constitutes the identifying sign of the character. In spite of the complexity and contradictions of the chronology from one book to the other,[13] it appears certain that the woman who managed to 'steal' Michael Richardson from Lol V.Stein, that evening at the ball, several years ago in *Le Ravissement*, was Anne-Marie Stretter. One can indeed recognize the same strange presence through her detachment in relation to her environment. Thin already at that time, with this "non-regard" (RLVS p.6), her presence would provoke uneasiness: "...son

---

[11]Madeleine Alleins, op.cit. pp.131-132

[12]ibid. p.132

[13]It is indeed extremely difficult to assert that the narrative content of *Le Vice-consul* is chronologically ulterior to that of *Le Ravissement de Lol V.Stein*. The temporal ambiguities of the texts suggest two alternative first encounters between Anne-Marie Stretter and Michael Richard/Richardson. They no doubt had a love affair, but did they meet for the first time in S.Tahla, at the time of the Ball, or in Calcutta as Michael Richard suggests (VC p.187)? Did they meet only two years before in Calcutta as the public voice asserts (VC p.137), or a long time ago in S.Tahla as her subsequent suicide attempt could suggest? In the latter case her daughters' age, adolescent in *Le Ravissement*, would contradict their state of childhood in *Le Vice-consul*.

élégance et dans le repos, et dans le mouvement...inquiétait" (RLVS p.15). She had this "obscure négation de la nature" (RLVS p.15) which recalled the grace of a dead bird. Such existential absence had already made Tatiana, Lol V.Stein's closest friend, conclude: "Rien ne pouvait plus arriver à cette femme...plus rien, rien que sa fin" (RLVS p.16).

Such an occlusion of self, so striking in Anne-Marie Stretter, is also reflected in her environment: apart from her bed and a piano in the bedroom, all furniture has been removed (VC p.188). Such bareness, such absence of an opulence that her status would perhaps justify, places her again on the side of the needy, of the Indians outside. This lack, be it external or internal, goes beyond the liberating feeling of the negation of the ego; it indicates already that Anne-Marie Stretter belongs to "un univers plus vaste où les limites de la personne ont cessé d'être sensibles."[14]

No doubt the vice-consul's attraction towards Anne-Marie Stretter corresponds to this latter realization. The vice-consul indeed tries to fuse himself with this power of lack/absence, of unreason suspected in Anne-Marie Stretter, in order also to become connected, through her, to this place of indistinction outside the Embassy. Sylvie Gagné rightly suggests that

> "Entre lui et elle, peut-être pas la fascination, mais un lieu sublime où il ne voit ni lui, ni elle, fusion effaçant les limites, chaos d'où on ne peut plus symboliser, d'où les rires, les pleurs, les cris ("Nous n'avons plus rien à nous dire")"[15]

Hence also the impossibility between them of naming and formulating, of using a language which would stop and rigidify everything. However, the vice-consul's attempt at fusing with this power of depossession, of unreason strongly sensed in Anne-Marie Stretter, also provokes, as we shall finally see, the latter's ruin as a person and as Ambassadress; as Gagné again mentions, he offers a mirror to Anne-Marie Stretter:

> "Intelligence qu'il a d'elle, d'Anne-Marie Stretter, comme si la rencontre de ce même...qu'est le Vice-consul, appelait sa mort, la conduisait jusqu'à la mer

---

[14]Alleins op.cit. p.132
[15]Gagné op.cit. p.108

> tandis que lui se voit 'photographié au bord de la mer d'Oman...'"[16]

They both recognize the power of unreason in the other, and we can conclude the analysis of the relationship between the two characters in Gagné's terms:

> "La rencontre entre le vice-consul et Anne-Marie Stretter aura lieu en miroir; les regards seront 'échangés', glissés dans la dépossession, chacun fixant l'autre soi-même.".[17]

As a result of her encounter with the vice-consul, Anne-Marie Stretter will start to abandon her role to follow unreason, to be fused into the figure of madness represented by the Cambodian beggar-woman outside the gates. By allowing herself to become sensitive to the vice-consul's presence, to the impact of his pleas and shouts, Anne-Marie Stretter has therefore lost her once-acquired immunity, to have gradually reactivated her own latent lack of reason.[18]

4 Anne-Marie Stretter's passage to Unreason

We shall now examine more closely how the passage from reason to unreason[19] finally takes place in Anne-Marie Stretter,

---

[16]ibid. p.106

[17]ibid. p.107

[18]It is worth noting that this phenomenon, where a male character appears responsible for another character's passage to unreason, is almost unique in Duras' writing. In all other Durasian texts, with the exception of the character of the sailor in *Le Marin de Gibraltar*, it is the woman (the woman of *L'Amour*, Alissa in *Détruire Dit-elle*, the women of *La Maladie de la Mort* or *Les Yeux Bleus, Cheveux Noirs*) who gives the men access to unreason. Such an exception asserts in my view the function of the character of the vice-consul as agent of contagion. As distinct from other Durasian figures, the vice-consul does not fully embody the state of unreason: we have shown in the previous chapter that he only exists as a man of passage whose insistent presence reactivates Anne-Marie Stretter's inner mode of being.

[19]The word 'unreason' does not here refer to the way it has been apprehended for some centuries by society, which Foucault defines as "l'envers simple, immédiat, aussitôt rencontré de la raison; et cette forme vide, sans contenu ni valeur, purement négative, où n'est figurée que l'empreinte d'une raison qui vient de s'enfuir, mais qui reste toujours pour la déraison la raison d'être de ce qu'elle est" (HF p.192). As we shall see, the term 'unreason' is to be understood here in

and how, as a result of the encounter with the vice-consul, she alternates between the two poles before finally submitting to unreason.

From activity to passivity

Tears and sleep constitute the main occurrences which, as usual, in Duras' texts signal the passage to the authenticity of unreason. Such features start occurring in Anne-Marie Stretter immediately after the reception evening marked by the vice-consul's fit of madness and his exclusion. She accompanies Rossett outside the palace at dawn and unexplained tears come to her eyes.

> "...il (Rossett) voit que dans ses yeux clairs le regard danse, s'affole, il voit tout à coup, voilà, c'est vrai, les larmes.
> - Que se passe-t-il?
> - Rien, dit-elle, c'est la lumière du jour, quand il y a du brouillard, elle est si pénible..." (VC p.164)

The plausibility of the explanation offered by Anne-Marie Stretter, "c'est la lumière du jour", disappears when later, in the Islands, the same scenario recurs:

> "elle a pleuré...sans raison visible...elle n'a pas dit pourquoi...ce n'est pas lui, il en est sûr, qui a fait pleurer Anne-Marie Stretter" (VC pp.171-172).

The following evening during their journey and arrival at the Islands, Anne-Marie Stretter's mode of presence starts to alter noticeably, as absence and passivity take over. During the conversation which precedes the dinner at the Prince of Wales, Anne-Marie Stretter appears absent: "Anne-Marie Stretter paraît ne pas entendre" (VC p.181), and soon returns to a state of sleep: "Anne-Marie Stretter dort, elle ne peut pas répondre" (VC p.181). Her absence, though lasting only for the duration of a conversation, nevertheless asserts what Marcelle Marini expresses in these terms:

> "Du rôle d'utilité - détentrice d'un secret qu'elle ignore, témoin, approbatrice - miroir de leurs propos - elle

---

the meaning of 'breakthrough'.

passe au rôle d'inutilité." (TF p.120)[20]

Indeed the passage from activity to passivity soon seems definite and inescapable on that same evening in the Islands: a chapter (VC pp.185-200) which also clearly shows the transition of Anne-Marie Stretter from a state of presence to one of absence.

That evening Anne-Marie Stretter performs her duties in her usual calm and rational manner. Lucid and determined, she opposes Rossett's idea of meeting the vice-consul again by faithfulness to her world: "Si je me forçais à le voir, Michael Richard ne me le pardonnerait pas" (VC p.194). Identified with her major role as preserver of the existing order, she calmly tries to appease Rossett and to bring him back to reason: "Ne pensez pas à lui. Il va partir très vite, mon mari fera le nécessaire" (VC p.194). Anne-Marie Stretter seems that evening to have regained her usual self: welcoming, calm, rational and wise, she remains the reassuring centre of this European nucleus, a presence which allows Michael Richard to say jokingly: "C'est tout ce qu'il y a, ici...Anne-Marie, rien d'autre" (VC p.194).

Heat, as so often in Marguerite Duras' narratives, constitutes a contributing factor in the emergence of unreason and indeed, under the effect of the distressing heat, Anne-Marie Stretter's appearance alters under Rossett's very eyes. In a fit of frightening overbreathing, she suddenly loses all attractiveness in the mens' eyes. As she is taken by an inner struggle, an "insupportable bien-être" (VC p.196), the unexpected occurrence of tears is again devoid of any psychological relevance: "Est-ce sûr? Oui ce sont des larmes...Elles sortent de ses yeux et roulent sur ses joues, très petites, brillantes" (VC p.196). They become the tangible sign of her impending and unavoidable absence. Rossett, enlightened, will later suspect: "Est-ce que ce sont les larmes qui privent de la personne?" (VC p.201).

Anne-Marie Stretter's tears indeed signal her total loss of consciousness, away from her everyday life; when the tears have

---

[20]Respecting the plurality of meaning, the present reading really doubles, rather than annihilates Marini's feminist interpretation, according to which Anne-Marie Stretter reacts with sleep to the male appropriation by discourse of her once-lived encounter with a beggar-woman in Savannakhet: "...elle est condamnée comme la mendiante à être discours inutile et silence profond" (TF p.120).

dried up, she returns to her world "comme après une absence réelle" (VC p.196). She herself admits:

> "Je pleure sans raison que je pourrais vous dire, c'est comme une peine qui me traverse, il faut bien que quelqu'un pleure, c'est comme si c'était moi" (VC p.198)

The pain experienced by Anne-Marie Stretter can, in the context of *Le Vice-consul*, be identified with that of Indian suffering and the necessity of crying; "il faut bien que quelqu'un pleure" again stresses her greater involvement with the problematic of India outside the palace.

However, such enigmatic occurrences are in fact common to all Durasian beings taken by the mode of unreason. We have seen above that tears can replace the inadequacy of language and help establish intimacy between characters, a feature strongly present in *Les Yeux Bleus, Cheveux Noirs*.[21]

As for Anne-Marie Stretter, I would agree with Marcelle Marini to assert that tears emanate from this internal shadow, "l'ombre interne" (TF pp.50-51), which resists conscious discourse, communication or social relationships, and, as Marini continues, madness appears to be the result of the complete passage to the outside of this internal reality.[22]

Initiated by tears, Anne-Marie Stretter's attitude soon alters irremediably. Affected by this anonymous external suffering force and in a state of absence now similar to sleep, she not only becomes withdrawn from 'her' world, but also attains a regressive state on Michael Richard's knees:

---

[21]"Ils se mettent à pleurer. Les sanglots sortent de leurs corps (...) Ils sont dans un bonheur qu'ils ne connaissent pas encore (...) Ils voudraient que les sanglots sortent de leurs corps sans qu'ils sachent pourquoi. Il pleure tandis qu'il le lui demande (...) Ils pleurent comme ils s'aimeraient" (YB p.112).

[22]In the passage referred to, "l'ombre interne" is further defined as "cette région écrite où se situent les archives du soi"...as "la fomentation du moi par moi", or else as a "corps pulsionnel, 'le chaudron des sorcières' dont parle Freud, corps toujours déjà texte-texture de traces innombrables qui débordent sans fin, lieu insituable de l'inconscient, hiéroglyphes de son histoire ou tout événement vient prendre forme" (TF p.51). Marini continues by asserting that the mad have replaced this internal shadow with a dazzling light; everything is outside, hence the absence for them of any possible discrimination among the different elements of reality. "La suppression de toute différence et repère fait le vide partout."

> "Elle s'est assise sur lui, les jambes relevées...comme elle est rajeunie assise ainsi dans une pose enfantine, disloquée, sur ses genoux" (VC p.197).

Abandoned to sleep or to a state of semi-consciousnes, she soon becomes pure passivity, objectified, like the women of *L'Amour, La Maladie de la Mort* or *Les Yeux Bleus, Cheveux Noirs*, by the male look of her two male companions:

> "(elle) va vers le lit, se repose...son corps allongé apparaît privé de son volume habituel. Elle est plate, légère, elle a la rectitude simple d'une morte...le visage lui-même est modifié, différent, il est ramassé sur lui-même, vieilli" (VC p.197)

"Séparée d'elle-même, là-hors" (TF p.107), Anne-Marie Stretter is given to her own suffering: "Elle donne le sentiment d'être maintenant prisonnière d'une douleur trop ancienne pour être encore pleurée" (VC p.198).

The impact of the beggar-woman on Anne-Marie Stretter

Filled by her own unreason and taken over by this newly-realized inner dimension, Anne-Marie Stretter makes her final move onto the side of unreason. This step, which seems intimately linked to the presence of the beggar-woman outside the palace, marks, for Anne-Marie Stretter as for Morgan's fictionalised Cambodian woman's journey into madness, the beginning of a marginalising process.[23] In a move originally initiated by her encounter with the vice-consul, Anne-Marie Stretter has gradually become vulnerable to the beggar-woman's song, which pursues her and repeatedly penetrates the walls of the palace or of the hotel. Marcelle Marini rightly states:

> "Une partie de la fiction est construite sur le cheminement d'Anne-Marie Stretter vers la mendiante qui est autant cheminement de son chant en elle." (TF p.102)

---

[23]Morgan for instance is eager to add the character of Anne-Marie Stretter to his fictionalised account of the beggar-woman's journey into madness (VC p.183). "Progressivement" remarks Marini, "Anne-Marie Stretter est assimilée à la mendiante. De qui parle-t-on? D'elle où toutes deux se confondent" (TF p.120).

The insistent, loud presence of the beggar-woman outside the hotel:- "un chant s'élève tout à coup...c'est cette femme de Savannakhet...c'est vrai on dirait qu'elle la suit" (VC p.199) - reactivates, from the depths of Anne-Marie Stretter's sleep, her sensitivity to this woman who constitutes, as we shall see, the principal and true embodiment of madness itself.

After her passive resistance to the male discourse earlier in the sequence, and her acceptance of subjection to an objectified state, Anne-Marie Stretter suddenly transgresses the implicit law which had maintained her securely behind the gates or the walls of her various residences.

> "Anne-Marie Stretter sort, elle ne les (les amants) voit pas derrière la grille; elle va calmement vers la mer" (VC p.199).

As Marini remarks, she responds, attracted by the voice of the siren who inhabits the lagoon, "la femme de Calcutta, son double, la femme de son adolescence" (TF p.127).

Indeed an inverted movement between the presences of the two women can finally be noticed, as Marini again observes, by which Anne-Marie Stretter's irretrievable slippage into absence becomes inversely proportional to the beggar-woman's increasingly pregnant presence. Such a phenomenon happens not only, as Marini suggests it does, through the male discourse which repeatedly assimilates Anne-Marie Stretter to the beggar-woman:

> "présence (Anne-Marie Stretter) qui est faite absence au fur et à mesure que l'absente (=la mendiante) est faite présente par-dans le discours des amants" (TF p.120).

The occurrence also signals the mechanism of Anne-Marie Stretter's progression into madness. As her mode of rational presence gradually becomes crippled by absence, the impact of the beggar-woman's mad presence is in turn increasingly felt.

We have already recalled that Anne-Marie Stretter was the only person capable of identifying the origin and language of the mad woman outside the gates of the palace. Though no possibility of dialogue exists between Anne-Marie Stretter and the beggar-woman, the latter nevertheless does represent for Anne-Marie Stretter - even in the midst of her fully rational social existence - the promise of her true identity,[24] of the irrational force which motivates her in her more intimate life. She not only reminds her of her lost origin, of her secret existence in Savannakhet; she also appears to hold the key to her personal history. Anne-Marie Stretter, disturbed by the woman's song, one day declares: "C'est cette femme...qui chante sur le boulevard...écoutez... Il faudra que je m'arrange un jour pour savoir quand-même..." (VC p.156). In spite of Morgan's rational answer, "Mais tu ne sauras rien...elle est tout à fait folle" (VC p.156), Anne-Marie Stretter remains quietly faithful to her secret wish, unconsciously awaiting the appropriate moment to fulfil her promise.

Anne-Marie Stretter lets herself become vacant, awaits another reality. Freed from any ideological function, she abandons herself to sleep; emptied of any language, she falls into silence. Driven outside by the beggar-woman's Savannakhet song, she ends up leaving her residence like "...la reine qui a abandonné son royaume pour venir en l'allée"...(TF p.112).

> "Elle ne va pas jusqu'à la plage, elle s'allonge dans l'allée, la tête sur la paume de sa main, accoudée sur le sol, dans la pose d'une liseuse, elle ramasse du gravier et le jette au loin. Puis elle ne jette plus de gravier, elle déplie son bras, elle pose son visage sur ce bras allongé et elle reste là." (VC pp.199-200)

A convergence of the movements of the two women takes place by which Anne-Marie Stretter, who has even become physically similar to the beggar-woman - "elle est devenue subitement celle que, laide, cette femme-là aurait été" (VC p.197) -, goes outside to meet the woman who dares to follow her wherever she goes. Lying on the park which goes to the sea,[25]

---

[24]Marini's thesis sees in the beggar-woman the representation of the quest for an origin and links this search for identity to the discovery in Anne-Marie Stretter of sexual difference: "Le chant sans cesse l'éveille au désir de savoir ce qu'il en est en vérité d'elle-même en son sexe, des premiers temps de son histoire dont toute sa vie depuis lors l'a fait dévier." (TF p.127)

[25]Marcelle Marini, playing on the French word-association 'mer/mère', sees in Anne-Marie Stretter's movement towards the sea something very similar to Morgan's beggar-woman's attempt to fuse herself with the mother. "Le retour à la mère, c'est se main(tenir) au dessus de l'eau, noyée à chaque vague, endormie peut-être, ou pleurant dans la mère" (TF p.128). She also continues: "le voyage

Anne-Marie then remains totally dispossessed. Like Lol V.Stein, who does not talk any more and lives with the mad on the beach, Anne-Marie Stretter is, as Duras puts it, "déjà atteinte définitivement".[26] Emptied of all rational drive, she remains in agreement with this obscure reality, having now become pure enigma for the outside. Totally given over to the world of unreason, in a movement of opening through which outside reality penetrates her entirely, Anne-Marie Stretter, finally fused with the beggar-woman, has become, through the loss of her rational ego, pure desire.

> "Elle est le désir Anne-Marie Stretter...Ça lui permet une fusion...un abandon à la douleur de l'Inde...comme un abandon à la mort"[27]

Anne-Marie Stretter has therefore entered what Deleuze and Guattari would call the process of 'desiring-production'. In the anti-Oedipal strategy,

> "if man is connected to the machines of the universe, if he is in tune with his desires, if he is 'anchored', he ceases to worry about the fitness of things, about the behaviour of his fellow-men, about right or wrong, and justice and injustice (...) The life that is in him will manifest itself in growth, and growth is endless eternal process. The process is everything."[28]

---

d'Anne-Marie Stretter au pays du féminin la conduit au royaume de la mère dont elle attend qu'elle lui transmette la représentation et le signifiant de son sexe qui lui permettent d'articuler leur relation entre elles et leur relation à l'autre des sexes, d'ordonner son imaginaire en un système propre, de trouver forme pour son désir et son plaisir" (TF p.131).

This interpretation, which fits logically with Marini's otherwise convincing feminist and psychoanalytic approach by which there is no possible feminine subject in the phallic system, however restricts the impact of Anne-Marie Stretter's movement of liberation by reducing it too much to a symptom, a kind of mirror of an occidental patriarchal system. In turn I would again argue that the unreason of the Durasian being exists as an alternative conception of desire, rather than as a symptom promoted by the inadequacy of a societal system.

[26] Duras, in *Marguerite Duras à Montréal*, p.40

[27] Duras, in *Les Parleuses*, p.215

[28] Mark Seem, in the Introduction to Gilles Deleuze & Felix Guattari, *Anti-Oedipus* (Minnesota Press 1983) p.xxiii

In her 'vital progression' towards the outside, Anne-Marie Stretter has therefore met the schizophrenic state by which a being becomes "touché par la vie profonde de toutes les formes ou de tous les genres."[29] She has escaped the false consciousness of what Deleuze and Guattari see as the 'capitalist being', to situate herself in "l'éclatante et noire vérité qui gît dans le délire" by which "il n'y a pas de sphères ou de circuits relativement indépendants".[30] In so doing, she has become this "sujet nomade et vagabond" since "le désir (...) manque de sujet fixe; il n'y a de sujet fixe que dans la répression".[31]

Anne-Marie Stretter's movement towards Unreason finally seals her ambivalence between life and death. One can indeed say that her rational being succumbs to her encounter with the vice-consul:

> "Anne-Marie Stretter meurt peut-être ainsi, d'être restée à l'écoute du regard et du cri du vice- consul, sur l'amour, le désir, la passion au coeur desquels elle se trouve comme en un vide. Ne coïncide-t-elle pas alors à ce point au désir, à cette place intenable, à corps perdu, faute de distance".[32]

"Car", as Deleuze and Guattari recall, "le désir désire aussi cela, la mort, parce que le corps plein de la mort est son moteur immobile, comme il désire la vie...".[33] And Anne-Marie Stretter does end up adhering to this urge to be totally traversed by the outside world. She has relinquished her public envelope, which maintained her, dead, stultified in the boredom of the indefinite realm of desire.[34]

---

[29]Deleuze & Guattari op.cit. (*L'Anti-Oedipe*) p.10

[30]ibid. p.9. We may continue with Deleuze and Guattari and assert that her state contrasts sharply with that of the "schizophrène artificiel, tel qu'on le voit à l'hôpital, loque autistisée produite comme entité". (ibid. p.11)

[31]ibid. p.34

[32]Gagné, in *Marguerite Duras à Montréal*, p.105

[33]Deleuze & Guattari, op.cit. p.14

[34]We must, however, continue to bear in mind that Anne- Marie Stretter's new state of awareness, when apprehended from a psychoanalytic-adaptive perspective, can only be viewed as a symbol of autism and as a sign of schizo-phrenia. Forgetting that schizophrenia is a mental state which mainly exemplifies the process of production of desire, such a state is explained in the above instit-

5 The impact of Anne-Marie Stretter's unreason on the white circle of the Embassy

There is no doubt that Anne-Marie Stretter's desertion of her public position has a profound effect on the society of *Le Vice-consul*. To complete the examination of the way in which madness contaminates the European world of Calcutta, I propose finally to consider how Anne-Marie Stretter's passage to unreason in turn affects the inner circle of the Embassy.

The impact of the first contact with madness through the vice-consul's mental crisis and exclusion is all the more disturbing for Anne-Marie Stretter's private circle since it happens in a general climate of fear of contagion. Encircled by leprosy, famine and the repeated outcry of madness, they cannot forget that Europeans who are unable to stand the stress regularly commit suicide: "les suicides d'Européens pendant la famine qui jamais ne les touche, pourtant, c'est curieux" (VC p.161).

With Anne-Marie Stretter's altered presence, however, they gradually approach the nature of Unreason itself. They are sensitized to it by their trips to the Blue Moon. In spite of her reassuring commentary: "Vous savez...le Blue Moon c'est un cabaret comme un autre. Les Européens n'osent pas y aller à cause de la lèpre, alors ils disent que c'est un bordel" (VC p.158), they all confusedly know that in these escapades away from the security of the palace, to which she drags them after her carefully planned receptions in the Embassy, what is really at stake, beyond the transgressive sensual freedom, is the transgression of the limit between reason and unreason. Attracted by this woman who does not fear contagion, they end up being exposed not only to the physical contagion of leprosy - "les blancs n'associent-ils pas la lèpre au Blue Moon, ce bordel où iraient les amants, Anne-Marie Stretter et M.Richard?" (TF p.105) - but also to the threat of sexual laxity and ultimately unreason: "Bordel", continues Marini,

---

utional perspective in terms of the ego, and "on ne peut plus que 'goûter' une essence ou spécificité supposées du schizo, fut-ce avec amour et pitié, ou pour la recracher avec dégout. Une fois comme moi dissocié, une autre fois comme moi coupé, une autre fois (...) comme moi qui n'a pas cessé d'être, qui était là spécifiquement, mais dans son monde, et qui se laisse retrouver par un psychiatre malin, un sur-observateur compréhensif, bref un phénoménologue." (Deleuze & Guattari op.cit. p.31) "bord d'elle. (Ils) disent tous que c'est le bord d'elle qui vous contamine" (TF p.105).[35]

Well before Anne-Marie Stretter's encounter with the vice-consul and her final passage to the side of Unreason, however, she had already represented the ideal instrument for the transgression of reason, a certain form of contagion, for the men around her.

Recalling the impressive effect of the vice-consul's fit of madness, her attractive presence carries, also, an obsessional power. We have already mentioned that her music deeply impresses the men with an effect similar to that of the beggar-woman's song. Though still distanciated, Crawn appears addicted to her musical charm: "Quand je serai sur le point de mourir, je te ferai prévenir, tu viendras me jouer le Schubert" (VC p.161). As for Michael Richard, he now remains as if mesmerised, glued to her within the Embassy:

> "D'où vient-il? Il n'habite pas à Calcutta. Il y vient pour la voir, rester près d'elle. C'est près d'elle qu'il désire être" (VC p.151).

It is through music that Anne-Marie Stretter,

> "...la musicienne de Schubert, a enlevé Michael Richard au monde du 'boulevard' pour lui faire découvrir que le désir peut se vivre aussi au coeur des ambassades...". (TF p.106)

Rossett also succumbs to her spell: her music provokes in him phantasms of Anne-Marie Stretter herself:

> "Charles Rossett reconnaît tout de suite le morceau de Schubert (...) Il voit dans un éclair blanc: Anne-Marie X..., dix-sept ans, frêle et longue, au conservatoire de Venise, c'est le concours de fin d'études, interprète l'oeuvre de Schubert qu'aime George Crawn" (VC p.186)

---

[35]Sexuality is indeed constantly linked with unreason in Duras' narratives. It is "une chose malfaisante qui porte au crime et à la folie" (YB p.51)

Rossett, deeply disturbed by the strange occurrence of the tears, at dawn after the reception evening, soon becomes obsessed by the enigma of Anne-Marie Stretter's presence:

> "Il pense aux larmes. Il la revoit pendant la réception, essaie de comprendre, frôle des explications, ne les approfondit pas" (VC p.164).

Finally, with Anne-Marie Stretter's altered mode of presence, the men progress in the intelligence of unreason. Her absence, in spite of the uneasiness it produces, forces them to distance themselves from their own rational or patronizing discourse: "discours inutile" remarks Michael Richard. No doubt influenced by Anne-Marie Stretter's total passivity, they become increasingly aware of her identification with the beggar-woman, to the point where Morgan suggests adding the character of Anne-Marie Stretter to his book, and where Crawn manages to contemplate how madness can be felt as an ultimate fulfilment; referring to the beggar-woman, he does not hesitate to suggest:

> "...elle a trouvé comment se perdre il me semble, elle a oublié, ne sait plus qu'elle est la fille de X ou de Y, plus d'ennui pour elle (...) Jamais, jamais le moindre soupçon d'ennui" (VC p.181).

The full effect of Anne-Marie Stretter's contagion can be best seen, however, in her impact on Richard and on Rossett. In remaining open to everyone,[36] she contaminates them with her mode of absence:

> "son contact sans l'intermédiaire de mots agit comme un révélateur. Qui l'approche est privé de la personne et donc de l'illusion amoureuse qui croit qu'un être est capable de monopoliser l'attention entière, d'occuper tout le présent. Et pourtant à voir cette femme sombrer

---

[36]"Les gémissements de l'humanité blessée, niée, étouffée, sont trop présents en elle, pour qu'elle puisse s'attacher à la fugacité de ses mouvements personnels, aux préférences passagères du sentiment...L'accès de cette femme est libre. Elle est place traversée. Immergée dans une compassion générale, elle ne peut plus s'arrêter à une relation exclusive" (Alleins op. cit. pp.131-132)

loin de l'instant, on n'en éprouve, semble-t-il, nul sentiment de frustration, nulle tristesse."[37]

Indeed Richard and Rossett share with her the disturbing experience of her tears: "On dirait que l'ivresse gagne, que l'odeur d'une femme qui pleure se répand" (VC p.196) and, powerless in the face of this progression of unreason, Richard also experiences suffering. The two mens' closeness and direct contact with Anne-Marie Stretter are soon a danger to their own lives. Michael Richard had long before become Anne-Marie Stretter's prey. Does one not expect that, deeply identified as he is with her, his fate will one day be linked with hers?

> "On pense qu'il n'est pas impossible, qu'un soir, ils soient retrouvés morts ensemble dans un hôtel de Chandernagor, après le Blue Moon, une nuit...on dirait: pour rien, par indifférence à la vie" (VC p.152).

Rossett, the newcomer, also contaminated through his intimacy with Anne-Marie Stretter, experiences the contagion of the same void when he kisses her:

> "...voilà que dans le baiser - il ne s'y attendait pas - il entre une douleur discordante, la brûlure d'une relation nouvelle entrevue mais déjà forclose...". (VC p.189)

Soon Rossett finds himself deprived of all desire: "il se trouve à la fois privé d'elle et privé de désir" (VC p.202). Assailed by vivid fantasies about Anne-Marie Stretter, soon tired and disturbed, he is sent back towards the Other, the mad woman outside the gates who perhaps retains the secret of Anne-Marie Stretter's absence.

Unreason has thus accomplished its work by claiming Anne-Marie Stretter, via the effect of the vice-consul's contagious presence, and her passage into Unreason constitutes the final proof of the ineffectiveness of the gates. The function of the gates has turned against the whites, not only by their failure to separate, but also by the setting up of an enclosing device. They have now also metaphorically allowed Anne-Marie Stretter to escape.

In sensitizing her companions to unreason, Anne-Marie Stretter destabilises them but, in deserting them, in abandoning

---

[37]ibid. p.132

them to their world, she moreover creates a void in this already crumbling world.

With the contagion of unreason from the vice-consul to Anne-Marie Stretter, the circle is closed. The main historical stages of the meaning given to madness, stressed by Foucault, can be found in the narrative of *Le Vice-consul*: from the tragic and ancestral fear prevalent in the 15th century,[38] to the reduction of madness to a human scale with the character of the vice-consul, and finally to a return of unreason in its cosmic configuration with the fusion of Anne-Marie Stretter and the beggar-woman.

The white socius of *Le Vice-consul* represents a confrontation of two very different social investments, which correspond to the two aspects of the social machine, as defined in Deleuze and Guattari's *Anti-Oedipe*. Though we have few overt signs in *Le Vice-consul* which would enable us to say to which type of social formation that white socius belongs, we can still recognize what Deleuze and Guattari would describe as a modern state, marked, though removed from the metropolis, by a capitalist formation. Deleuze and Guattari have shown that in a modern social system, two major types of social investment, the segregative and the nomadic, both corresponding to unconscious investments in the social field, can be identified, and that they both correspond to positions of desire. The white group of Calcutta can be seen to correspond to a segregative mode and as such to constitute a subjugated group, in which Anne-Marie Stretter's central figure tends to occupy the mother position, with the female gender situated in the place of the lack. The oedipal structure remains a means of integration within the group. "Aussi Oedipe fleurit-il dans les groupes assujettis, là où un ordre établi est investi dans ses formes répressives elles-mêmes. (AO p.123). To follow Deleuze and Guattari's line of thought, we can also say that the Europeans' libidinal investment in the social field corresponds to an unconscious investment of a revolutionary type. But the major segregative mode of the white society pictured in *Le Vice-consul* seems gradually to be penetrated by the 'nomadic' mode represented by the Indians and by the successive figures of

---

[38]Such fear is recognizeable in the whites' reaction to the presence of the Indians outside the palace: lepers, beggars and mad people are embodied in the figure of the beggar-woman.

madness of the vice-consul, Anne-Marie Stretter and the beggar-woman. The nomadic mode, which corresponds to a 'revolutionary' unconscious investment and follows the lines of escape of desire, proceeds in a fashion inverse to that followed by the segregative mode.

> "L'investissement révolutionnaire inconscient est tel que le désir, encore sur son mode propre, recoupe l'intérêt des classes dominées, exploitées, et fait couler des flux capables de rompre à la fois toutes les ségrégations et leurs applications oedipiennes, capables d'halluciner l'histoire, de délirer les races et d'embraser les continents." (AO p.125)

Indeed reason in *Le Vice-consul* increasingly appears in a position of defeat. Unreason finally accomplishes its work in claiming Anne-Marie Stretter, chief representative of the white community.

Chapter 6

THE SPATIALISATION OF DESIRE

> "L'histoire...devient maintenant visible. C'est sur le sable
> que déjà elle s'implante,..." (*L'Amour* p.13)

Space is a prerequisite of fiction, the story needs a setting, a "map-space" in order to unfold. In realistic narratives, "the existence of such a map attests to the readability of the text with which it is coextensive, to its naturalness as a supposed mirror of reality."[1] In modern fiction, however, this space is often shattered or called into question. The space of *L'Amour*, which we shall consider with frequent reference to *Le Ravissement de Lol V.Stein* (the two pieces of writing may be seen as versions of the same text), participates in this problematisation, in which language asserts its different status. But, more to the point here, I propose to cast light upon how the space of *L'Amour* is constructed; a space which mostly allows for the representation of madness. To carry out this task I shall adopt a semantic approach supported by textual and intertextual considerations.

> "The empty hall and dining rooms of a 'fin-de-siècle' hotel near a beach or a forest, tennis courts echoing with the bounce and pock of fuzzy balls, bay windows from which light pours onto terraces and dark gardens,

---

[1]Solomon in Foreword to *Yale French Studies* no.57 (1979): *Locus: Space, Landscape, Decor in Modern French Fiction.* p.3

the fading splendour of reception rooms flooded by the light of glycerine chandeliers, and where, to a plaintive tune, ill-defined figures slowly abandon immobility."

Verena Andermatt evokes in these terms[2] the landscapes and decor "familiar to the readers of Marguerite Duras' novels". While acknowledging that in later works, namely *Le Ravissement* (1964), *L'Amour* (1971) and *India Song* (1973) there is a change in the way in which these decors function in the text, Andermatt sees Duras' earlier writing as a mirror of "a post-war situation of a predetermined and insurmountable alienation"[3] in which landscape and decor simply underline the solitude of the characters.

The disquieting effects produced by the distortion of spatial perspective in *Le Ravissement*, mentioned also by Andermatt, extend to *L'Amour*. However, in spite of textual operations which create 'non-realistic' effects, it appears that the living-space of *Le Ravissement* remains familiar, still largely derived from the necessities, however thin, of the plot.

The descriptive account of S.Tahla, mostly realistic, provides an accurate topography complete with social strata (RLVS p.40) - delimitation of town centre, residential and industrial areas - by which the reader can construct an exact mapping of the space which supports Lol's walks. The realism of the town is reinforced by the allusions in the characters' conversation to the modernisation which the town has experienced over the last ten years (RLVS p.77). This space also evolves mainly around the characters: background details serve to fill up the "space" of Lol's existence and most of the spatial metaphors can be explained in terms of the characters rather than of the space itself. Andermatt's study, based almost exclusively on the passages in which the fragmentary contrastive style calls into question the rest of the text, ignores the superposition of two types of space in *Le Ravissement*: the realistic setting, a filled space - town, the house in which Lol arranges her objects - , and the phantasmatic space, the space of madness or the empty space, which gradually invades the whole text. During her walks Lol phantasmatically reconstructs the space of the ballroom; in J.Hold's terms "ce qu'elle rebâtit, c'est la fin du

---

[2]Verena Andermatt, 'Rodomontages of *Le Ravissement de Lol V.Stein*' in ibid. p.23
[3]ibid. p.23

monde" (RLVS p.47): the instant of separation between her fiancé and herself, between day and night.

We propose to show in this chapter how, in a process of integration of these two kinds of space, *L'Amour*, while being a variation of *Le Ravissement*, effectively marks itself off from it. Although on one level *L'Amour* can be read as the spatial actualisation of Lol V.Stein's madness, the enclosed space of *Le Ravissement*, symbolised by references to "l'enceinte du bal" and to the sense of emptiness issuing from the rigidity and immobility of a space filled by objects, has been replaced, in *L'Amour*, by an infinite outside space without clear demarcation, where emptiness, the very metaphor of madness, originates in the void of space itself.[4]

Indeed the setting of *L'Amour* corresponds to a flattened out space, a process of laying bare. Thus the seascape, a setting of universal value which everybody 'knows', is stripped of its familiarity by a certain use of language to produce an atmosphere of atemporality. For Duras, "le paysage de la fin ou du début du monde, peu importe, c'est la mer".[5] Infinity and its connotation of eternity is indeed suggested by a space where the sea and the beach extend endlessly.

I propose to consider the way in which the geographic space of *L'Amour* reflects Lol V.Stein's phantasmatic space in three phases. First I shall concentrate on the spatial imagery used in the text. We shall see that many of the images used to picture the setting of *L'Amour* establish a geometrical graphic configuration. This topography - often pictured in movement - appears concomitant to a simplification of space, a thinning-out process which forms a counterpoint to what happens in *Le Ravissement*.

Thematic considerations derived from Bachelard's approach will then allow us to examine the passage from the relatively solid tangible world of *Le Ravissement* to a liquid universe more appropriate for translating the incessant movement of desire central to *L'Amour*.

---

[4]We have shown in the study of *Le Ravissement* in Chapter 3 that madness corresponds precisely to a void, to an emptiness which cannot be represented; hence Lol pictured as a figure of void by J.Hold.

[5]Michelle Porte, in *Le Camion: entretien avec Michelle Porte* (Minuit, Paris 1977) p.129

Finally a consideration of the nature of the locations found in *L'Amour* will allow us to cast light upon a space which functions as a hieratic space. *L'Amour* shows a strong predilection for places which function as boundaries or as 'in-between' spaces, but in so doing seems only to transgress or abolish limits previously erected. A circular equivalence between origin and end, imbued with religious overtones, brings into existence the atmosphere of the end of the world, which is referred to in *Le Ravissement*.

1   The spatial imagery and the geometrical representation of Lol's sexual desire

In many ways the landscape of *L'Amour*, centred predominantly around the flattened surface of the beach, embodies the space described in *Le Ravissement*. However, a process of simplification has occurred in the passage from one text to the other at both the referential and the structural level. As mentioned above, the two works could be read as variations of the same text. The coexistence of two specific settings can be noted: the seascape and the urban landscape. The few allusions to the sea in *Le Ravissement* could easily be extracts from *L'Amour*: an empty beach, ..."la plage vide était autant que si elle n'avait pas été finie par Dieu" (RLVS p.172), disturbed only by the noise of the seagulls, "la mer est très basse, étale pour le moment, au-dessous des mouettes idiotes piaillent"(RLVS p.183)[6]. On several occasions the two works refer to the same dark ballroom, circularly arranged, with drawn curtains, green plants and an empty stage. Common features exist between the arrangement of Lol's lounge in her house in S.Tahla and the hall of the hotel in *L'Amour* (RLVS p.90 & A p.68), both furnished with armchairs strictly lined up along the white walls. References to buildings which carry over from one text to the other are common, though identity of the two can never be total. Houses in *L'Amour* are often outlined briefly. The inhabited villa noted in *L'Amour* (A pp.75-76), with the mention of one or

---

[6]The seascape is not, however, specific to *Le Ravissement* or to *L'Amour*. As Duras mentions in *Au delà des pages* (TF1 episode 4, February 1988), "...tous mes livres se passent au bord de la mer (...) tout est au bord de la mer". Indeed the seascape is a constant reference in Duras' novels, from *La Maladie de la Mort* to *Les Yeux Bleus, Cheveux Noirs*. Even in *Emily L.*, where the main constituent of the setting is the river, the sea is recalled by the blue and white colours of the seagulls: "les mouettes filent avec le vent, des folles" (EL p.20).

two descriptive elements - its gardens ('parc') and terrace - , recalls Tatiana's villa in *Le Ravissement* (RLVS p.68). One of the sparse details used to picture another building, the abandoned house (A p.55), situated on a hill ('hauteur'),[7] alludes also to Tatiana's villa, which is said to be situated on "une légère hauteur" (RLVS p.68). Indeed places tend to merge into each other in the descriptive accounts, not only when compared across the two texts, but also within one text. Thus the ballroom of *L'Amour* contains certain elements which bear a very close resemblance, both in nature and arrangement, to those in the hall of the hotel:

> "Il y a des glaces, elles sont ternies. Des fauteuils sont rangés face aux glaces, le long des murs clairs. Les socles de plantes vertes sont vides." (A p.128)
> "Le hall a changé d'aspect. Les glaces se sont ternies. Les fauteuils sont face aux glaces, rangés le long des murs blancs. Seules les plantes noires sont encore à leur place..." (A p.68)

Word for word, sentence for sentence, an identity between these two places is established: common allusions to the tarnished mirrors, to the armchairs arranged along the white walls, the presence or absence of plants...

This lack of descriptive discrimination, which assimilates places as varied in nature as Lol's lounge, the hall of a hotel or a ballroom, characterises Duras' texts and exemplifies one aspect of the simplification of space observable in *L'Amour*.

The most obvious indication of the similarity of space in the two texts, however, rests in the naming activity. S.Thala is the predominant location in the two works. Its name takes on particular importance in *L'Amour* since it is the only name used in the whole text. But as the orthographic variation in the passage from one text to the other indicates - S.Tahla in *Le Ravissement* has become S.Thala in *L'Amour* - the town of *L'Amour* carries in its signifier the mark of its similarity and of its dissimilarity to the town which Lol traverses in her walks. S.Thala presents a simplified space which has occurred through a shift of emphasis from the relatively spread-out decor of *Le Ravissement* to a unique

---

[7]'La hauteur' is also a recurrent feature in *L'Après-midi de Monsieur Andesmas*, where the terrace fulfils a key function.

place named S.Thala. Indeed we can barely discover any allusion to the T.Beach or the U.Bridge of *Le Ravissement* in the reference made to other towns in *L'Amour*:

> "Au-delà de la digue, une autre ville, bien au-delà, inaccessible, une autre ville, bleue, qui commence à se piquer de lumières électriques. Puis d'autres villes, d'autres encore: la même" (A p.11)

This operation of reduction to a single space exists together with a process of extension within *L'Amour*. The name S.Thala does not apply only to the town(s) in *L'Amour*; its denomination increasingly extends to the larger referential space: sea as well as town: "Tout ici, tout c'est S.Thala" (A p.66). This phenomenon is echoed lexically through the increasing presence of the word S.Thala. From p.15 onwards, the word S.Thala begins obsessively to replace other signifiers like "l'espace" or "l'ensemble". It recurs, for example, twenty times in the journey sequence (A pp.110-122).

The major device which brings about the simplification of space in *L'Amour*, however, is the use of recurrent imagery. Duras' texts always contain a certain degree of geographical imprecision; the country of *India Song*, for instance, is to a large extent the result of Duras' invention; the towns of S.T(ah)la, T.Beach, U.Bridge could not be found on any map. Within the textual topography of a given space like that of *Le Ravissement*, however, detailed accounts of the places mentioned can often be found:

> "Le centre de S.Tahla est étendu, moderne, à rues perpendiculaires. Le quartier résidentiel est à l'ouest de ce centre, large, il prend ses aises, plein de méandres, d'impasses imprévues. Il y a une forêt et des routes, après ce quartier..." (RLVS p.40)

For this structuration of space *L'Amour* substitutes a geometrical configuration, a schematised presentation of decor where "l'effet de réel" is kept to a minimal level. The text creates a neutral space defined geographically only by recurrent diagrams, mainly rectangles, quadrilaterals, triangular and circular patterns.

The rectangular imagery

In contrast to the detailed references to the successive houses inhabited by Lol, to the many streets and boulevards followed in her walks, the urban setting of *L'Amour* is described in its basic outline only. The houses are frequently alluded to as amalgamated with the town, elements fused into the general topography of "l'épaisseur de pierre" (A p.32). The textual space of *L'Amour* also reflects this lack of structured physical space: chapters are not clearly marked; instead the text unfolds with sequences of uneven length.

When individually described, buildings are presented as basic shapes, chiefly rectangular, within a static geometry. As its etymology indicates (rect/angle=straight angle), the shape of the rectangle carries the sign of its fixity. When explicitly named, the image of the rectangle serves to outline a schematised decor:

> "La maison est un rectangle gris aux volets blancs" (A p.55)
>
> "Devant eux la maison grise, le rectangle aux volets blancs, perdue au milieu du vertige de S.Thala" (A p.111)

The grey rectangle recalls a child's drawing, in which a few lines, transformed by imagination, suffice to create a referential world, a world whose fixity is nevertheless threatened by the polysemy of the descriptive activity. In the second example, the house is referred to a few lines later as a rectangle with white shutters. Another example adds to this impression of cardboard decor:

> "Entre lui et eux, il y a un rectangle de soleil découpé par l'ouverture du balcon. Personne ne franchit le rectangle de lumière" (A p.96)

The rectangle of light[8] which signals the opening of the balcony creates an impression of cut-out space. The rectangle explicitly referred to as "découpé" appears in a general context of stillness - "Il fait à S.Thala ce jour-là une grande chaleur immobile" (A p.85) - and symbolises in the anecdotal context separation, lack of communication between characters, since nobody in the

---

[8]The rectangle of light is a direct reference to the erection of a space which functions as a stage or as a filmic location. This aspect is examined in the last chapter of this study, in the section entitled 'Theatricality or the didactic dimension of Duras' texts'.

sequence dares to infringe the rectangular shape which separates the traveller from his wife and children.

Adventures of a quadrilateral shape

As an alternative to the rectangular imagery, the quadrilateral figure in its generic plurality, referring to various possible shapes: square, rectangle, rhomboid..., incidentally corresponds to the passage from the urban to the natural setting, from geometrical stasis to geographical mobility. It still alludes, however, to a human-made space, as shown in the following sequences from *L'Amour*.

> "Régulières, sans à-coups, les larmes coulent des yeux. Il se bâtit sur la mer un grand quadrilatère de lumière" (A p.102)
> "Il voit que le sable, sous ses yeux, s'éclaire. Il lève la tête, il aperçoit de la lumière sur la mer" (A p.103)
> "Il se bâtit sur la mer un grand quadrilatère de lumière blanche...Sur la mer le grand quadrilatère de lumière est bâti" (A p.103)
> "Le quadrilatère de lumière pluviale a disparu" (A p.105)

These sequences could be entitled "the adventures of the quadrilateral", the existence of which appears naturalised through its link with the apparition of light and the production of rain on a stormy day. Because of its recurrence, the quadrilateral figure structures the sequence in which it appears. The presence of this pattern is also treated anecdotally since the quadrilateral gradually shapes itself in the sky, remains there, then disappears. From this treatment the figure acquires not only its dynamism but also its narrative impact: the characters' behaviour mirrors the modifications of the setting linked to the presence of this pattern: the rain is echoed by the woman's tears, the light seems to emanate from her eyes.

The image of the quadrilateral serves mainly to demonstrate the unstable, though still recognizable, nature of Duras' settings, be they human or natural. On the other hand the use of the verb "bâtir", which primarily relates to the human activity, implies a certain degree of permanence. Paradoxically what is built up in *L'Amour* is doomed to disappear. The apparent stability of the image is just an illusion as 'le bâti-ment'..."de forme indéfinissable"

(A p.120), referring to the casino of S.Thala, seems to indicate. In contrast to *Le Ravissement*, which alludes to a process of reconstruction of the end of the world as a result of Lol's fantasy, *L'Amour* asserts a construction process existing of its own accord: "Il se bâtit sur la mer un grand quadrilatère de lumière...cela se bâtit" (A p.102). This points up the extreme versatility of a natural space in which natural 'events' such as the appearance of light, colour, or the movement of the sea, are treated as episodic. From the moment of their appearance these elements are doomed to sudden eclipse.

Rectangular shapes therefore create a simplified setting defined by its geometrical relations, in which the static quality of its cut-out decor, with its box-like houses of unspecified location hardly integrated into the surroundings, is compensated for by natural movement, although this too is occasionally represented in a geometrical mode.

The triangular geometry of desire

The main function of the geometrical vision of space in *L'Amour*, however, is the translation into graphic terms of the problematic of Lol's sexual desire[9] in *Le Ravissement*. The obsessive nature of Lol's phantasmatic quest, expressed in *Le Ravissement* by the distances relentlessly covered in the streets of S.Tahla, is expressed in *L'Amour* by a triangular geometry. This geometry reproduces the terms of Lol's desire, described by J.Hold in his narration of *Le Ravissement*.[10]

Lol's mental pursuit, originating in the trauma which followed the physical separation from her fiancé who abandoned her in order to dance with another woman during a ball at T.Beach, corresponds to a phantasm of identification doubled with an attempt at partial substitution. The identification is with the sexual desire observed between the lovers (Michael Richardson and Anne-Marie Stretter), whose relationship appears reenacted later

---

[9]This is a desire which, as has been shown in the study of Lol's madness in Chapter 3, is based on a different epistemology, which represents an impossibility for the bourgeois society of *Le Ravissement*.

[10]Even though, as we have seen in Chapter 3, doubt can be cast on J.Hold's narration, mainly through the use of external testimony and hypotheses, we may nevertheless trust his awareness of the problematic of Lol's desire to justify the analysis which follows.

in the couple J.Hold/Tatiana, and the substitution mechanism involves the woman who has taken her place: "Une place est à prendre, qu'elle n'a pas réussi à avoir à T.Beach" (RLVS p.60). The substitution in Lol's case can never be total since the origin of her phantasm lies in the necessary triangular relationship between lovers.[11] The fantasy of "enfermement à trois" has been lived once in the darkness of the walled-in ballroom:

> "Elle sourit, certes, à cette minute pensée de sa vie...Il ne reste de cette minute que son temps pur, d'une blancheur d'os...
> Et cela recommence: les fenêtres fermées, scellées, le bal muré dans sa lumière nocturne les aurait contenus tous les trois et eux seuls. Lol en est sûre: ensemble ils auraient été sauvés de la venue d'un autre jour, d'un autre, au moins." (RLVS p.47)

With the arrival of dawn, which signals the end of the ball, Lol predicts the imminent departure of the lovers. This event duly puts an end to the phantasmatic relationship, then amplifies Lol's desire and initiates a relentless mental quest for the reenactment of the short-lived moment.

> "Elle se voit...au centre d'une triangulation dont l'aurore et eux deux sont les termes éternels" (RLVS p.47)

Lol recreates the terms of her desire in *Le Ravissement* by her repeated walks through S.Tahla. Inhabited by her memories, she throws herself into errant pursuits which lead her to cover the different areas of the town from the centre to the suburbs (RLVS p.59) or to the residential area in the south of S.Tahla where Tatiana lives (RLVS p.68). The vagrancy in the recognizable structured space of S.Tahla is replaced in *L'Amour* by a gratuitous circulation on the neutral plane surface of the beach, on which the triangular shapes formed by the characters' movements signify the representation of desire laid bare in geometrical terms.

The image of the triangle functions as a focal point in the opening sequences of *L'Amour*; it is presented as an assertion of movement, pure geometry in action:

---

[11]Let us recall that what is at stake for Lol, both in T.Beach and in the reenactment of the trauma in S.Tahla, resides primarily in the relationship to the other woman.

"entre l'homme qui regarde et la mer, tout au bord de
la mer, loin, quelqu'un marche" (A p.87)
"Le triangle se ferme avec la femme aux yeux fermés"
(A p.8)
"Du fait de l'homme qui marche, constamment, avec
une lenteur égale, le triangle se déforme, se reforme
sans se briser jamais" (A p.8)
"Le glissement régulier du triangle sur lui-même prend
fin" (A p.9)
"Le triangle se défait, se résorbe. Il vient de se défaire"
(A p.10)

The triangle, evoked in its materiality as an outline traced in
the sand, embodies the main aspect of Lol's desire. The three
angles - and the suggested three sides - formed by the respective
positions of the characters represent diagramatically the triadic
relationship between lovers, whilst the constant shifting of position
(A p.8) and the circular repetition of movement parallel the
obsessive circulation of desire among the protagonists. The triangle
represents an enclosed structure reminiscent of the "bal muré" in
which Lol was prisoner of her own desire. The figure of the
triangle therefore establishes the passage from the mental space,
the triangulation in which Lol V.Stein imagines herself and which
is at the origin of her 'madness', to a flat projection on the
referential plane of this mental operation.

A phenomenon of 'mise en abyme' linked to the triangular
representation of space takes place later in the text. The triangle
appears in the referential structure of the setting: the island where
the woman sleeps is pictured as a triangle encased between the
two tributaries of the river: "la rivière se sépare. C'est là, entre les
deux bras de la rivière" (A p.43). The triangular island evokes in
physical terms the separation of the three lovers from the outside
world which is necessary to the existence of Lol's phantasm, and
which is expressed in *Le Ravissement* by the security of darkness.
The 'mise en abyme' effect is produced by the triangular position
adopted by the characters within this triangular setting. The
woman sleeps on a step, leaning against the prison wall, the walker
stands at the extreme point of the land while the traveller sits on
a bench twenty metres away from the woman.

"Il s'assied sur un banc, à mi-distance entre elle qui dort
et celui qui parle à la pointe de l'île" (A p.44)

This isosceles triangle formed within the triangle of the island reinforces the inescapable confinement of a relationship which holds the three characters together. In addition, the graphic layout of the island can be seen to refer metaphorically to the female sexual organ. This image allied to the insistent references to the tumultuous movement of waters at the rivermouth in this sequence alludes to the problematic of female erotic desire. Triangular patterns in *L'Amour* thus serve to make visible and to translate the terms of the female phantasm into material configurations.

Circular layout, or the circulation of desire

Circular graphics in turn structure the whole space of *L'Amour* and provide the support necessary for the circulation of desire. In *L'Amour*, gaze and space engender one another; the look exists in relation to space, and vice-versa. Topological and anthropological interdependence create a circular spatiality where the character constitutes the pivot around which space unfolds. If, however, we concentrate only on the spatial images used to picture the setting, we notice a proliferation of circular figures. This phenomenon asserts "ce royaume percé de toutes parts" (RLVS p.49) mentioned in *Le Ravissement*. The setting becomes the metaphorical representation of this "mot-absence" which motivates Lol's quest:- "Un mot-trou, creusé en son centre d'un trou, de ce trou où tous les autres mots auraient été enterrés" (RLVS p.48). Here again the very essence of Lol's sexual desire is laid out in referential terms: round elements of the setting indeed behave as in "ce royaume percé de toutes parts à travers lequel s'écoulent la mer, le sable" (RLVS p.49)

Roundness is obvious in the representational structure of the landscape: evocation of muddy water-holes and springs emptying onto the beach (A p.8), repeated reference to the abyss of the sea - "le gouffre" - and the river-mouth. Circular 'graphics' can alternatively be used to depict the urban decor, evocatively 'full', or to refer to the natural milieu made of 'empty' circles opening onto the surface.

The urban setting illustrates in an exemplary way the first type of circular shape; houses in *L'Amour* are inevitably surrounded by walls, fences, gardens:

"Une allée est devant elle. Au bout une grille blanche.
Le parc s'étend, vertes pelouses, jusqu'à la grille fermée"
(A p.78)

The emphasis on the circularity of the space around the
house signifies enclosure, doubled with ambiguous semes of threat
and separation.

"L'épouvante passe, terrasse, parc, lieux d'épouvante
tout à coup...Elle montre autour d'elle l'habitation, le
parc, l'espace clos de murs, de grilles, les défenses" (A
p.83)

'Full' circles, however, are deceptive, their plenitude is only
illusory. The emphasis on circularity blots out the centre, imposing
a landscape metaphorically structured in a similar way to the
"mot-trou" which constitutes Lol's quest in *Le Ravissement*. The
walls of the few houses alluded to in *L'Amour* all surround gardens
which in turn surround other buildings; the house itself is hardly
depicted at all, as if the inside of the circle had been eaten away.

The town S.Thala illustrates further the deceptiveness of the
'full' circle. By the repeated use of the word "contourner" S.Thala
becomes circularly enclosed. The sequences which retrace the
journey in S.Thala (A pp.110-122) present, in contrast to repeated
references to the volume or thickness of the town which represent
the external vision, a town riddled with holes in a general
atmosphere of emptiness. After a deceptive reference to plenitude
at the beginning of the sequence - the villas touch each other, the
parks are smaller - houses come to stand in the middle of a
vertical void, "le vertige de S.Thala", as so many holes from which
the inhabitants emerge: "Les voici tout à coup surgis de la ville, des
trous, de la pierre..." (A p.117). At the heart of S.Thala, the casino,
a 'quasi-no'; an almost-nothing, stands at the centre of the spatial
configuration of the town. A hole dominates the sea, and the fact
that its openings have been nailed up does not alter the
significance of this but rather reinforces the meaning of emptiness.

'Empty' circles, however, often referred to in conjunction with
a descending swallowing movement, connote depth, and become
direct representations of this "mot-trou creusé en son centre d'un
trou (...) où tous les autres mots auraient été enterrés" (RLVS
p.48). The abyss or whirlpool, metaphorical signifier of the sea in
L'Amour, becomes, at the referential level, a "mise en abyme" of

this phenomenon of engulfment of other elements: "...une flaque se vide, une source, un fleuve, des fleuves, sans répit, alimentent le gouffre de sel" (A p.8)

Graphically and lexically, the textual space of *L'Amour* reinforces the significance of the referential space. Andermatt notes in *Le Ravissement* "the prevalence of the letter 'o', as absence, as opening, as containing a missing term within its circumference". Present not only in Lol's name, it can also be seen in some passages where by a "repetition of similar sound-images the eye perceives, in the 'o', the plenitude and perfection of the circle reversible into nothingness".[12] Repetition of words, sounds and letters is much extended in *L'Amour*: "source", "gouffre", "embouchure" all contain the 'o', the sign of the void, at their centre. And as the text unfolds, the hole suggested by the letter 'o' and by its associated sound u pervades the whole of the text. In a mirroring effect the descriptive evocation of the gestures and the movements of the characters reveals a proliferation of the 'o/ou' which again defines space as circular. The words "autour", "partout", "tout", "tout autour", "montrer autour", "tourner", "contourner" are rife.

Metaphorical figures, though limited in number in *L'Amour*, also allude to a landscape pierced with holes:

> "Au-delà de la digue...une autre ville, bleue, qui commence à se piquer de lumières électriques" (A p.11)
> "Il (le cri) a lacéré la lumière obscure, la lenteur" (A p.12)

In the first of these examples a semantic proliferation is taking place. "Se piquer" can be read as 'to be spotted', as if by rust or mould. The light, thus connotatively treated as equivalent to mould, and reminiscent of another example in which the light oxidises the sea and the sky, "la mer est déjà oxydée par la lumière obscure, de même que le ciel" (A p.9), has a pervasive effect on the landscape. In several passages in *L'Amour*, space behaves as in chemical reactions where elements react with each other. Thus elements such as light or colour appear suddenly and act upon

---

[12]Verena Andermatt quotes J.Hold's description of Lol and Tatiana at the dinner party (RLVS p.147), where both women wear black and appear more similar in the eyes of the men. (op.cit. p.28)

other elements of the setting before disappearing, unexpectedly, by absorption or dissolution.

The unusual redundance of stylistic figures in a short space - a metaphor and an oxymoron in "Il a lacéré la lumière obscure" - produces a somewhat phantasmatic effect in the second example above. Light is made tangible by the use of the word "lacéré" - it is lacerated by sound - and is thus extended to become the symbol of the whole space. Elements which operate as threats for other spatial elements - here the sound threatens the light - are not unusual in *L'Amour*.

Circular graphics therefore delineate a space in a state of constant instability. In a text which elaborates constantly upon 'o'/the hole, the plenitude and perfection of the circle are readily reversible into nothingness.

In the movement from *Le Ravissement* to *L'Amour*, a reduction in the complexity of space has therefore taken place. The setting has acquired the characteristics of Lol's madness itself in becoming, like unreason which cannot be apprehended by the 'fullness' of reason, a representation of the void. It furthermore reflects Lol's sexual fantasy in giving priority to a mobility which ensures the circulation of desire.

Geometrical patterns enhance the nature of space in *L'Amour*, a space in a constant process of structuring/destructuring. *L'Amour* presents a space conceived of as emptiness, in which the shapes of rectangles - houses, quadrilaterals of light -, the triangular patterns traced on the sand, and the circular swallowing up of spatial elements all contribute to the filling of a void. An important characteristic of space thus emerges: space exists prior to its constitutive elements. "la mer, le ciel, occupent l'espace" (A p.9). "L'espace...occupé ou vide" (A p.12).

This repeated movement of inclusion/exclusion in space of geometric forms or of other spatial elements (sound, light) engenders a phenomenon of successive construction and destruction of space in *L'Amour*. Lol V.Stein's belief in a time always ready to be used, a basic feature of her fantasy world, reappears transferred onto the referential plane and is realized in the spatial configurations of *L'Amour*.

> "Elle croyait qu'un temps était possible qui se remplit et
> se vide alternativement, qui s'emplit et se désemplit,

puis qui est prêt encore, toujours, à servir..." (RLVS p.159).

This aspect, linked to the concentration on the spatialisation of the characters' looks - "ils déchiffrent l'espace" - , suggests that space has become, in *L'Amour*, one of the active elements of the fiction.

2   Liquidity as actualisation of Lol's fantasy

"L'eau et la folie sont liées pour longtemps dans le rêve de l'homme européen" (HF p.22)

Inspired by Gaston Bachelard's work, I now propose to show how a dominant element of the landscape, water, shapes the space of *L'Amour*, secures a demarcation from *Le Ravissement* and in so doing becomes more suited to the actualisation of certain aspects of the phantasm.

In *Le Ravissement* allusions to liquidity remain episodic and easily circumscribed. References to phenomena of liquefaction are mostly attributed metaphorically to the characters, or alternatively to evocations of the phantasm of the ball. The characters' subjectivity in *Le Ravissement* is frequently presented in images of viscosity. Forgetfulness is alluded to as "engluement" (RLVS p.135), emotions are compared to a greasy substance: "Partout le sentiment, on glisse sur cette graisse" (RLVS p.159). Yet free-flowing emotions can also occur in the text:

"Elle (Lol V.Stein) baigne dans la joie. Les signes de celle-ci sont éclairés jusqu'à la limite du possible, ils sortent par flots d'elle-même tout entière" (RLVS p.165)

In *L'Amour*, spatial configurations correspond to the transposition into external space of the characters' internal moves. The movement of waters in *L'Amour* expresses the emotionality of the characters in a manner comparable to that in *Le Ravissement*:

"Je (J.Hold) vais tomber. Une faiblesse monte dans mon corps, un niveau s'élève, le sang noyé, le coeur est de vase, mou, il s'encrasse..." (RLVS p.111)
"La mer monte entre les berges de vase" (A p.43)
"La mer monte toujours. La rivière se remplit. Les berges sont noyées..." (A p.48)

Feelings and emotions expressed in liquid terms in *Le Ravissement* are presented as a threat to the characters' existence, as potentially destructive as are the sea's waters for the setting of *L'Amour*:

> "...des mouettes sont mortes sur la plage. Du côté de la digue, un chien. Le chien mort est face aux piliers d'un casino bombardé...C'est après l'orage, la mer est mauvaise" (A p.33)

This observation correlates with the point made above in chapter 3, that Lol's alternative mode of existence can only be actualised beyond the limits of subjectivity.

The liquid setting of *L'Amour* confirms the shift which has taken place from the characters of *Le Ravissement* to the composition of the new landscape. This displacement accounts at the anecdotal level for the characters' extreme concentration on the setting of *L'Amour*: "Ils déchiffrent l'espace"; emptied of themselves, the characters direct their attention towards the outside.

References to liquidity in *Le Ravissement* can also occur in the irruption of the phantasm. A marine vocabulary develops when the memory of the phantasmatic ball is evoked: the ball becomes "une épave dans un océan" (RLVS p.45) or

> "ce navire de lumière sur lequel chaque après-midi Lol s'embarque mais qui reste là, dans ce port impossible, à jamais amarré et prêt à quitter, avec ses trois passagers, tout cet avenir-ci..." (RLVS p.49)

The specific use of liquidity in the reference to Lol V.Stein's phantasm of the ball also alludes by comparison to a world in *L'Amour* which, as we shall see, is by its very nature more consistently suited to expressing the terms of the phantasm.

Passage from the tangible world of Le Ravissement de Lol V.Stein to the liquidity of L'Amour

One extract from *Le Ravissement* embodies in its reference to liquidity the operation which takes place in the movement from *Le Ravissement* to *L'Amour*: the emigration of substance from the characters to the setting, and the loss of 'objective' meaning which supports the emergence of the phantasm. In this passage, Tatiana's nudity acquires such a perspective for the characters that it stands out against the other elements of reality.

> "La nudité de Tatiana déjà nue grandit dans une surexposition qui la prive davantage du moindre sens possible. Le vide est statue. Le socle est là: la phrase. Le vide est Tatiana nue sous les cheveux noirs, le fait. Il se transforme, se prodigue, le fait ne contient plus le fait. Tatiana sort d'elle-même, se répand par les fenêtres ouvertes, sur la ville, les routes, boue, liquide, marée de nudité" (RLVS p.116)

Through a pouring-out process which affects the setting - "Tatiana sort d'elle-même", "se répand" -, factual reality (here Tatiana's nudity) empties itself of meaning: "le fait ne contient plus le fait". As a consequence of the outflowing of the signified, emptiness is instituted: "le vide est statue". *L'Amour* extends to its own space the significance of this passage. As we have seen in the first part of this section, circularity, by its very nature and also by the establishment of a constant flowing of waters from the pond to the abyss, from the river to the sea, constructs a space which functions as a void. Its continuous movement alludes only to its own emptiness.

The space of *L'Amour* establishes the abolition of a tangible, solid world in favour of a liquid universe. *Le Ravissement* presents a world which does not flow. The structure of its decor is fixed in its spatial configurations as a contrast to a world which is in constant flux in *L'Amour*. Allusions to water in the referential setting construct a frozen world. S.Tahla is submitted to a "quotidienne glaciation" through Lol's lack of memory (RLVS p.61), and J.Bedford, in the cold order of Lol's house, "guette le craquement des glaces de l'hiver" (RLVS p.34). Water takes the form of a hard surface, like the sea in the mirror, "la glace", "la mer était dans la glace de la salle d'attente" (RLVS p.171).

As a contrast to this fixed world, there is a loss of solidity in *L'Amour*, the threat of friability, concomitant with the displacement from the urban setting to the granular texture of the sand. The town S.Thala itself evokes the crumbling of a world covered in white ashes (A p.112). Mineralisation has replaced any sign of life. The casino, in *Le Ravissement*, is untypically evoked through liquidity. "Sa blancheur toujours de lait, de neige, de sucre" (RLVS p.176) pictures a world which flows or dissolves. In

L'Amour the casino has become chalk-like: "c'est un bâtiment indéfinissable de la blancheur de la craie" (A p.120). Organic matter has disappeared in favour of extensive mineralisation: chalk, dust, ashes, elements which become the signs of a desolate universe, and which anecdotally justify at the end of the sequence (A p.121) the return of characters from the town to the sand. The sand indeed asserts the realm of the formless. Its friable substance constitutes a threat to stability, and its flowing nature, "écoulement de sable, continu" (A p.63) announces the transition to liquidity.

> "L'histoire.   Elle   commence...mais   elle   devient maintenant visible. C'est sur le sable que déjà elle s'implante, sur la mer" (A p.13)

The sea or the sand cannot be trusted to support writing which can disappear, liquefy, at any moment. *L'Amour* constitutes the passage to a liquid universe in which the predominance of waters (sea, river...) remains constant throughout the text.

Liquidity and female desire

In giving priority to water over other elements (fire, air, earth), the text of *L'Amour* enhances a liquid 'rêverie' which takes on feminine configurations. the threat to this 'rêverie', however, lies precisely in the ambivalent masculinity of water, or else in the possible reversibility towards solidification.

A poetic imagination may see in the essential components of the landscape of *L'Amour* the predominance of a feminine world. Genette recalls Bachelard's attention to the importance of word gender[13] in the sexualising reverie of things. The liquid components of space in *L'Amour* are mostly of female gender: la mer, la rivière, la flaque, la source, l'embouchure; the passage to the masculine in 'le gouffre', for example, implies, as we shall see later, a threat to the feminine.

L'Amour includes the two types of water: soft water - "l'eau terrestre" - and, predominantly, sea water, "l'eau lourde de sel". The evocation of the island banks provides an image of sexualised water which metaphorically represents the feminine sex through the triangle-shape (cf. p.167 above) and through the evocation of "la trouée", "l'embouchure" (A p.44). The soft waters in *L'Amour*

---

[13]Gérard Genette, *Figures II* (Coll. Points 1969) p.119

also carry the traditional connotations linked to femininity: calm and passivity are present in the evocation of "les surfaces d'eau calme, isolées". The circumvolutions of the river which are the geological basis for the island where the woman can sleep, "entre les bras de la rivière", produces the image of a maternal refuge, a cradle, in contrast to the increasingly violent movement to which the waters of the river are submitted. 'Soft' waters, in their sacrificial passivity, can become grist for the salted monster, the sea:

> "Une flaque se vide, une source, un fleuve, des fleuves, sans répit, alimentent le gouffre de sel" (A p.8)
> "Il croit réentendre la coulée, la descente continue des eaux vers le gouffre de sel" (A p.27)

One particular reference to the sea in *L'Amour* refers to female fecundity (A pp.23-26). "Pregnant waters" can be linked closely with the woman's situation. The repeated references to the nauseating movement of the swell in the sequence, and the presence of white 'eruptions' - "les éclatements blancs" -, introduce the 'nutritious' image of milk.

> "Le mouvement de la mer commence à se voir, la houle affleure et se résout en éclatements blancs"(A p.26)

However, as the word "éclatement" suggests, the nutritive liquid can become violence, at the same time soft and bitter. Soft water performs in accordance with the connotations implied in its particular signifier in so far that it becomes soft to the point of sacrifice, while the sea, in spite of its attempt to soften and become "la mer...verte, fraîche" (A p.59), remains most often not "la mère" but "l'amer" with its "âcre odeur déterrée des eaux" (A p.109).

Thus the sea represents violent waters in *L'Amour*. "La mer est une ennemie qui cherche à vaincre et qu'il faut vaincre"[14]. Lafourcade's comment is echoed by Marguerite Duras:

---

[14]Gaston Bachelard, *L'Eau et les Rêves* (Corti, Paris 1968) p.225. Lafourcade's original comment can be found in *La Jeunesse de Swinburne*, vol.1 p.50. It is a conclusion which, if we take into account the plurality of meaning contained in the homonym mer/mère, fits well with the representation of the mother in Duras' fiction: whenever she is represented, as in *Un Barrage Contre le Pacifique*, *L'Amant* or in the beggar-woman's story, the mother contains a threat to the children.

"La mer me fait très peur, c'est la chose au monde dont j'ai le plus peur...Mes cauchemars, mes rêves d'épouvante ont toujours trait à la marée, à l'envahissement par l'eau" (L p.84)

Hardened by its masculine element, salt, which by its very nature counteracts any 'dream of softness', the sea enters into sexual conflict with land waters. Bachelard points out that

"C'est une perversion qui a salé les mers. Le sel entrave une rêverie, la rêverie d'une douceur, une des rêveries les plus matérielles et naturelles qui soient"[15].

Incidentally the recurrent image of the abyssal swallowing, "l'engouffrement", used to typify the action of the sea, corresponds to another displacement which takes place in the transition from *Le Ravissement* to *L'Amour*. The swallowing which characterises the wind in the former work shifts to the sea in *L'Amour*, indicating again the passage to a liquid universe.

"L'engouffrement du sel" however corresponds to a sexual assault upon soft waters, the feminine principle in the text of poetic imagination; the sequence in which the characters intensely watch the interpenetration of the sea and the river waters (A pp.43-55) is the retracing of a sexual scene. The threatening rise of the sea - "la mer monte entre les berges de vase" (A p.43) - with the noise and the movement of aggressive insertion between the river banks, sexually referred to as "la trouée de la mer", culminates in an intense disarray, a whirlpool or "le désordre des embouchures" (A p.46). The climatic intensity soon gives way to the calm resulting from the interpenetration of the waters.

"il montre la rivière envahie, les déchirures de l'eau, la remontée brutale du sel vers le sommeil" (A p.47)

The ambivalence of the sea (sometimes maternal but most often performing as masculine waters) exemplifies the sense of threat which pervades the text. Thus a threat to the landscape occurs when water becomes mixed with solid substances and consequently tends to lose its fluidity.

The sea can become a threat since it performs above all as "un gouffre de sel", an abyss of salt. In providing the sea with a

---

[15]Bachelard op.cit. p.211

solid substance, the salt guarantees its aggressiveness. Sea waters indeed are often maleficient, mischievous. Changes of mood constitute a menace to the landscape as the angry waters, in an example already cited, devastate the beach, and litter it with dead seagulls and a dead dog, near a semi-derelict casino.

However, when the sea allies with the sand, it becomes 'water of death': "vase noire". "Le ciel noircit. La mer basse s'alourdit, elle devient vase noire" (A p.137). Another example of water whose thickening carries the meaning of death is provided in *L'Amour* by the viscous gas-oil indirectly referred to in "la fumée des pétroles" (A p.28). Indeed as Bachelard observes, for material imagination "tout liquide est une eau; ensuite toute eau est un lait"[16] and oil, as a contrast to the white nutritious image contained in "les éclatements blancs", represents the black milk, the "aliment du feu".

> "C'est peut-être l'idée que le feu s'alimente comme un être vivant qui tient le plus de place dans les opinions que s'en forme notre inconscient".[17]

Bachelard notes that one can find in the chemistry of fire all the characteristics of digestion,[18] and in *L'Amour* as in many other texts smoke becomes an excrement of fire:

> "La ville, là-bas, est invisible, engluée dans ses excrétions" (A p.101)

Organic imagination creates in the town S.Thala a morbid space, a landscape of death. The menace lies in the viscous nature of the black liquid, oil, which sustains the existence of another element, fire, the (exact) opposite of water. The subsequently dried-out space of the town, which has become ashes, dust and chalk under the combined action of fire and sun, has become a still universe which, though circumscribed within the town, nevertheless functions as a threat to the moving liquidity which guarantees the existence of a phantasmatic space. However the connotations of the name S.Thala tend to reestablish the predominance of a liquid milieu. The phonetic nature of S.Thala, marked by the repeated 'a'

---

[16]ibid. p.158

[17]Gaston Bachelard, *La Psychanalyse du Feu* (Idees, 1949) p.109

[18]ibid. p.110

and the labial 'l' posited as a hinge at the centre of the word, thus preventing accumulation, points to this "psychisme hydrant" which characterises the text of *L'Amour*:

> "...la voyelle 'a' est la voyelle de l'eau. Elle commande aqua, apa, wasser. C'est le phonème de la création par l'eau...".[19]

In this section we have attempted to indicate the major importance of one of the components of the landscape in *L'Amour*: of water. We can conclude that not only does liquidity generally allude to the very desire of language which aspires to flowing, "le langage veut couler",[20] but that in the context of *L'Amour* liquidity serves to connote a feminine desire, Lol's desire, threatened by masculinity, itself the representation of an ideological order, taken as a loading of substance. Waters need to remain pure, calm water being crucial to the preservation of femininity. Moreover liquidity secures movement against solidification. The transitory nature of water corresponds to the need for a phantasmatic world which must remain fluid and in movement, floating above a fixed reality like the phantasm of the ball.

3 The setting of *L'Amour* and the reconstruction of the end of the world

As a result of her fantasy, Lol attempts to reconstruct the atmosphere of the end of the world which she experiences in the traumatic scene of the ball. Emptiness constitutes the means by which the reconstruction can happen. This is done in *Le Ravissement* by a formal, fixed arrangement of Lol's house, which becomes "un univers aux confins vides" (RLVS p.45), and later by a mental process of forgetfulness: "elle commence à marcher dans le palais fastueux de l'oubli de S.Thala" (RLVS p.43).[21]

---

[19]Bachelard op.cit. (*L'Eau et les Rêves*) p.253

[20]ibid. p.251

[21]This process, which constitutes a prerequisite for the Durasian mode of being (that of freed desire apprehended by Reason as madness), is didactically mentioned by the woman of *L'Homme Atlantique* to the actor: "vous oublierez...que c'est vous, vous l'oublierez (...) Je crois qu'il est possible d'y arriver, par exemple à partir d'autres approches, de celle entre autres de la mort, de votre mort perdue dans une mort régnante et sans nom" (HA pp.7-8).

The actualisation of the phantasm, referred to as the reconstruction of the end of the world, comes into existence in *L'Amour* through means which work at the level of the constitution of the setting itself. We have already shown in the first part of this section that *L'Amour* presents in its spatial imagery a space structured as a void. We shall be more concerned here with the nature of the places which constitute the landscape of *L'Amour*. A marked predilection for space as opposed to places will become evident, as will a valorisation of places which function as limits and hence initiate a paradoxical play on the nature of boundaries. We shall see that such a structuration of space serves to support the symbolic status of a setting which asserts itself as a hieratic space.

The cosmic value of space

The nature of the places to be found in *L'Amour* most often supports the priority given to space; space understood here in the two distinct etymological senses of the space-in-between (l'écart, l'intervalle) and of its more general, cosmic meaning. Possibly as an echo of the place Lol occupies in the ball scene - she stands between the two lovers -, the text of *L'Amour* reveals a high incidence of places which function as transitory loci or 'écarts référentiels'. Most of the 'human' settings in which the characters meet refer to mutually adjacent places: hallways, balcony, hotel forecourt, stairs, terrace. Such locations appear to be not unlike those insubstantial places - "lieux sans lieux" - mentioned by Foucault in referring to Blanchot's fiction.[22] Indeed the transitory value of such places is reinforced by the limited episodic function they perform in the text. They appear in short sequences to stress for instance the passage of a character through the hallway (A p.56) or the position of a protagonist: the traveller repeatedly stands at the window or on the balcony (A p.73).

The evacuation of places in favour of space is however more significant in the shift towards the sand which typifies the setting of *L'Amour*. If one can find places representative of themselves in *L'Amour* such as houses, a cafe, the casino, S.Thala, the island, such places nevertheless exist isolated in the landscape, carefully enclosed or circumscribed in their particular sequences. The exploration of a house by one character or an escape towards the

---

[22]Michel Foucault, 'La Pensée du Dehors' in *Critique* no.229 (1996) p.529

town, often scrutinized by the other protagonists, are presented as a threat. Contrary to the Proustian space, however,[23] which appears deprived of space in its fragmented presentation of places, the setting of *L'Amour* provides a non-restrictive, often panoramic view of its diegetic space. The sea and the beach provide in their anecdotal relevance the physical support for this infinite surface which characterises space in its cosmic mode. Consistently present throughout the text - the characters converge, evolve on the beach...echoed in conversations "c'est un pays de sables...de vent" (A p.53) -, the sand asserts in *L'Amour* the displacement from the urban setting to the spatiality of the beach. This is a shift already announced at the end of *Le Ravissement* by Lol's journey to the sea. "L'investissement des sables" (A pp.106- 107) corresponds, as the word 'investissement' suggests, to the assumption of power by the sand. *L'Amour* presents the story of a shift from a limited place to a cosmic one, from the "Babylone délaissée" of S.Thala (A p.106) to the surface of the sand. Similarly one can say that the true inhabitants of *L'Amour* are the voices coming from the sand rather than the ghost-like inhabitants of S.Thala. The depersonalisation process in which the characters are reduced to voices points, in *L'Amour*, to a dematerialised world and to the actualisation of the imaginary world of *Le Ravissement*.

The stress placed on the infinity of landscape, and as a corollary on its emptiness, through the valorisation of the sand, is reinforced by the priority given to referents such as "l'espace", "la totalité", "le tout", "l'ensemble". Table 2 (p.182) gives as an example the list of instances in which the word "espace" or one of its composites is used, be it referentially or metaphorically.

A semantic contamination occurs at the lexical level which underlines the bias towards a panoramic view of the world. Space in its function of support for characters' actions is minimised in favour of its more cosmic value. "...regarder la mer, c'est regarder le tout. Et regarder le sable, c'est regarder le tout, un tout." (L p.86)

The priority given to the unity of substance indicates a homogenous view of the world. Such an emphasis corresponds to a principle of spatial continuity, to a philosophy of space in which space is presented as an abstract reality;

---

[23]George Poulet, *L'Espace Proustien* (Gallimard, Paris 1963)

Table 2   *List of instances in which the word "espace" is used in
            L'Amour*

page no.	
12	"Le cri a été proféré et on l'a entendu dans l'espace tout entier, occupé ou vide"
15	"Elle montre autour d'elle, l'espace..."
18	"...le voyageur lève la main et montre autour de lui, l'espace."
29	"...son regard bleu inspecte à son tour l'espace..."
32	"Ainsi chaque jour doivent-ils couvrir la distance, l'espace des sables de S.Thala"
40	"Il entre dans l'espace clos..."
50	"le silence commence par un espacement des départs de bateaux...le silence commence par un espacement des temps...la plainte vient de s'espacer"
54	"...Il regarde vers la mer, au fond de l'espace"
64	"...elle déchiffre lentement l'espace..."
69	"...Il s'immobilise au milieu de la piste, montre l'espace, décrit l'espace entre les fauteuils alignés et les piliers..."
70	"...Puis, de nouveau, montre l'espace, décrit l'espace entre les fauteuils alignés."
72	"le voyageur ne les voit nulle part dans l'espace, le temps, de S.Thala"
84	"Dehors. L'espace..."
107	"Elle regarde au-dela de l'hôtel et des parcs, l'enchaînement continu de l'espace"
133	"Il n'y a que lui de vivant dans tout l'espace visible..."
142	"La lumière monte, ouvre, montre l'espace qui grandit."

"Pour le philosophe, l'espace est ce qui précède les lieux. Ce qui à priori se trouve là pour les recevoir."[24]

A writing practice based on such a philosophy in which space in its cosmic dimension has become the main locus of the fictional world, reinforces the uniformisation process taking place in the passage from *Le Ravissement* to *L'Amour* exemplified in the first part of this section. An infinite space indeed constitutes a prerequisite for this 'end of the world' universe, in which, as we shall see later, can be discerned an equivalence, both in spatial and temporal terms, between the concepts of beginning and end.

The uniformisation of the setting resulting from the referential priority given to 'space as such' appears, however, to be at least partly compromised by a certain structuration of the background through a paradoxical play on the nature of boundary.

The problematic of transgression: places as limits and boundaries

An emphasis on what functions as a limit in the setting of *L'Amour* can be detected in the repeated use of sequences in which geographical landmarks are stressed. A proliferation of prepositional morphemes throughout the text serves to designate spatial relations. Examples of this are: "vers" (A pp. 14,15,20,23,24,25,33,44,51,54,etc.), "jusqu'à" (pp.15,78,etc.), "autour" (pp.15,19,46,51,55,73,83,89,etc.), "derrière" (pp.28,29,4042,76,etc.), "devant" (pp.14,29,42,47,55,74,76,etc.), "au-dessus" (pp.28,33,84,102, 104,105,etc.). Two short extracts, which recall filmic writing, exemplify the high concentration of spatial determinants:

> "Au matin, des mouettes sont mortes sur la plage. *Du côté de* la digue, un chien. Le chien mort est *face* aux piliers d'un casino bombardé. *Au-dessus*, le ciel est très sombre, *au-dessus* du chien mort." (A p.33)
> "*Devant* lui, la route vide, *derrière* la route, des villas éteintes, des parcs. *Derrière* les parcs, l'épaisseur, insaisissable, S.Thala dressée."(A p.42)
>
> (*my emphasis*)

Similarly a wider vocabulary emphasises in relay-like fashion the limit-line in the idea of going along or around. A referential

---

[24]Poulet op.cit. p.58

demarcation is rendered through repeated expressions such as "longer" (pp.92,106,etc.), "border" (pp. 43,74,etc.), "contourner" (pp.58,106,etc.), "aller le long de" (pp.43,62,67,68,etc.): "Le voyageur passe le long de la mer. Il longe l'hôtel derrière le mur" (A p.55).

Moreover a semantic barrier is established through the repeated use of privatives: "inaccessible" (pp.11,12), "impossibilité" (p.18), "indéfini" (pp.7,8,20), "illimité" (pp.21,73), "insaisissable" (pp.42,43), "infatigable" (p.58), "innombrable" (p.73), "invisible" (p.101), "inexplicable" (p.117), "indéchiffrable" (p.134), "indiscernable" (p.142).

The following extract exemplifies the cumulative effect of such expressions over a sample passage:

```
1    "Jour.
     L'homme marche de nouveau au bord de la mer.
     Elle est là de nouveau, contre le mur.
     La lumière est intense. Elle est sans mouvement
5    aucun, ses lèvres sont serrées. Elle est pâle.
     Il y a sur la plage une certaine vie.
     A l'approche du voyageur, elle ne fait aucun signe.
     Il va vers le mur. Il s'assied à côté d'elle. Il regarde ce qu'elle
     veut, semble-t-il, éviter de voir: la mer, le mouvement
10   nauséeux de la houle, les mouettes de la mer qui crient et
     dévorent le corps du sable, le sang...
     ...Elle se tourne vers lui.
     Là-bas l'homme s'arrête au milieu des mouettes. Puis
     repart, va vers la digue...Elle se tient, le visage vers le sable.
15   Lui regarde vers la digue celui qui s'éloigne." (A p.23)
```

The presence of "une certaine vie" is central to the passage. It refers directly to the child the woman is carrying, who in order to be born will have to break free from the mother's physical boundaries. But it also alludes metaphorically to the liberatory process the female character herself has to go through, in Duras' fictions, in order to live more fully. This manifestation of life at the heart of the passage, reinforced by references to nausea (line 10), to blood (line 11) or to the body,[25] is contained or repressed. The

---

[25]The anthropomorphisation of the setting is obvious at this point. It is reinforced by a set of isotopies which, in the passage, oppose proximity ("il s'assied à côté d'elle... elle se tourne vers lui...le visage vers le sable...") to distance

sense of the limit as interdiction runs through the passage via the chain of privatives and the reference to the woman's avoidance of speech (line 5) and of seeing (line 8-9).

A thematisation of the limit can also occur in the referential setting. The demarcative line allied to a sense of interdiction is emphasised in the references to walls and to gates. "Elle montre autour d'elle l'habitation, le parc, l'espace clos de murs, des grilles, les défenses" (A p.83).

The erection of limits or boundaries thus apparent in the text of *L'Amour* constitutes an ultimate attempt[26] to counteract the uniformisation of the setting, and establishes a tension between the assertion of boundaries and their negation.

In an infinite background, elements have a tendency to fuse into each other, and we have seen in the section on objects that the sea and the town take on common characteristics. The inside tends to merge with the outside and the prison, for instance, becomes 'dehors les murs' (A p.54). Consequently the attempt to separate spatial elements from each other by erecting demarcation points justifies the insistent gaze of the characters upon the setting.

However the emphasis on boundaries, with its subsequent tension between erecting and negating them at the textual and referential levels, gives rise to a real questioning of the notion of limit when dealing with referential places which - often explicitly in the text - act as physical boundaries (the sea wall, S.Thala). Such a questioning directly reflects the problematic of madness, and the tension between free expression and repression which constitutes the dilemma of deviancy in relation to the accepted limit or norm.

After erecting S.Thala and the sea-wall as limits or interdictions

"Ici c'est S.Thala jusqu'à la rivière" (A p.19)

("là-bas...l'homme va vers la digue..."), or the inside ("le corps du sable...le sang") to the outside ("la mer...la houle"), and exemplifies at a spatial level the dynamic of the characters' quest inscribed between nothingness and infinity.

[26]An attempt also present in *L'Homme Atlantique*: "vous penserez que le miracle n'est pas dans l'apparente similitude entre chaque particule de ces milliards du déferlement continu, mais dans la différence irréductible qui les sépare..." (HA p.11) I shall return to the significance of this in terms of the characters' mode of existence in the final chapter of this study.

"Il a atteint la digue. Il ne l'a pas dépassée" (A p.11)

the arbitrariness of the demarcative line appears to be explicitly pointed out:

"Après la rivière, c'est encore S.Thala" (A p.20)
"C'est vrai que je me suis perdu...j'ai dépassé la distance...Il indique du geste la direction solitaire de derrière la masse noire de la digue" (A p.41)

The recognition of borderlines and their subsequent negation establishes a problematic of transgression. Indeed there is no simple negation; an emphasis on negation is set up in which the limit previously asserted serves to uphold the interrelated meanings of interdiction/transgression. The overstepping of the limit, seen as the transgression of what is implicitly forbidden and therefore avoided, becomes an issue repeatedly mentioned in the text, and metaphorically reinforces the dilemma between Reason and Unreason as experienced by the characters.

"Je la cherche, il explique - quelquefois elle dépasse les bornes de S.Thala, mais il suffit de le savoir" (A p.87)
"...Elle dit:
- quelquefois il dépasse S.Thala mais il suffit de le savoir, elle ajoute - d'attendre...
Le voyageur dit
- On ne peut pas dépasser S.Thala, on ne peut pas y entrer.
- Non, mais lui - elle entend - lui quelquefois, il se perd" (A p.29)

To ignore or transgress the limit which exists as a metaphor of reason does not make it disappear since, as Sollers mentions, "La transgression...lève l'interdit sans le supprimer."[27] Rather a meaning of loss of identity felt as the ultimate danger is elaborated. "Il remonte vers la ville de S.Thala et cette fois il se perd dans son épaisseur" (A p.138). The prohibition experienced as danger produces the characters' anxious wait and gaze. In contrast to *Le Ravissement*, in which transgression does not occur - places like the forest, symbolic locus of interdiction, are never penetrated by Lol -, *L'Amour* erects places of interdiction such as

---

[27]Philippe Sollers, *L'Ecriture et L'Expérience des Limites* (Points, 1970) p.108

the sea wall and, more particularly, S.Thala, as focal points in the landscape, and after an initial avoidance, the characters enter the forbidden area, the space of madness.

In terms of its plot, the sense of transgression gives the text its dramatic overtones and creates a tension explicit in the characters' expectations. The text establishes transgression as a necessity in which we recognize various features reminiscent of Bataille's modern conception of "texte-limite". To a certain extent, *L'Amour* can be seen as an example of what, according to Sollers, Bataille conceives of as the passage from the discontinuous to the continuous:

> "Le passage du discontinu (du monde significatif formé d'individus et de choses) au continu (manifesté par la mort, la violence, la révolution) recouvre le jeu fondamental de l'interdit et de la transgression".[28]

What proves more relevant for our concerns here is the relationship between reason and unreason which increasingly appears, from *Le Ravissement* onwards, as a common relevant feature of Duras' texts. In accordance with Bataille's 'continuous world', *L'Amour* gives importance to such values as animality, alluded to in "Elle fonce, bestiale, elle va" (A p.73), madness, an important element in the typification of the walker designated as "le fou", or death, with the dead dog and the deserted space of S.Thala. These aspects emphasise features of unreason alluded to by Foucault as "le néant au coeur de l'existence", except that with Duras' texts the concept of nothingness has also to do with a necessary abandoning of reason in order that another state of being may be reached.

The spatialisation of Lol's madness, or the search for an 'elsewhere'

The transgression of limits metaphorically announces a world which exists beyond the recognized boundaries or the established values of reason and which culminates in its hieratic dimension.[29]

---

[28]Sollers ibid. p.106

[29]Leslie Hill, in an article entitled 'Marguerite Duras and the Limits of Fiction' (*Paragraph* (Oxford University Press no.1 March 1989)), has drawn attention to the fact that as a result of "the preoccupation with limits and borders", the hieratic dimension for Duras extends to the act of writing itself, which acquires "a kind of transgressive potential" (p.2).

A dialectic of the sacred develops in *L'Amour*, anticipated in *Le Ravissement* through several explicit references to God: "Puis un jour ce corps infirme remue dans le ventre de Dieu" (RLVS p.51). The text of *L'Amour* erects a hieratic space based partly on Christian mythology. Allusions to one episode in the New Testament can be discerned; thus semantically one passage combines certain features of Christ's retreat to the desert with the resurrection scene. The walker, followed by the woman, disappears into the sand:

> "Ainsi chaque jour doivent-ils couvrir la distance, l'espace des sables de S.Thala" (A p.32).

They disappear for three days:

> "Ils disparaissent, ils tournent du côté de la rivière...C'est avec le soir qu'elle reparaît...ils sortent de trois jours d'obscurité, de nouveau on les voit dans la lumière solaire d'un S.Thala désert" (A pp.32-33)

The processes "disparaître", "reparaître" which punctuate the passage reveal the symbolic code. The characters' disappearance, although it is justified by the peculiarity of their activity - they must cover the surface of the sand - , added to the sudden reappearance of the woman after three days of obscurity, creates religious overtones which take the event outside the normal so that it becomes chiefly answerable to the symbolic code. This meaning is reinforced in the final evocation of solar light in a desert-like S.Thala, which reinforces an atmosphere of unreality.

However, the text of *L'Amour*, which at the semantic level can be seen to reflect the Judaeo-Christian foundations common to Western societies, paradoxically also refutes this obvious interpretation. In the space of the text, God is not apprehended as the Great Signifier, "ce mot qui est censé mettre fin aux mots",[30] but is instead, somewhat derisorily, negated; pre-established meaning or absolute principle becomes "ce truc", a human

---

"a kind of transgressive potential" (p.2).
[30]ibid. p.117

invention. "Après seulement elle entendra le bruit, vous savez? de Dieu? Ce truc?" (A p.143).[31]

The sacred dimension of *L'Amour* lies not so much in an external meaning but rather reflects the problematic of Lol's phantasm, the phantasm which initiates the search for an 'elsewhere' - "un ailleurs" -, experienced as the reconquest of an original situation. Similarly the 'sanctification' of space in *L'Amour* stems above all from the perception of the origin.[32] In *Le Ravissement*, the theme of origin is repeatedly fictionalised as social determinants which add to the typification of characters:- S.Tahla is described as Lol's native town and the characters are in turn classified as "l'homme de T.Beach", "l'homme de S.Tahla" etc. In *L'Amour* the concept of origin is more directly thematised through various allusions to originating situations such as birth or the mythical/biblical moment of creation. These situations echo the terms of Lol's original trauma in the scene of the ball, a 'primal scene'.

> "In many ways the ball scene has the status of an original fantasy, a kind of primal scene of the Indian cycle, in which a scene is reconstructed 'après coup' across the imaginary registers of seen and heard, by people who may or may not have seen or heard anything. Like the primal scene, then, the ball scene is first of all a fantasy".[33]

Here the concept of origin is closely related to the meaning of end. Separation in its final sense lies at the heart of these 'originating moments' in the same way as Lol's fantasy stems from the irremediable separation from her fiancé, from this 'end of the world' in which the end stems from the beginning of a day:

> "dans les multiples aspects du bal de T.Beach, c'est la fin qui retient Lol. C'est l'instant précis de sa fin, quand

---

[31]Leslie Hill's reading is that God in Duras is linked to what cannot be represented. "God, in Duras, is the name for this impossibility of naming, and functions as a sign of the fundamental confusion and precariousness that exists at all boundaries and margins." (op.cit. p.3)

[32]This is a feature which fully fits the findings of Chapter 1, where it has been shown that unreason in the woman is primarily to do with a quest for origin.

[33]Elysabeth Lyon, 'The Cinema of Lol V.Stein' in *Camera Obscura* no.6 p.9

l'aurore arrive avec une brutalité inouïe et la sépare du couple que formaient Michael Richardson et Anne-Marie Stretter, pour toujours, toujours" (RLVS p.46).

Indeed as Elysabeth Lyon recalls,

"The fantasy, in psychoanalytical terms, originates in the continually repeated moments of separation ...The fantasy is the 'mise en scène' of the subject in relation to loss - to the experience of separation and to an impossible desire for a lost object".[34]

However, as we have seen in Chapter 3 above, Lol's fantasy is not strictly to do with the loss of the love object, but rather with the emergence of a new epistemology based on fusion beyond the realm of subjectivity.

Birth is presented in *L'Amour* as a definitive separation from the mother, an abandonment behind the sea wall: "Ses enfants sont là-dedans, (...) la ville en est pleine, la terre" (A p.52).

The following passage fuses evocations of the creation of literary space with the emergence of a referential universe and pictures creation primarily as a result of physical separation:

"Le voyageur désigne le perron. Il demande:
- Dites-moi quelque chose de l'histoire.
...Il répond:
- A mon avis, l'île est sortie en premier - il montre la mer - de là. S.Thala est arrivée après, avec la poussière - il ajoute - vous savez? le temps...
Le silence commence par un espacement des départs de bateaux. Il dit:
- Le silence commence par un espacement du temps"
(A pp.49-50)

Separation as the principle of creation appears spatialised in the last sequence of *L'Amour*:

"Ils se taisent. La lumière augmente de façon indiscernable tant son mouvement est lent. De même la séparation des sables et des eaux.

---

[34]ibid. p.25

La lumière monte, ouvre, montre l'espace qui grandit ...
- Qu'arrivera-t-il lorsque la lumière sera là?
On entend:
- Pendant un instant elle sera aveuglée. Puis elle recommencera à me voir. A distinguer le sable de la mer, puis, la mer de la lumière, puis son corps de mon corps. Après elle séparera le froid de la nuit et elle me le donnera. Après seulement elle entendra le bruit vous savez? de Dieu?...ce truc...?
Ils se taisent. Ils surveillent la progression de l'aurore extérieure." (A pp.142-143)

This evocation of dawn, which accompanies the regained visual perception of the various spatial elements, can be read as the spatialisation of the original trauma, and echoes referentially the original dawn interiorised by Lol, and the separation of bodies which ensued from it: M.Richardson from A-M.Stretter, Lol from the couple.

However, the sequence mostly takes on the meaning of an anamnesis.[35] Its religious overtones lie in the quasibiblical allusion to the re-creation a world with the emergence of light, the successive separation of elements: the sand from the waters, the sea from the light. The mastery of time expressed in the supervision of "la progression de l'aurore", whereby time is lived as a spaced-out dimension rather than as a continuous, intangible one, adds to the meaning of liberation.

The search for an 'elsewhere' which commands the hieratic quality of space in *L'Amour* is also rendered by the textual and anecdotal importance given to the dimension of what is beyond. Considerations of the nature of what is beyond help to make more remote the link with the concept of origin and to further intertwine the meanings of beginning and end.

The dimension of the beyond dominates the text through a varied vocabulary, as we observed when dealing with the abolition

---

[35]I would, with Christiane Makward in her article 'Structures du Silence/du Délire', assert that "le tableau de clôture de *L'Amour* est une ouverture sur laquelle il ne faudrait pas 'fermer les yeux'. Lol V.Stein s'éveille à la lumière du jour, l'autre fait lever son corps. Elle a entraîné dans son anamnèse, dans sa régression à la mer/mère originelle, deux autres êtres humains et désormais c'est elle qui 'fera' car elle a atteint la capacité d'intelligence de la vie, ce que Duras métaphorise en quadrilatère de lumière sur la mer" (op.cit. p.317)

or subversion of limits. References to the invisible, the unlimited, the indiscernible, the inaccessible or the ungraspable all stress a dimension which escapes the characters' gaze and knowledge, and are formulated in terms of the symbolic code. In addition, the proliferation throughout the text of the adverbial syntagm "au-delà" reinforces such a symbolic reading:

> "*Au-delà* de la digue, une autre ville, bien *au-delà*, inaccessible, une autre ville, bleue..." (A p.11)
> "Il cherche à S.Thala. *au-delà*" (A p.74)(*my emphasis*)

An opposition between the 'here' - "l'ici" - and the 'there' - "l'au-delà" - develops in one section of the sequence in the cafe which the traveller and the woman enter:

> "Il cherche à voir *au-delà* de l'endroit enfermé, *au-delà* des vitres.
> Elle, elle est à regarder *ici*, l'endroit enfermé. *Au-delà* des vitres, du chemin de planches, de la plage, quelqu'un passe, une ombre marche d'un pas égal...
> ...Il dit
> - Il vient de passer *là-bas*..." (A p.36)
> "...le bruit *ici* décroît encore." (A p.37)
>
> (*my emphasis*)
> "...Le bruit, ici, a cessé. Le rongement incessant, là-bas, recommence" (A p.38)

The 'here' of the text - "l'ici" - which refers to the spatial enclosure of the cafe can also be read symbolically as limitation, as opposed to the referential opening of the beyond:- "l'au-delà des vitres". Beyond its spatial configuration and beyond its obvious mystical connotation, the "au-delà" constitutes the 'privileged' locus where a search, metaphorically synonym of loss of identity, can take place and hence guarantee the phantasmatic dimension of the text. The "au-delà" also becomes the locus for the celebration of origin as witnessed by the end of the following passage:

> "Le rongement incessant, là-bas, recommence. Il grandit. Il se transforme.
> Il devient un chant. C'est un chant lointain. Les populations de S.Thala chantent...
> ...C'est une marche lente aux solennels accents. Une danse lente, de bals morts, de fêtes sanglantes. Elle ne

bouge pas. Elle écoute l'hymne lointain."

(A pp.38-39)

It is from the place beyond that the distant song can be heard. In a ritualistic vocabulary tinged with religiosity, the song is presented as a hymn and the slow march with a solemn rhythm celebrates the Origin. Origin of humanity in the evocation of these "fêtes sanglantes" in which the moment of birth appears identified with pain as well as with joy, origin also of the story of Lol's phantasm - this 'already-there' of *Le Ravissement* and of *L'Amour* - in the evocation of "ces bals morts", which become at the same time celebration of an end, that of the story itself. Through this passage an essential aspect of the sacred space of *L'Amour* emerges in which origin and end - life/death but also joy/sorrow -, in ceasing to be perceived as contradictory, tend to fuse together.

Moreover the journey to S.Thala undertaken by the woman and the traveller anecdotally encourages the recognition of an end. Repeatedly announced at the beginning of the text, this journey, referred to as "le dernier voyage", takes on the symbolic meaning of death. As such it asserts the end of a known world circumscribed by reason - a meaning reinforced by the descriptive allusion to a ruined town - and the beginning of another world in the infinity of the sand. This other world can also be revealed in the comparative examination of the incipit and the excipit of the text of *L'Amour*:

"Un homme.
Il est debout, il regarde: la plage, la mer."(A p.7)
"Ils se taisent. Ils surveillent la progression de l'aurore extérieure." (A p.143)

Apart from the common situation of male character(s) watching the setting, a shift has taken place from the spatial dimension of the beach/the sea to the temporality of the progression of dawn, a passage from the 'here' of space to the 'beyond' of time. The explicit of *L'Amour* which concludes a sequence celebrating the rebirth of a day, the recreation of a world, symbolically asserts an attempt to escape the contingencies of the spatial and to enter the dimension of an eternal temporality.

In this section we have attempted to show that in *L'Amour* the emptiness of the referential space, which results from an evacuation of specific locations in favour of space itself and which reinforces the uniformisation process discussed in the first section, occurs in order to favour a particular locus: that of 'madness'. The characteristics of an imaginary space, defined in terms of Lol's fantasy, structure the setting of *L'Amour*, and constitute the transposition at the referential level of the problematic of Lol's madness.

The limited move towards a spatial structuration through the recognition of places which function as limits or boundaries serves chiefly to sustain Duras' project in *L'Amour*. Indeed the text of *L'Amour* exemplifies an attempt to go beyond the referential limits towards another dimension which gives the text its hieratic value, a dimension which again echoes the configurations of the phantasm. The 'sacralisation' of *L'Amour* results in the recognition of a 'beyond', characterised by a return to the Origin taken in its universal mythical sense. In the temporal circularity which ensues the two concepts of end and origin become fused, as if the setting of *L'Amour* had moved outside Space and Time, and as such had become a prerequisite for the actualisation of Unreason.

At the completion of this chapter, then, it appears that the spatial shift which has taken place in the evolution from *Le Ravissement* to *L'Amour* is the result of a complex process of simplification. This process is to be seen at work in the loss of discrimination between places themselves in favour of a schematised topology, as well as in the abandonment of a tangible world in favour of liquidity/fluidity. Finally we examined the evacuation of places and the abolition of limits circumscribing the privileged locus of Space.

From such a uniformisation of the setting emerges an increased degree of topological mobility and flexibility: a result of the graphic structure of the setting, of its liquidity, and of the abolition of limits. Such physical features appear to be essential to the development of a setting which expresses the workings of a mental space. In a mirroring effect the title of the text, *L'Amour*, becomes just another name for the same mental space, the only important locus in this whole oversimplified decor. Through its setting, the text of *L'Amour* proposes a journey into the imaginary, the 'sacralisation' of which parallels the quest for a world beyond Reason which can permit the fusion of beginning and end. The concomitant uniformalisation of time, in which the 'here' in the text functions as an essential link in the fusion of past and future, asserts a universal temporality which, like the ball at S.Tahla, "a scene which is at once 'eternity' and eternally absent",[36] exists through the meaning of eternity, emblem of the cosmic value of the text.

But, in spite of its universal dimension, the simplified yet nonetheless mobile setting of *L'Amour* appears to be particularly suited to expressing the pathos of the impossible encounter between the characters. The various appearing and disappearing images of resistance, particularly obvious in the geometrical vision of space, mirrors the dilemma of the difference of sexes, and Lol's madness indeed has greatly to do with the knowledge of that unavoidable conflict of human existence.

---

[36]Lyon, op.cit. p.7

SECTION III

"LE SEXE EST FOLIE"

Chapter 7

THE UNREASON OF LOVE, OR 'L'ESPOIR RETROUVÉ'

1 Sexual desire and madness

Love and sexuality constitute the subject-matter of most of Duras' narratives from *La Vie Tranquille* to her most recent productions; hence the temptation to view her novels as banal romantic narratives. Each Durasian text deals (primarily) with one or more love stories which repeat, overlap or interact with one another, often at an inter-textual level. The predominance of sexual desire is constantly restaged, be it for instance Anna's desire for the sailor in *Le Marin de Gibraltar*, or that of the actress of *Hiroshima Mon Amour* for her Japanese lover, Lol V.Stein's love for Richardson, the vice-consul's attraction to Anne-Marie Stretter or else the captain's wife's love for the house guardian in *Emily-L*. Examples are numerous.

Sexuality (even) becomes blatant eroticism in some of the more recent Durasian production. In *La Maladie de la Mort*, the characters' behaviour is openly divorced from sexual desire as such, through the presence of a prostitution contract in which the woman fulfils the historical role of the 'whore'. In *Les Yeux Bleus, Cheveux Noirs*, sexual activity has more to do with fantasy, and the black silk of a scarf laid over the female body feeds eroticism, reinforced by a sado-masochistic practice of physical or verbal violence: "il l'insulte avec les mêmes mots (...) c'est ainsi souvent avec les hommes (...) elle le leur demande" (YB. p.126). Durasian eroticism can also become pornographic, as some passages of

L'Homme Assis Dans le Couloir or of *Les Yeux Bleus, Cheveux Noirs* exemplify, in which sex becomes "le lieu de la jouissance" in particularly concrete terms.

Sexual desire in Marguerite Duras' texts is a most ambiguous and paradoxical reality, since it signals in many cases the individual's most radical perdition, while, as will be shown later in this chapter, at the same time remaining the only possible hope for humanity. Sexuality is perdition for the individual insofar that sexual desire often leads to madness:

> "Elle dit que c'est un velours, un vertige, mais aussi, il ne faut pas croire, un désert, une chose malfaisante qui porte aussi au crime et à la folie" (YB p.51)

Stories of criminal passion underlie several of Duras' narratives, as in *Dix Heures et Demie du Soir en Eté* with Rodrigo Paestra, and can become a fascination for characters like A.Desbaresdes in *Moderato Cantabile*. Sexual desire can become irresistible attraction at the risk of losing one's own reason. Lol's madness is linked to the loss of her lover and to her desire for fusion with Tatiana and J.Hold. In his quest for love, the vice-consul is ready to follow Anne-Marie Stretter into unreason, while we are led to understand that J.Hold has abandoned the mental security of writing about Lol V.Stein in *Le Ravissement de Lol V.Stein* to become the traveller in *L'Amour*, ready to follow the woman and the mad man in the journey to the end of reason. Sexuality tends to lead to madness in Duras, which is hardly surprising since

> "dans un contexte névrotique courant, sexuel est synonyme de folie. On peut même établir une équivalence imaginaire entre sexe, folie et mort."[1]

2 Sexual madness and world madness

> "L'événement aujourd'hui, c'est la folie humaine. La politique en fait partie, particulièrement dans ses accès meurtriers (...) Le monde moderne, le monde des guerres mondiales, le tiers-monde, le monde souterrain

---

[1]Guy Rosalato, 'Culpabilité et Sacrifice', in *Psychanalyse et Sémiotique* (10/18, 1975) p.76

de la mort qui nous agit, n'ont pas la splendeur policée de la cité grecque. Le domaine politique moderne est massivement, totalitairement social, nivelant, tuant. Aussi la folie est-elle un espace d'individuation antisociale, apolitique, et, paradoxalement, libre."[2]

If sexual desire has to do with madness in Duras' texts, it nevertheless represents and signals a type of unreason different from that of society.

"Pour aborder le politique -qu'il s'agisse de la vacance ou de la violence feutrée des sociétés bourgeoises, de l'horreur d'Hiroshima comme des camps de concentration,etc-l'écrivaine agit de biais, en mettant toujours au centre une histoire d'amour, sans se soucier de se faire taxer de futilité"[3]

And indeed, if Marguerite Duras keeps to her promise "je ne veux pas être déclarative" (P p.184), we still find constant references to the madness of the world and an uncompromising recording of societal failure, both in her fictional texts and in her journalistic and other media activity.[4] There is a displacement of the concept of madness in its relation to society, through which madness is no longer situated outside but becomes society itself. Julia Kristeva concludes that

"...La puissance des forces destructrices n'est jamais apparue aussi incontestable et aussi imparable qu'aujourd'hui, au-dehors comme au-dedans de l'individu et de la société"[5]

Duras' texts situate themselves in this problematic, but what is also at stake in them in my view is fully dependent upon a social and political awareness: as Duras has said,

---

[2]Julia Kristeva, op.cit. (*Soleil Noir*) (Gallimard 1987) p.242

[3]Marcelle Marini, 'L'Autre Corps', in *Ecrire, Dit-Elle* (Université de Bruxelles 1985) p.30

[4]Indeed it cannot be forgotten that Duras' fictions are only one aspect of her multifarious creative practice. Her main articles, written over the years in *L'Autre Journal, Libération* or *Le Nouvel-Observateur*, reinforced by her renowned television interventions from *Apostrophes* to her later *Au Delà des Pages* programmes, have expressed her political and ideological commitment.

[5]Kristeva op. cit. (*Soleil Noir*) p. 229

"tout est faux, toute notre société est fausse...La vue exacte, c'est la vue terroriste du monde. Excusez-moi, c'est celle-là...Il n'y en a pas d'autres. C'est scandaleux; la société est scandaleuse."[6]

The injustice of the social system,[7] where the poor coexist next to the rich and are kept in endemic poverty, is pictured in the colonial reality of *Un Barrage Contre le Pacifique Le Vice-consul*, *L'Amant* and later *L'Amant de la Chine du Nord*: "Il y avait dans le Barrage un programme politique tout simple" writes Duras. "C'était: on se taille, on laisse la colonie - l'Indochine - aux indigènes".[8] She asserts of *L'Amant*: "il n'y a pas une virgule qui soit inventée, tout a existé, tout".[9] *La Douleur*, Duras' war diary, not only constitutes a testimonial to the resistance movement but is also an uncompromising denunciation of the madness of the extermination camps.

"Ce qu'ont subi les juifs est ce génocide (...) l'horreur absolue, indépassable. Ça n'a pas laissé que de la douleur dans le monde. Ça a laissé de l'antisémitisme".[10]

She also asserts that the characters of Anne-Marie Stretter and the vice-consul are jews. (YV p.76) The condition of the jews becomes for Duras that of madness: this state of non- belonging, this errance and exclusion, "dimension illimitée, égarée, propre aux juifs". (YV p.27)[11]

---

[6]Marguerite Duras, *Au Delà des Pages*, programme 1 (February 1988) Leslie Hill rightly defines Duras' politics of writing as "a politics of revulsion based on an apocalyptic rejection of political faith." (op.cit. p.11)

[7]The consciousness of social injustice accounts for Duras' political positioning: "Il nous reste la conscience permanente de l'inadmissible de l'injustice sociale et l'inadmissible encore une fois c'est aussi une idéologie. C'est celle de ces quelques poignées d'hommes dont la perte défigurerait le monde. Abandonner la gauche, c'est abandonner le poème, la folie, la raison de vivre." (*Au Delà des Pages*, programme 1)

[8]'Duras Toute Entière', in *Le Nouvel Observateur*, 14-20 Nov. 1986 p.115

[9]ibid. p.115

[10]*Au Delà des Pages* (programme 1)

[11]Referring to the text of her latest production: *Yann Andrew Steiner* (P.O.L. Paris 1992), Marguerite Duras stresses her attraction towards the Jewish state: "C'est ma seule nostalgie, J'aurais voulu être juive. Je n'en ai jamais parlé." (*Le Nouvel*

The dying world of S.Thala, the evacuation of the social in *L'Amour*, the enclosement of the palace and the degradation of life inside it in *Le Vice-consul*, the claustrophobia of city life, all present a vision of a doomed civilization, a 'fissured' social world which is denounced in Duras' journalistic practice:

> "On est en train d'atteindre au désespoir concret, actif".[12]

Duras' texts go against the insufficiency of a cultural theory which considers that society is always normal. We find in her 'fictional' production the strong assumption, reiterated in autobiographical writing such as *La Vie Matérielle*, that "il existe des sociétés 'malades', celui qui introjecte les normes du groupe, introjecte en lui des normes morbides".[13]

3 The failure of gender politics and the irreconcilability of the sexes

In an alienated world, in which social madness predominates and interaction between sexes leads only to stories of murder and separation, the female character in the Durasian text occupies the centre of sexual economy - an economy which remains primarily heterosexual. At the risk of going against critics such as Trista Selous, who sees in the female Durasian figure a passive representation of femininity, "un objet d'investigation lié au désir de l'homme",[14] I would see the role of the female character in Duras as absolutely crucial, insofar that, despite appearances, it is the woman who leads the game of the sexual adventure. I fully support Marcelle Marini's claim that in Duras "la figure féminine, à la fois mise en résidence surveillée et exclue - répudiée - est porteuse de la plus forte potentialité de changement".[15] The woman takes on an increasingly initiatory role in the sexual interaction. "Le rôle d'amour qui a été le malheur de la femme est

---

Observateur, 'Les nostalgie de L'amante Duras', 25th June-1st July 1992, p.54).

[12]Marguerite Duras, in 'Les Chiens de L'Histoire' in *L'Autre Journal* no.6 (3-8 April 1986) p.6

[13]Devereux's theory of cultural relativism, in *Essais D'Ethnopsychiatrie Générale* (Gallimard, Paris 1970), cited by R.Jaccard, *La Folie* (P.U.F 1979) p.33

[14]Selous op. cit. p.211

[15]Marini, 'L'Autre Corps', in *Ecrire, Dit-elle* p.28

maintenant son terrain de départ" (L p.30). Paradoxically, and particularly if one thinks in feminist terms, this status rests on a fundamental loss of identity representing the very guarantee not only of her power but of another state of being.

An evolution in the centrality of the female character can be observed throughout Duras' production. In some narratives, as in *La Vie Tranquille*, the woman is pictured as active, as the desiring subject of the text. Gradually, and probably from *Les Chantiers*, the representation of women changes and the female characters become silent and enigmatic. They are no longer produced as subject(s) of the narration; they become objects of the male scopic drive. Such is the situation of Anna in *Le Marin de Gibraltar* or of Maria in *Les Petits Chevaux de Tarquinia*. The passage towards a total loss of identity culminates with the characters of Lol V.Stein (in the first love-episode at the ball), Anne-Marie Stretter or the woman of *L'Amour*, later followed by the women of *Aurélia Steiner* and of *Emily-L*, who become 'destroyed figures', absence/presence without apparent desire, often given to endless sleep.

The feature common to all these absent women resides, according to Kristeva, in "un ravissement dissimulé et anérotique" The women remain separated from the male Other, enclosed in their frigidity. One is dealing with a desire which cannot find satisfaction, which remains "dans les délices narcissiques et auto sexuels de la souffrance féminine". Kristeva sees in the sensual pleasure of the Durasian female figure "une mythification du féminin inaccessible".[16] This claim is in my view misleading since it restricts the dimensions of the text and does not take into account the strength which emerges from these 'absent' women. The meaning of liberation is dominant in Duras' texts, and saves the Durasian woman from complete despair, even if it means going through solitude, suffering and the 'experience' of death. I shall return to this aspect at a later stage; let us note here that if the existence of these absent women does not make sense in relation to the logic of the world, their renunciation of the status of active subject hides another power. The woman has a hold on the man and seduces him through her alternate state of presence/absence. Her power is neither logical nor external, but remains silent and

---

[16]Kristeva op. cit. (*Soleil Noir*) p.251

stems from another kind of knowledge. It is rather an intuitive awareness issuing from an inner coherence:

> 'quelque chose' d'infini et donc d'inarticulable (...) énergie tapie là et qui 'jaillit' dès que s'offre à elle un espace désert".[17]

In Duras' texts, the absent woman is, unlike the man, the one who knows. Her cognition does not exist in terms of social codes, in fact it cannot be expressed in words: "Vous lui demandez comment elle sait" we read in *La Maladie de la Mort*; "elle dit qu'on le sait sans savoir comment on le sait" (MM p.24). The woman remains in contact with darkness: "elle est là dormante, dans ses propres ténèbres, abandonnée, dans sa magnificence"(MM p.33). The female knowledge thus constitutes a sort of preconsciousness which cannot be apprehended by language or recuperated by the usual forms of power: it is below and beyond any possible recuperation. We read in *Emily-L* of that other destroyed character, the captain's wife:

> "-La force qu'elle porte en elle, elle doit la ressentir comme une sorte d'intelligence perdue qui ne lui sert plus à rien.
> -Vous voulez dire, comme un terrible défaut aussi qu'elle aurait attrapé au-dehors de sa vie, elle ne savait pas quand, ni comment, ni de qui, ni de quoi...?
> -Un défaut qui se serait logé là, au creux de son corps et que toute sa vie durant elle aurait fait taire pour rester là où elle voulait se tenir, ces régions pauvres de son amour pour le Captain." (EL p.121)

In spite of their absence to the world, innocent and ignorant of their own power, these female characters are, for the men of Duras' texts, supreme objects of sexual attraction. The woman of *L'Amour* is the most accomplished stereotype of this kind of being, to which the semio-narrative structure of "corps émouvant/corps ému" identified by Denis Bertrand can be validly applied:

> "Au corps émouvant, on peut assigner la position du destinateur (sujet manipulateur: il fait faire ou fait sentir, il fait loi) mais aussi celui de l'objet (il est

---

[17]Michel de Certeau, 'Marguerite Duras: On Dit' in *Ecrire Dit-elle* p.262

selectionné par un sujet) qui, surinvesti et modalisé, se trouve en quelque sorte 'activé'."[18]

At this point of the Durasian production, female passivity is at its maximum. Perhaps this is why, after *L'Amour* and especially from *Aurélia Steiner*, the female character once more acquires a more active position in Duras' texts. We can observe the passage from the existential level to a more concerted, instrumental and socially identifiable role. In *L'Homme Atlantique*, the woman director teaches the actor how to lose his identity, via the presence of the camera. In *Aurelia Steiner*, desires and values are produced by the first female figure, who spends her time writing; symbolisation takes place around the male body. In both *La Maladie de la Mort* and *Les Yeux Bleus, Cheveux Noirs*, the female character (in one case the woman-writer, in the other the young teacher) unreasonably accepts a prostitution contract with the man: "Il aime bien cette idée de la folie à partir de quoi elle est venue habiter la chambre et elle a accepté l'argent" (YB p.67). The woman does not hesitate to claim what the man owes her:

> "Vous dites qu'elle devrait se taire comme les femmes de ses ancêtres, se plier complètement à vous, à votre vouloir, vous être soumise (...) Elle dit que dans ce cas, c'est encore plus cher. Elle dit le chiffre du paiement" (MM pp.10-11)

As in *L'Homme Assis dans le Couloir*, where the woman leads the sexual interaction on equal terms with the man, the woman expresses sensual pleasure, while in *Les Yeux Bleus, Cheveux Noirs* the woman is the only one able to experience sexual orgasm:

> "Elle le fait elle-même avec sa propre main devant lui qui la regarde. Dans la jouissance elle appelle on dirait, une sorte de mot très bas, très sourd, très loin. Une sorte de nom peut-être, c'est sans aucun sens" (YB p.46)

Paradoxically, the active position regained by the female figure in Duras' later narratives does not fundamentally alter her social and individual predicament. Her renewed activity stresses

---

[18]Denis Bertrand, 'Le Corps Humain. L'Absence, Proposition pour une Sémiotique de L'Emotion', in *La Chouette* no.20 p.50

only the madness of a gender politics based on an impossible duality; and indeed,

> "la différence sexuelle apparaît toujours à la croisée des séries de déterminations aliénantes, comme le lieu fondamental de la différence: lieu mythique et ensemble socialement et culturellement repérable dans chaque situation historique concrète (...) lieu énigmatique, tant il sert de modèle occulte, voire dénié, à tous les autres dispositifs de la différence"[19].

Whatever she does, the woman ultimately remains superfluous in a society which fundamentally functions without her and which remains, in Marguerite Duras' own view, given to male homosexuality. Hence the typically extreme Durasian statement:

> "Tous les hommes sont en puissance d'être des homosexuels, il ne leur manque que de le savoir, de rencontrer l'incident ou l'évidence qui le leur révèlera (...) si vous êtes un homme, votre compagnie privilégiée dans l'existence, celle de votre coeur, de votre chair, de votre race, de votre sexe (...) c'est celle de l'homme" (VM p.45)

The woman becomes a double danger for the man; touched by her, he not only becomes aware of his lack of sexual desire, but also fears the state of non-identity, of internal death, offered by the woman: "c'est là en elle que se fomente la maladie de la mort" (MM p.38). The female body remains external, invites violence.[20]

---

[19]Marcelle Marini, 'L'Autre Corps' in *Ecrire, Dit-elle* p.28

[20]The sado-masochistic trend which can be regarded as a disturbing element of Marguerite Duras' fiction, already present in *Le Ravissement de Lol V.Stein* and *L'Amour*, translates a compulsion to ally the extremes of pleasure/suffering, life/death, to express the paradox of sexual desire. The extreme nature of these contradictions, recurrent as a 'trademark' in all of Duras' writing, reveals that the Durasian enterprise is primarily rooted in the pulsional world, in this "lieu où la contradiction est possible, ignorant le temps et la mort" (R.Menahem, *Langage et Folie* p.167).
However, I also see, in the sadistic male activity and in the passivity of the woman, the sign of the irreconcilability of sexes linked to social conditioning. In *Les Yeux Bleus, Cheveux Noirs*, the man is looking for a woman because he is

When pleasure is possible for the man, as in *L'Homme Assis Dans Le Couloir*, it becomes "bonheur intolérable" (HA p.30), and reduces the male figure to tears. Sexuality becomes "une chose infecte, criminelle, une eau trouble, sale, l'eau du sang" (YB p.51). The woman tells the man in *Les Yeux Bleus, Cheveux Noirs* that "un jour il devra bien le faire, même une fois, fourrager dans ce lieu commun, qu'il ne pourra pas l'éviter toute sa vie".(YB p.51)

In the latest Durasian texts, men are blatantly blocked in their lack of desire, condemned to the logic of the male economy. Homosexuals, and therefore all men in the Durasian logic, are sexually dead; hence the title *La Maladie de la Mort*, which applies to the male figure: "vous ne connaissez que la grâce du corps des morts, celle de vos semblables" (MM p.37) says the woman to the man of *La Maladie*. Hurt to have lost his sexual power, overcome by "ce chagrin mortel", (YB p.15) the male character is condemned to the limitations of his own logic; the woman in *La Maladie de la Mort* continues:

> "je ne voudrais rien savoir de la façon dont vous, vous savez...avec cette certitude issue de la mort, cette monotonie irrémédiable, égale à elle-même chaque jour de votre vie, chaque nuit, avec cette fonction mortelle du manque d'aimer" (MM p.50)[21]

A new conception of illness thus emerges in the Durasian text. Illness is no longer defined primarily in social terms, as had been the case for Lol V.Stein's madness, but in terms of the economy of desire itself, of the human being condemned to the logic of the 'Same Other', unable to have access through heterosexuality to another reality. In this dilemma, the man relies on the woman who, helped by her own historical position of exclusion, can indicate a new way of being.

---

afraid of the madness linked to his own social condition: "...il fallait payer les femmes pour qu'elles empêchent les hommes de mourir, de devenir fous" (YB p.24)

[21]This state of death is different from that of the woman: "Vous annoncez le règne de la mort. On ne peut pas aimer la mort si elle vous est imposée du dehors. Vous croyez pleurer de ne pas aimer. Vous pleurez de ne pas imposer la mort" (MM p.48). The state of being offered by the woman makes death itself superfluous and is linked to the loss of personal identity and to maximum availability: "celui qui en est atteint, ne sait pas qu'il est porteur d'elle, de la mort. En ceci aussi qu'il serait mort sans vie au préalable." (MM p.24)

For Marguerite Duras, homosexuality constitutes the death-seal of a society: "Le passage d'un homme de l'hétérosexualité à l'homosexualité est une crise très violente (...) ce sera la grande catastrophe de tous les temps" she asserts in *La Vie Matérielle* (VM p.46). Such a statement contains all the ambiguity of Durasian thought. It is possible to read such a conception of sexual politics as a strong valorisation of heterosexuality, as the sign of a rigid and conventional view of sexual identity. To apprehend the Durasian ideology in this way is in my view disputable since the 'homosexual' character in most of Duras' texts - be it the man of *L'Amour*, the Vice-consul, the sailor of *Aurelia Steiner* or the man of *Savannah Bay* - remains the male figure closest to the woman and therefore most open to personal liberation.[22] Homosexuality corresponds to this "peuple égaré" with which the woman identifies: "vous n'avez pas de place" asserts the woman of *Les Yeux Bleus, Cheveux Noirs* to the man, "vous ne savez pas où trouver une place. Et c'est de ça que je vous aime et que vous êtes perdu" (YB p.81). The 'condemnation'[23] of homosexuality can also be viewed as part of a process through which the woman, in spite of the failure between sexes, not only reclaims her place in the sexual economy, but also acquires a dominant position in gender politics with her role of initiator to sexual desire. Such a view would help to account for Duras' feminist position.

It can be argued, however, that Duras' feminism is not really at stake here. In her texts, the non-sense of gender politics is more radical and devastating. Ultimately the failure between the sexes does not stem from homosexuality, but rather from the irremediable impossibility of love between sexes. Not only can we read "la passion de l'homosexualité c'est l'homosexualité" (VM

---

[22]The men who interest Marguerite Duras "acceptent de voir leur parole minée, contaminée ou contrariée par celle de l'autre". Indeed one can note with Marcelle Marini that from *La Maladie de la Mort* especially, "Peu à peu émerge une autre figure masculine qui accepte de porter en son corps la blessure de la différence des sexes" (*Ecrire, Dit-elle* pp.38-39)

[23]The word 'condemnation' is in fact incorrect. Indeed just as the woman of *Les Yeux Bleus, Cheveux Noirs* speaks of the male lack of desire, one does not find in Duras a condemnation of homosexuality: "Votre détestation de moi, elle ne me regarde pas. Elle vient de Dieu, il faut l'accepter comme telle, la respecter comme la nature, la mer" (YB p.49)

p.41), but the woman herself can be reduced to the same predicament, enclosed in her own desire.

> "Là où l'imaginaire est le plus fort c'est entre l'homme et la femme. C'est là où ils sont séparés par une frigidité dont la femme se réclame de plus en plus et qui terrasse l'homme qui la désire. La femme elle-même, la plupart du temps, ne sait pas ce qu'est ce mal qui la prive de désir (...) là où on croit que l'imaginaire est absent, c'est là qu'il est le plus fort. C'est la frigidité. La frigidité c'est l'imaginaire du désir par cette femme qui ne désire pas l'homme qui se propose à elle (...). La frigidité c'est le non-désir de ce qui n'est pas cet homme (...). La vocation à un seul être au monde, incontrolâble, elle est féminine" (VM pp.39-40).

Paradoxically, and in spite of the many love stories which haunt the narratives, the impossibility of love remains at the heart of the Durasian text: "Dans l'hétérosexualité il n'y a pas de solution. L'homme et la femme sont irréconciliables" (VM p.40).

4 The unreason of love, or 'L'Espoir Retrouvé'

> "Il est impossible de rester sans amour aucun, même s'il n'y a plus que les mots, ça se vit toujours. La pire chose, c'est de ne pas aimer, je crois que ça n'existe pas..." (VM p.148)

> "On ne croit plus à rien et on croit à tout. C'est comme ça que l'impossible s'est programmé"[24]

It is very tempting to approach Marguerite Duras' representation of sexual politics in terms of failure and pessimism. I would argue, however, that this constitutes a misrepresentation of what is at stake in the Durasian narrative, and ignores the end of the quotation:

> "l'homme et la femme sont irréconciliables et c'est cette tentative impossible et à chaque amour renouvelée qui en fait la grandeur" (VM p.40).

---

[24] *Au Delà des Pages* (programme 1)

The lucidity of Duras' texts, where fundamental and historical dissatisfactions between sexes are inscribed, does not in my view suppress the optimism of the content. To obliterate this meaning seems to be the most common flaw in recent critical writing, from Daniel Sibony in *Jeux d'Ombre*[25] to Julia Kristeva in *Soleil Noir*.[26]

Love represents, in Duras' world, the absurdity which challenges all possible reason. In the Durasian text love resides in the fascination which irremediably locks lovers like Lol V.Stein to their missing object or, when reciprocity exists, which encloses them in a mutual fusion: "Fondus ensemble en une seule couleur, une seule forme. Un seul âge (...) Ils étaient seuls, perdus (...) Ils ne voyaient rien" (EL pp.16-17). The conception of love without object, announced in *Le Ravissement de Lol V.Stein* and developed in *L'Amour*, fully asserts itself in the later fiction. "Je peux dire qu'il s'agit d'un amour absurde, sans sujets" (VM p.86), we read in *La Vie Matérielle* of the couple of *Les Yeux Bleus Cheveux Noirs*, and the same could be said of the relationship between the woman-narrator and her companion in *Emily-L*. The irrepressibility of love which, in spite of a more explicit concern for homosexuality, more clearly informs her recent fictions, thus represents an evolution in Marguerite Duras' writing. From *L'Homme Atlantique* onwards, the text is concerned not so much with the individuality of a love story, but rather with the attraction which exists between two human beings. The actualisation of love has become irremediably impossible, and forces the characters to go beyond the boundaries of personalised love and self-identity in order to realize the state mentioned in *La Vie Matérielle*:

> "Ils savent plus que les autres dans le sens du silence à faire sur l'amour mais ils ne savent pas le vivre. Ils vivent à la place une autre histoire comme s'ils étaient d'autres gens" (VM p.87).

---

[25]Daniel Sibony, 'Jeux D'Ombre, Littérature et Mélancolie' in *Nouvelles Littéraires* (July 1987) p.18

[26]"Duras choisit ou succombe à la contemplation complice, voluptueuse, envoûtante de la mort en nous, de la permanence de la blessure" (Kristeva op.cit. p.244)

In spite of the inherent difficulty between sexes, the characters not only take responsibility for their own sexuality[27] while waiting for love; they also accede to a sense of wonder in the awareness of the other's uniqueness:

> "Elle lui dit qu'il est beau dans une façon dont rien d'autre n'est beau dans l'univers, aucun animal, aucune plante. Qu'il pourrait ne pas être là. Ne pas être survenu dans la chaîne de la vie" (YB p.53)

This love exists in spite of the characters' inability to live it: "un amour qui aime déjà, qui envahit et qui reste en deçà de tout ce qu'on pourrait en dire, pour des raisons d'ordre religieux" (VM pp.86-87) and can be read as a provocation in relation to the madness of the world. The unreason[28] of love based on its impossible actualisation nevertheless remains the only solution outlined in Duras' fiction:

> "Je voulais vous dire ce que je crois, c'est qu'il fallait toujours garder par devers soi (...) une sorte d'endroit personnel (...) pour y être seul et pour aimer. Pour aimer on ne sait pas quoi, ni qui ni comment, ni combien de temps (...) pour garder en soi la place d'une attente, on ne sait jamais, de l'attente d'un amour, d'un amour sans encore personne peut-être, mais de cela et seulement de cela, de l'amour" (EL p.135).

Another logic, reminiscent of the relationship between sexes, can be discerned according to which "l'amour s'organise dans une sorte d'équation qui vous échappe".[29] 'Madness' ultimately remains inescapable in Duras' fiction; beyond the absurdity of sexual politics lies the unreason of the powerful instinct of love, which makes the characters "vivre l'amour comme le désespoir"

---

[27]"C'est vrai que je suis responsable de cet ordre astral de mon sexe au rythme lunaire et saignant. Devant vous comme devant la mer." (YB p.53)

[28]In order to avoid the negative connotations of the word 'unreason', the term 'non-reason' should perhaps be used. I do not here mean what Foucault describes as "l'envers simple, immédiat, aussitôt rencontré de la raison, et cette forme vide, sans contenu, ni valeur, purement négative où n'est figure que l'empreinte de la raison qui vient de s'enfuir, mais qui reste toujours, pour la déraison, la raison d'être de ce qu'elle est" (HF p.192).

[29]interview 11th April 1981 in *Marguerite Duras à Montréal* p.48

(EL p.40). And behind the unreason of love, which actualises Verdiglione's statement wherein "le sexe annonce toujours la perte du sens, un contresens",[30] lies a celebration of the libido and of the imaginary, whereby the difference between fantasy and reality has disappeared.

We reach at this point the concept of a pulsional body "qui n'est de l'un, ni de l'autre sexe, mais qui crie la demande de l'autre".[31] Love here explodes the usual limits to such an extent that it becomes lack of reason, beyond the common understanding of sexual desire. If in Duras' texts the female characters love a void, an absence, it is mainly to transcend individual boundaries in order to situate themselves in a state of desire. I would therefore at this point refute Kristeva's assertion about Duras' texts: "jamais, peut-être, art ne fut aussi peu cathartique".[32] A close and exhaustive reading of Duras' production, up to her latest texts, shows instead an optimism which sustains and inflates her writing.

I would further argue that this optimism, perhaps despite appearances, does not become mystifying or escapist. This is precisely because it does not, as Kristeva suggests, simply recognize the weight of human suffering, or "succombe à (...) la contemplation (...) envoûtante de la permanence de la blessure",[33] but integrates suffering and the consciousness of death into the state of love experienced by the characters.

5 The ambiguity of the Durasian conception of love and the diagnosis of melancholia

> "J'entends les gens dire elle est folle Duras. Ça m'est égal. Je ne suis pas sans folie non plus, comme tout le monde."[34]

Marguerite Duras' ambiguously painful apprehension of reality has provided a basis for Julia Kristeva and Daniel Sibony's approaches towards Duras' texts, whereby the texts are primarily

---

[30]A.Verdiglione, 'La Jouissance de la Matière' in *Psychanalyse et Semiotique* (10/18 1975) p.41

[31]Marcelle Marini op.cit. in *Ecrire Dit-elle* p.41

[32]Kristeva op.cit. (*Soleil Noir*) p.235

[33]ibid. p.244

[34]*Au Delà des Pages* (programme 4)

seen as broad manifestations of melancholia, as expressions of "cette soif de la douleur jusqu'à la folie".[35] I would like to discuss here the relevance of such claims.

> "Vous voyez comment sont les écrits de Duras: écriture savamment négligée, à l'instar d'une toilette ou d'un maquillage défait pour suggérer une maladie à ne pas surmonter."[36]

Sibony is echoed by Kristeva, who sees in Duras' texts

> "un univers de malaise troublant et contagieux. L'écriture (...) s'en tient à la mise à nu de la maladie. Sans catharsis, cette littérature rencontre, reconnaît mais aussi propage le mal qui la mobilise."[37]

Indeed one can detect pathological tendencies in the Durasian text,[38] incidentally as reminiscent of schizophrenia as of melancholia.[39] For instance Duras' apparent need to pervert the function of language by introducing her famous ellipses of meaning, these 'blancs', could perhaps be seen as the sign of a schizophrenic tendency, since

> "nommer les objets du monde d'une manière acceptable, c'est consentir à un compromis, à un contrat avec cette société".[40]

One can also guess, as the opening quotation for this section suggests, that there are in Duras herself, as in everyone moreover, the seeds of unreason: her irrepressible inner violence[41] and her

---

[35] Kristeva op.cit. (*Soleil Noir*) p.246

[36] Sibony op. cit. (*Jeux D'Ombre*) p.18

[37] Kristeva op.cit. (*Soleil Noir*) p.237

[38] cf. the more 'clinical' analysis of the Duras text in 'La Mise en Scène de la Folie', Chapter 1 above.

[39] As Guy Rosalato mentions, madness is indeed constituted of three psychoses: schizophrenia, paranoia and melancholia (depression). (cf. 'La Folie et le Sacré' in *Psychanalyse et Sémiotique* p.79)

[40] Salomon Resnick, quoted in Jaccard op.cit. p.89

[41] "Je ne sais pas ce que c'est la non-violence. Je ne peux pas me la représenter. La paix avec soi je ne sais pas ce que c'est. Je ne fais que des rêves tragiques, de haine. Ce qui me donne envie de pleurer c'est ma violence." ('Marguerite Duras: Moi', in *L'Autre Journal* 30th April - 6th May 1986)

dislike of social reality can also be interpreted as signs of morbidity. The Kleinian psychoanalyst Wilfred Bion has maintained that one of the essential characteristics of the schizophrenic personality is a hatred of reality.[42] The impossibility of consummation of love recurs in the Durasian texts; this can certainly be interpreted, as Kristeva proposes,[43] as an imbalance probably resulting from Duras' own mother's 'madness'; the maternal presence which has become "objet d'amour archaïque, immaîtrisable et imaginaire".[44] One can also wonder if the references to uncontrollable fear which recur in one book after another come from such mental difficulties: "Je suis quelqu'un qui a peur, continue Alissa, peur d'être délaissée, peur de l'avenir, de la faim, de la misère, de la vérité" (DDE p.46). The fear is echoed by the woman narrator *Emily-L*:

> "C'est en moi, secrété par moi. Ça vit d'une vie paradoxale,géniale et cellulaire à la fois. C'est là. Sans langage pour se dire. Au plus près, c'est une cruauté nue, muette, de moi à moi, logée dans ma tête, dans le cachot mental. Etanche. Avec des percées vers la raison, la vraisemblance, la clarté". (EL p.51)

As has already been mentioned in the study of *Le Ravissement*, where we saw that Lol can be apprehended as hysteric, it is important not to be drawn into what can be seen after all as a diagnostic bias. I would simply point out in the first instance that if one comes to see Marguerite Duras' texts as expressions of recognizeable pathological symptoms, then the creative power of her writing in relation to the sterility of the majority of so-called 'normal people' should bring us to question the very norms attached to mental illness. Recent critics of Duras' texts fall into an old trap once denounced by Laing and others of the anti-psychiatric movement. Such critics' attempts to understand Durasian production while situating it in the literary tradition of Nerval, Dostoyevsky, Flaubert, Valéry etc. remains limited to the

---

[42]Jaccard op.cit. p.83

[43]Kristeva's approach in *Soleil Noir* suggests that Duras' mother determined the sexuality of her children and motivated their incestuous desire - hence the later inability to love.

[44]Kristeva op.cit. (*Soleil Noir*) p.262

satisfying rationale of labelling what they see as signs of morbidity.[45] As Verdiglione signals, however, "L'impasse du psychiatrisme, justement, dérive de ce qu'on ne peut pas faire un diagnostic de la folie".[46] It is undeniable that artistic production partakes of madness; the 'artist' is

> "un individu capable d'établir et de maîtriser un rapport d'expression avec son propre inconscient, capable autrement dit d'actualiser et d'élaborer des potentialités psychotiques qui sont étouffées chez le commun des hommes".[47]

I would also agree with Michel Thevoz that, if one excludes here the mental disabilities of physical origin,

> "la folie ne saurait être affectée d'un caractère morbide, elle apparaît au contraire comme une exaltation, parfois féconde sur le plan de l'expression, de ressources psychiques qui existent peut-être, mais de manière latente, chez tout homme"[48]

If melancholia describes what is at work in Durasian prose, it may be according to the meaning given to it in the text of Greek antiquity *Problemata 30*, where melancholia appeared divorced from pathology and was considered as an extreme state of human nature, "comme une crise naturelle si on veut, revêlatrice par conséquent de la vérité de l'être".[49]

Secondly there is little doubt, in Marguerite Duras' case, that, independently of any clinical diagnosis, writing has become an effective means of control over her own inner unrest. Writing functions as a security device which helps her compensate for the painful apprehension of reality:

---

[45]To be fair to Kristeva, she does make an obvious link, in the first part of her article 'La Maladie de la Douleur' in *Soleil Noir*, between the symptoms of melancholia in Duras' texts and the state of the world: "la destruction de la nature, des vies et des biens se double d'une recrudescence ou simplement d'une manifestation plus patente, des désordres dont la psychiatrie raffine le diagnostic: psychose, dépression, manie, borderline, fausses personalités...etc." (op.cit. p.229)

[46]A.Verdiglione, *La Folie dans la Psychanalyse* (Payot

[47]Michel Theroz, 'Art et Folie' in Jaccard op.cit. p.119

[48]ibid. p.121. And, I would add, "chez toute femme".

[49]Sibony, op.cit. (*Jeux D'Ombre*) p.18

"quelquefois on dit je vais me tuer et puis on continue
le livre" (VM p.71)
"il me semble que c'est lorsque ce sera dans un livre que
cela ne me fera plus souffrir" (EL p.23).[50]

One would also have to recognize, with Sibony, that the
activity of writing repeatedly mentioned by Duras in *La Vie
Matérielle* is founded on a kind of narcissistic impulse.[51]

I would also accept the view that in the seemingly subdued
existence of Duras' heroines there is a sign of the threat posed by
the Other-woman to Duras (the writer) herself:

"Pour une femme la position déprimante est de buter
sur l'Autre-femme comme sur un roc: c'est de ne pas
être la première femme. Duras surmonte cette position
en étant la première de ses héroïnes, la
Femme-Ecriture qui se répond et correspond à
elle-même (...) Les héroïnes de Marguerite Duras sont
déprimées parce qu' elle les surmonte et les surplombe
totalement; comme une mère qui ne donnerait qu'un
peu de vie à ses filles, gardant pour elle l'essentiel en se
nourrissant de leur faiblesse".[52]

Such convincing explanations, founded on psychoanalytic
presuppositions, while having some relevance, nevertheless again
stop at the diagnostic level and rob the text of its wider ideological
dimension. As a counterweight, I would like to raise the following
questions about the Durasian text:

---

[50]In another very revealing utterance, Duras clearly states that the experience of
unreason imbues the personal fight against the invasion of creativity: "Quand
j'écris je suis parfois...véritablement envahie par la littérature. Envahie par l'écrit,
je ne peux pas aller aussi vite que lui. Alors je fais des phrases inachevées, je
pose des mots. Après coup quand je relis mes mots, je les rassemble avec des
phrases...c'est à dire que la correction de la phrase je m'en fous. On croit que j'ai
imposé un style, une liberté, une syntaxe beaucoup plus libre qu'avant...et bien
je ne l'ai pas fait dans ce sens là...Je l'ai fait parce qu'il ne pouvait en être
autrement, pour me dégager de l'écrit, pour lutter contre l'envahissement de
l'écriture" (op. cit. ('Duras Toute Entière') p.116)

[51]Sibony writes that in her texts Marguerite Duras "s'identifie à ce trou,
s'incarnant comme la Femme - creuset d'écriture, la donneuse de vie, creusée
d'écriture infinie" (*Jeux D'Ombre* p.56) 1977) p.24

[52]ibid. p.56

Why is the Female Other such a threat both to the
characters and to the writer herself?

Why is society given over to an economy of the Same,
be it of male or female homosexuality, and why is the
woman excluded from libidinal activity in the triangular
relationship?

Why is is impossible for both male and female
characters to find an object of love?

One may choose to see the female fear of the Other woman
as an inherent characteristic of femaleness, or as a sign of
fundamental morbidity through which Marguerite Duras' fictions
would remain "des romans au ras de la maladie".[53]

Such determinist positions seem, as I have indicated above,
rather limited, since they omit to consider that in Duras' texts the
leader of the new state of being remains the woman; a fact only
evasively hinted at by Kristeva in her expression "la passivité
froissée mais sournoisement puissante des femmes".[54]

If the woman is placed in a position of threat in relation to
the Same-Other, it principally reflects an ideological system based
on the economy of the couple, on the problematic of the
privatisation of love, and of irremediable exclusion. Sexuality is tied
to the economy of the Same because of a Western patriarchal
system whereby men are given power from birth and where
ultimately, and even after the positive wave of the feminist
movement, women still have no place.[55] Men can only love
themselves in the image of another man: "l'homosexuel porte le
deuil absolu de la femme, ce second terme" (VM p.38) Marcelle
Marini echoes this:

"les oeuvres durassiennes entrecroisent sans cesse les
différences de race, de culture, de classe, de nation, de

---

[53]Kristeva op.cit. (*Soleil Noir*) p.234

[54]Kristeva op.cit. (*Soleil Noir*) p.262

[55]"Je crois que c'est terrible la sujétion dans laquelle nous sommes" echoes Duras
in *Au Delà des Pages*, "dans laquelle ils (=les hommes) veulent nous mettre. C'est
épouvantable. La plupart des choses...la femme les ressent d'une façon lointaine,
comme un souvenir un peu, comme si les choses s'engloutissaient tout de suite
dans le temps dès qu'elles sont subies. C'est comme ça qu'elle se sauve la
femme...mais on se demande comment on peut subir ça; c'est toujours la mise à
mort, ça ne change pas du tout c'est terrible...c'est hallucinant" (programme 4)

langue, de génération et de sexe. Mais, au bas de l'échelle, c'est toujours une femme que l'on trouve, cumulant tous les rejets".[56]

The only solution left for women is to identify with the Female Other, be it the mother or the rival woman, in "une quête à jamais nostalgique du même comme autre, de l'autre comme même".[57] If it is impossible for Marguerite Duras to find an object of love, it is because the libidinal investments cannot be actualised in such societal limitations.

The object of love can ultimately only be imaginary, the woman being faithful to her own fantasy of a lover, while the man remains attached to his own image of power in the homo- sexual fantasy. And it is at this level, rather than, as Trista Selous sees it, at the level of female passivity, that an escapist dimension in Duras may come into play. But even here I would argue, along with Deleuze and Guattari and contrary to what psychoanalysis still tends to maintain, that there is no opposition as such between the so-called fantasy world and the 'real' external world, since fantasy constitutes one reality among others. Indeed

> "any attempt to label one phenomenon of human existence as 'more real' than another remains arbitrary. People who do so are employing a biased definition of reality"[58]

and reflect the establishment of a dualism between the 'real' object rationally produced and an "irrational fantasizing production". But "there is no such thing as the social production of reality on the one hand and a desiring production that is mere fantasy on the other". (AO p.28)[59]

It is at this level that I see Duras' prose as fundamentally optimistic, in this state of love experienced by the female characters which makes them transcend societal limitations and

---

[56]Marini, in *Ecrire, Dit-elle* p.27

[57]Kristeva op.cit. (*Soleil Noir*) p.262

[58]Klaus Theweleit, *Male Fantasies* (Polity Press 1987) p.219

[59]Klaus Theweleit makes the same point: "...the human unconscious (is) a force of production...what it produces is not a special 'psychic' reality, but social reality per se." (op.cit. p.255)

personal boundaries, in this "intelligence de l'amour" or unreason of desire, this

> "raison obscure d'avoir à souffrir pour se rappeler d'une absence sans image, sans visage sans voix mais qui emporte le corps tout entier, comme sous l'effet de la musique, vers l'émotion qui accompagne la délivrance d'on ne sait quel poids formel" (VM p.87).

6 Theatricality or the didactic dimension of the Durasian text

> "Ce n'est pas possible que vous ayez vu à travers ce que j'ai écrit les images indépendantes de leurs commentaires"[60]

The unreason of love is the result of a 'practice of the loss'. In some of the later Durasian fictions this practice becomes the object of a more evident didacticism, which shows that the concept of love exists in Duras as a possible alternative to the madness of the social scene.

In Marguerite Duras' earlier fictions, the didactic dimension of the texts was discernible in the existence of the woman in relation to the man, in her presence as initiator of another mode of being. With *L'Homme Atlantique* and *Les Yeux Bleus, Cheveux Noirs*, however, explicit didacticism becomes part of, or exists in parallel with, the fictional content of the text, through the references to theatricality.

Theatricality allows the staging of this alternative mode of being in a more concrete and explicit manner. Scenic indications, juxtaposed to or included in the fictional content of the texts as signs of an open external form of didacticism, have always been part of the Durasian practice of writing, be it in *L'Amour, Détruire Dit-elle, Savannah Bay* or elsewhere:

> "Elles encerclent et travaillent l'histoire. Méta-narratives à cet égard, elles ont pour objet la scène qui sert d'arène à des manipulations et dispositions commandées par une économie domestique de l'espace".[61]

---

[60]*Marguerite Duras à Montréal* p.39
[61]de Certeau op.cit. p.259

With *L'Homme Atlantique* and *Les Yeux Bleus, Cheveux Noirs*, scenic directives no longer refer 'only' to a plural practice of production, but become closely connected to the subject-matter of the narrative. Such an emphasis on the importance of theatricality supports Duras' programme of "la pratique de la perte", aimed at emancipation from the social via access to another mode of being. We find in these texts an equivalence between the scenic and the characters' fictional state of being. Theatricality becomes, as the characters' main mode of presence, an element of the fiction, while fiction tends to be represented in a media context.

Both texts, *Les Yeux Bleus* and *L'Homme Atlantique*, include two levels: that of the narrative, an attempt to enact/re-enact a love relationship, and that of description, with its cinematographic or theatrical representation. The two levels interpenetrate one another, especially in *L'Homme Atlantique*, which is fully situated in the development of the plurality of the Durasian mode of expression. Fragments and images from other Duras texts can be find in both books, again particularly in *L'Homme Atlantique*, which may be seen as another version of *L'Amour*.[62]

L'Homme Atlantique tells the story of a female film director who instructs a male film actor on how to lose his sense of self in order to re-enact "la comédie de la fin d'un amour" (HA p.19). In *Les Yeux Bleus, Cheveux Noirs* a woman who defines herself as an actor (YB p.16)[63] accepts a contract of prostitution with a homosexual man in order to teach him the access to love. She also complies with the man's wishes : "Chaque soir, elle amène son corps dans la chambre, elle défait ses vêtements, elle le place au milieu de la lumière jaune" (YB p.103). The actor-narrator in turn situates the elements of the fiction as scenic indications, and reflects on the theatrical adaptation of the story :

---

[62]Indeed we can find in *L'Homme Atlantique* and *L'Amour* not only the same typographic structure, but also related narrative situations and common textual fragments and images. Both texts seem to focus on this "moment inaugural" which is "pure madness" when apprehended from the side of reason. *L'Amour*, however, offers the perfect representation of the loss of identity, while *L'Homme Atlantique* presents its prescriptive aspect. In this sense *L'Amour* is more visual or cinematographic than is *L'Homme Atlantique*.

[63]The word 'actor' is deliberately used here in order to avoid certain sexist connotations associated with the word 'actress'.

"Il s'agit de tenir le récit initial dans un état agonisant, dans cette condition agonistique et frontalière par laquelle il devient l'excès de la perte (...) de ce qu'il ne peut dire."[64]

In both texts, various elements of 'mise en scène' - the setting, the camera or the look - are strongly present. The surface of representation is a common element in most Durasian fiction. Its actualisation takes various forms: the terrace in *L'Après-midi de Monsieur Andesmas*, "le chemin de pierre" in *L'Homme Assis dans le Couloir* or the beach in *Le Ravissement de Lol V Stein*, *Le Vice-consul* and especially *L'Amour*, where it is viewed as a liberating space allowing the characters' mode of presence. In *Les Yeux Bleus, Cheveux Noirs* and *La Maladie de la Mort*, the bedroom and the bed become metaphors of the stage.

"Elle dit qu'un jour elle fera un livre sur la chambre, elle trouve que c'est un endroit comme par inadvertance, en principe inhabitable, infernal, une scène de théâtre fermée" (YB p.40)

On this platform the characters are exposed: "Ils seraient aveuglés par la lumière, ils seraient nus, sexes nus, des créatures sans regard, exposées" (YB p.61). For the most part it is the woman who stands objectified in the enclosed space: "Elle est au centre de la chambre vide, sur les draps blancs étalés à même le sol" (YB p.22). "La flaque des draps blancs" becomes equivalent to the beach. The surface of representation pictured in the texts implies that a state of being has already been reached, usually by the female figure. She becomes the exclusive focus for her male counterpart.

The camera in *L'Homme Atlantique* is the chosen medium for promoting the sense of the loss. The instructions given to the film actor by the female director are transparent indications on how to achieve this "pratique de la perte", the sense of 'non-preference' without which the actor cannot identify with his role.

"Vous ne chercherez pas à comprendre ce phénomène photographique, la vie"(HA p.25)

---

[64]de Certeau op.cit. p.259

The juxtaposition of the filmic process with life in the above quotation clearly indicates the constant counterposing of two realities in *L'Homme Atlantique*; that of the discipline necessary for the actor's practice and that of the "être au monde" of the Durasian character. The representation of an actor's rehearsal at the primary level of the text provides a transparent metaphor of Marguerite Duras' paradoxical vision of existence.

> "Vous ne regarderez pas la caméra. Sauf lorsqu'on l'exigera de vous...
> Vous oublierez...
> Que c'est vous, vous l'oublierez...
> Vous oublierez aussi que c'est la caméra. Mais surtout vous oublierez que c'est vous. Vous." (HA p.7)

The loss of self-awareness can be achieved by lapses of memory - "vous oublierez" - and by a refusal to understand: "Vous ne chercherez pas à comprendre". Any preconceived way of being is thus abandoned in order to achieve this other state of non-existence, this "mort régnante et sans nom" (HA p.8), a state in which physical death becomes irrelevant. Paradoxically, forgetting one's ego brings a renewed awareness of the unicity of one's being in the world. To be is to be for the first time; this is a necessary condition if the actor's playing is likely to achieve any plausibility in *L'Homme Atlantique*, but is also the required mode of being for the Durasian character.

> "Le plus grand danger(...)c'est de vous ressembler" (HA p.23)
> "Vous penserez que...ceci est inaugural comme l'est d'elle-même votre propre vie à chaque seconde de son déroulement. Que dans le déferlement milliardaire des hommes autour de vous, vous êtes le seul à tenir lieu de vous même" (HA pp.5-10)

The camera, instrument of cinematographic reproduction and perhaps a metaphor of God, is consistently and ambiguously mentioned in the narrative.

> "Au bout du voyage, c'est la caméra qui aura décidé de ce que vous aurez regardé (...) Regardez là comme un objet de prédilection désigné par vous, attendu par vous depuis toujours, comme si vous aviez décidé de lui tenir

tête, d'engager avec elle une lutte entre la vie et la mort" (HA pp.25-26)

The camera gives relevance to the actor's movement and, as with the walker's incessant, erratic movement in *L'Amour*, the pacing movement in front of the camera facilitates the loss of self-identity.

"Vous verrez tout viendra à partir de votre déplacement le long de la mer, après les piliers du hall, du déplacement de votre corps dont vous aurez pensé jusqu'à cet instant qu'il était naturel" (HA p.13)

Through the camera, the actor reaches the state of presence/absence[65] which strikingly recalls the state of the female Durasian figure:

"Vous êtes resté dans l'état d'être parti et j'ai fait un film de votre absence" (HA p.22)
"Vous êtes à la fois caché et présent. Présent, seulement à travers le film, au delà de ce film, et caché à tout savoir de vous, à tout savoir qu'on pourrait avoir de vous" (HA p.27)

"La pratique de la perte" would not be sufficient without the attention paid to the look, which gives fuller meaning to the Durasian enterprise. Marguerite Duras' fictions are renowned for the constant reiterative emphasis placed on the scopic drive. The ternary structure of the narratives, which often comprises a character or two observing another couple, encourages the pre-eminence of the look. Such is the case for example for Lol V.Stein in relation to Tatiana and J.Hold, or for the man of *Les Yeux Bleus, Cheveux Noirs* watching the young foreigner and the woman in the hall, or again for the woman-narrator and her friend

---

[65] *In L'Homme Atlantique*, the mode of presence/absence is reached through the logical implications linked to the presence of the camera. In *Les Yeux Bleus, Cheveux Noirs*, presence/absence is inscribed in the logic of theatricality with the importance of the light which allows the surface of representation to come to life. The constant contrast between the lit central area of the bedroom, where the woman stands when she fulfils her contract with the man, and the darkness around, is echoed by the changes in the intensity of the light during the suggested performance of the text. The absence of the actor's play, through silence and sleep, coincides with the decline of the light.

in *Emily-L*, observing the captain and his wife. Looking constitutes one of the main activities in Duras' fictions, and through it the characters become alternatively subject and object of the scopic drive.

However, behind what can be seen as an objectifying look, often that of a male character over a female body,[66] stands another scopic dimension where the look has more to do with creativity and a sense of essentiality. If the look of the (often male) Other in Duras' narratives apparently constitutes an objectivisation of the observed character, its impact on the character in question is in fact very different. It is the scopic drive of the Other which gives recognition to the state of being achieved by the female figure, a recognition which is also the sense of "inaliénable royauté" to be reached by the actor:

> "Durant votre passage il vous faudra donc croire à votre inaliénable royauté (...) Vous marcherez comme vous le faites quand vous êtes seul et que vous croyez que quelqu'un vous regarde, Dieu ou moi, ou ce chien le long de la mer..." (HA p.12)

In the Durasian perspective, to be seen is not a sign of alienation from the Other, but is lived as an indication of one's "inaliénable royauté", a recognition of one's fundamental importance, a coronation of one's own presence in the world through the Other's scopic preference.

For the character her/himself, the activity of looking has to do with intensity, a characteristic which is constantly referred to in Marguerite Duras' narratives,[67] and which paradoxically prevents one from seeing:

> "Ce que vous serez en train de voir là, la mer, les vitres, le mur (...) Vous ne l'aurez jamais vu, jamais regardé" (HA p.9)
> "Vous regarderez ce que vous voyez. Mais vous le

---

[66]The objectifying process has been denounced by a number of critics of the Duras text. As already mentioned, they mainly see in the Durasian narrative a depiction of women as passive and dependent.

[67]If our postmodern period is indeed 'visual', as it is often said to be, then this would be another reason for asserting that Marguerite Duras is definitely a contemporary writer!

> regarderez absolument. Vous essaierez de regarder
> jusqu'à l'extinction de votre regard, jusqu'à son propre
> aveuglement et à travers celui-ci vous devrez essayer
> encore de regarder." (HA p.8)

Through the intensity of this new way of looking, ambiguously described as the loss of the ability to see, the dissolution of boundaries in what is seen of the world becomes possible:

> "Vous et la mer, vous ne faites qu'un pour moi, qu'un
> seul objet (...) Je la regarde moi aussi, vous devez la
> regarder comme moi, comme moi je la regarde de
> toutes mes forces, à votre place" (HA p.14)

Access to an awareness of one's own "inaliénable royauté"[68] can be gained through a perception of self and of the world which goes beyond appearances, through the ambiguous and paradoxical double movement of loss of identity and a renewed sense of one's own uniqueness. In a passage from *L'Homme Atlantique* which reaches biblical overtones and which is reminiscent of the final passage of *L'Amour*, the access to this inaugural moment is thus pictured:

> "Vous penserez que le miracle n'est pas dans
> l'apparente similitude entre chaque particule de ces
> milliards du déferlement continu, mais dans la différence
> irréductible qui les sépare, qui sépare les hommes des
> chiens, les chiens du cinéma, le sable de la mer, Dieu de
> ce chien ou de cette mouette tenace face au vent, du
> cristal liquide de vos yeux de celui blessant des sables,
> de la touffeur irrespirable du hall de cet hôtel passé de
> l'éblouissante clarté égale de la plage, de chaque mot de
> chaque phrase, de chaque ligne de chaque livre, de
> chaque jour et de chaque siècle, et de chaque éternité
> passée où à venir et de vous et de moi.
> Durant votre passage, il vous faudra donc croire à votre
> inaliénable royauté" (HA pp.11-12)

This passage carries all the optimism of Marguerite Duras' prose. Through his practice, the actor of *L'Homme Atlantique* reaches the state of unreason experienced by the Durasian female

---

[68] - though one can legitimately wonder: at what cost?

character; through a mode of absolute presence which implies a loss of one's social sense of self, the world is recreated via a new way of looking. Paradoxically, *L'Homme Atlantique*, one of Duras' shortest texts, offers a synthesis of her ideological programme.[69] The optimism of the prose lies in her belief in a permanent renewal of existence against any kind of predetermination, either by God or by society, which would prevent individual freedom. Such a position may of course appear utopian or idealist[70]. It is rather the sign of a positive and courageous vision of the tragic dimension of existence: from suffering arises life, absence makes love possible. Behind the unreason of the Durasian mode of being we can detect a philosophy of existence which metamorphoses everyday living in order to allow the miracle of the 'event' to appear; suffering is transcended in an increased consciousness of life.

To limit Marguerite Duras' texts to the level of a simple recording of societal failure constitutes a limitation of the potentiality of her narratives. "Le public lit des choses qu'au cinéma il refuserait. C'est par le livre que la forteresse sera minée".[71] Indeed there is in Duras' production a belief in another order of reason, "la pratique de la perte", evoked in her fictions through the unreason of love and described in her articles, with the same typically Durasian ambiguity, as a political loss:

> "Pour moi la perte politique, c'est avant tout la perte de soi, la perte de sa colère autant que de sa douceur, la perte de sa haine autant que de sa faculté d'aimer" (YV p.7)

---

[69]At the risk of being carried away by the false reassurance of a certain conceptualising vocabulary, I would like to point out here that if *L'Amour* does present the actualisation of desire, and *L'Homme Assis dans le Couloir* its sexualisation, then *L'Homme Atlantique*, through its prescriptive dimension, offers a synthesis of the possibility of desire itself.

[70]This position, dependent on a 'pratique de la perte', can indeed be seen as a utopian vision. But, as Margaret Whitford recalls (*Luce Irigaray*, 'Philosophy in the Feminine', Routledge, London 1991, p.19), it has been argued that "we 'need' utopian visions, that imagining how things could be different is part of the process of transforming the present in the direction of a different future". This is a view expressed by M.Marini in different terms: "The value of utopia is not to programme the future but to help to change the present" (in *Lacan*, Paris Belfond, 1986, p.621).

[71]Marguerite Duras, in *L'Autre Journal* (no.11) p.28

Paradoxically, such a practice fully supports the optimistic view of Duras' writing which can be expressed in these terms:

> "je ne crois plus à rien du tout, seulement à l'individu et à sa propre survie, à sa propre liberté, à sa propre sauvegarde, et à sa propre grâce, à sa propre immensité"[72]

[72]*Marguerite Duras à Montréal* p.47

CONCLUSION

This exploration of the concept of madness and unreason present at the heart of Marguerite Duras' texts from 1964 onwards has shown that signs of clinical madness are indeed detectable in the Durasian text. Nevertheless madness here has little to do with the "auto-référence vide" mentioned by Foucault (HF p.581) and present in Raymond Roussel or in Artaud, by which the impossible and contradictory statements "j'écris" and "je délire" remain linked. Madness in Duras' prose remains mediated by writing, by the object of a story to be told.

The examination of the reception of Marguerite Duras' texts has shown how the unreason of the Durasian female character lies at the root of the feminist conception which views Durasian production as a whole as an articulation of the feminine. This explains the fact that feminist critics have seen Durasian prose mostly as a reflection of womens' repressed position in the ideological order, and have therefore often reduced the impact of Duras' writing. It has also been established that unreason, the non-clinical form of madness, is reflected in the presence of the gaps and holes which disrupt the chain of meaning in Durasian fiction and account for the frustration of reason in certain readers. Against Selous' interpretation, it has also been argued that the experience of the female characters, designated as 'mad' or absent, is relevant not so much in terms of passivity as in terms of a power beyond rationality and knowledge. In that sense one can indeed conclude that Duras frees reason from the myth of signification, by recognizing that at the heart of discourse lies a void or silence.

Madness does not constitute another type of reason, it is coherent within its own discourse.

The study of the novels of the cycle of Lol V.Stein, namely *Le Ravissement de Lol V.Stein* (1964), *Le Vice-consul* (1965) and *L'Amour* (1971), has brought to light an evolution in the concept of madness closely interlinked with an alteration of the social perspective from one text to the next. *Le Ravissement* deals with a Western apprehension of madness, that of mental illness situated primarily in the individual. In *Le Vice-consul*, which has a lot in common with 'third world' literature, the structure of exclusion from a social setting serves as a framework for the perception of reason. The text of *L'Amour* largely evacuates the social aspect and madness becomes an experience broadly linked to a universal problem.

Throughout this evolution, madness takes on three alternative meanings which nevertheless tend to overlap from one text to another:

1.   The sense of abnormality, which implies a ruling reason through which madness becomes a negatively loaded concept.
2.   The signification of difference or absence of reason with the emergence of madness as a vital force, whereby exclusion from the social structure tends to become strength.
3.   Finally madness becomes a liberating experience of unreason which functions in a mode of inclusion and which corresponds, as exemplified in the characters, to a phase of ego dissolution.

Duras' treatment of madness in these three texts can be summarised as follows. Though *Le Ravissement* treats madness as illness - and I have argued that it is so mostly as an effect of the repressive social structure -, Marguerite Duras' writing in *Le Ravissement* does not evacuate "cette vérité de soi-même, lointaine et inverse" (HF p.576); on the contrary, through the emergence of Lol's desire and its effect on Jacques Hold, it puts this other form of human existence at its centre. With *Le Ravissement de Lol V.Stein*, Duras does not fix madness in a unitary meaning, but overcomes the fear of its recognition. She welcomes madness and unreason instead as a positivity at the heart of human interaction.

Le Vice-consul embodies in turn a presentation, not so much of unreason - in that it constitutes the Other in relation to Logos -, but of the dialectical dilemma which exists between the two. With the narrative of *Le Vice-consul*, the reader witnesses how the repressive principle of logocentrism, historically exemplified in the common practice of exclusion, fails to function, and how the white society which is represented becomes completely split by the increasing infiltration of unreason via the arrival of the vice-consul. The unreason apparent in the successive characters of the beggar-woman, the vice-consul and Anne-Marie Stretter nevertheless happens at most times to be circumscribed by reason.[1] There is in fact no real dialogue with madness in the narrative of *Le Vice-consul*, no expression of unreason as such, or any recognition of its possible language. Lack of reason is instead perceived against a rational background in which reason remains the norm. Madness is experienced in the mode of a felt opposition:

> "région du langage où se trouvent et se confrontent à la fois le sens et le non-sens, la vérité et l'erreur...les limites du jugement et les présomptions infinies du désir" (HF p.186)

L'Amour corresponds to the positive pole of madness, with the characters' liberation from the constraints of society and the actualisation of another mode of desire.

In *L'Amour*, however, beyond the abandonment of reason to be observed in the characters, the new social order constitutes a simple reversal, still based on exclusion, in which the so-called 'normal' people find themselves interned within the town of S.Thala. If the end of *L'Amour* evokes the advent of an alternative mode of being, the thematic of separation and exclusion still counteracts such a reading, and indicates that in fact reason has not disappeared. What predominates in *L'Amour* is the destruction of a civilization punctuated by the sirens of *S.Thala*, in favour of a cosmic, universal space. In spite of a return to the myth of unity or origin, the text of *L'Amour* presents only an individual solution. It is as such opposed to ancestral myths in which madness was not

---

[1] Let us recall, for instance the vice-consul's exclusion. The account of the story of the beggar-woman by Peter Morgan shows that language asserts its dominance over an objectified madness.

evacuated but, on the contrary, included within the social group by a kind of alliance which secured a system of common beliefs. The mad characters of *L'Amour* do not establish any 'alliance' with the rest of the community.[2] Their group constitutes instead a kind of elite which has access to a certain 'truth'. Rather than being shared or accepted by their group, their unreason remains an individual and punctual liberation, and cannot as such constitute any alternative to the social context. The text indeed offers no indication which would allow us to infer the presence of a new social order. At most we can assert that the text of *L'Amour* corresponds to the triumph of the repressed of society over Reason, and that in this process the individual solution given to the mental conflict becomes political. In the implied refusal of a society ruled by frustration, the myth of normality is transgressed. Bourgeois order, represented in *L'Amour* by the town, annihilates itself from within. It no longer functions as a defence against anguish, as in *Le Vice-consul*, or as a safeguard for identity, as in *Le Ravissement*. The fear of lack and of disorder is overcome; hence the failure, albeit relative, of the dominant order.

The collective solution pictured in *L'Amour* therefore remains primarily symbolic in the sense of a fusion which takes on the characteristics of a reintegration with nature. But because of the repression of reason which operates in *L'Amour*, the problem of madness in relation to the question of its historicity can find no solution. Ultimately Marguerite Duras falls under the same criticism as that addressed to Foucault by Derrida. In staging madness in *L'Amour*, she has in fact interned Reason, in "un acte de renfermement du Cogito qui serait de même type que celui des violences de l'âge classique".[3]

However, in spite of the various interactions observed in the texts of the cycle of Lol V.Stein between the characters' madness and their social context, their unreason does not exist so much as a symptom provoked by the inadequacy of a social system; in this it is different from many other lived experiences of madness. It primarily stems from an alternative conception of desire. The

---

[2]What happens in *L'Amour* is in fact very different from what occured in the Laingian home mentioned in Chapter 1, where the community would take part in the staging of delirium.

[3]Jacques Derrida op.cit. p.88

implications of such desire not only constitute a challenge in relation to the conception of a gender politics based on the economy of the couple, but ultimately also question the position of humanity in the world. The coherence created by the recurrence of the same figures from one text to another indicates that characters such as Anne-Marie Stretter, Lol V.Stein or the vice-consul fulfil a textual function in the Durasian world. Not only do these characters motivate Duras' writing; they also promote the enigma of a scenario constantly restaged from one text to the next. The reader is in fact confronted with the same scenario, be it on a Normandy beach, in Calcutta or in the enclosed space of a bedroom. Beyond textual variations, these presences from *Le Ravissement* to *Emily-L* deal with the same quest or dilemma: that of the impossibility of desire.

This quest for the impossible may appear to exist in the Duras text at the cost of the evacuation of any social relevance. Indeed the narratives do not directly reflect the problematic of a modern Western society or the situation of women at the end of the 20th century.[4] It may also appear that Duras' texts only reproduce the most glaring stereotypes ranging from bourgeois adultery or the problematic of a love story to prostitution, incest or proxelitism which are to be found predominantly in the tabloid press.[5] To view Duras' texts in relation to their ability to 'reflect' reality in a transparent mode is once more to reduce considerably their inner coherence and literary power.[6] Not only are Duras' texts all situated in close connection with the evolving social

---

[4]It is at this level of criticism that Selous' argument in *The Other Woman* (op. cit.) mostly lies, and the popular reception of both *L'Amant* and *La Douleur*, for instance, has a lot to do with the fact that these two texts have been received by readers at a realistic level, as transparent confession or as straightforward testimony.

[5]This view is possibly reinforced by Duras' interventions as a public figure in issues such as "l'affaire Grégory".

[6]Such a reduction is comparable to the critical strategy denounced in this study, namely that which applies a diagnostic/medical approach to the characters in order to retrieve for Duras' texts some 'realistic' value. On the other hand, if Duras' texts are not realist texts, one could argue that they are ultimately more realistic than realist writing, insofar that they overtly reflect the unavoidable impossibility of translating lived reality into language, and denounce as such the illusion of transparency which lies at the root of realist writing.

problematic of their time;[7] they also stem from the intensity of what is lived, sometimes desperately, at the sexual and interrelational levels. This experience remains at the limits of sanity, too often impossible to express, be it the desire for fusion with the other, an attraction towards the same other or the possible irresistible impulse to relinquish self-identity. Indeed we can hear in Duras' texts "l'inavouable de toute une société".[8]

The exposure of this troubled and obscure reality which lies at the heart of human experience defies any everyday logic or known coherence. Lol's knowledge indeed has to do with this realisation, with the irremediable absence of any possible conceptualisation which could translate such experience. The relentless confrontation with the absence of the Signifier, metaphorised in Duras' texts by the recurrent reference to God, "Dieu?...ce truc?..." (A p.143), is enough to be (or to appear to be) mad.

It is also at this point, in this politics of the impossible, that the logic of Marguerite Duras' writing can be found, and I would, with Marty, assert that her texts do not present "une figuration pathétique de l'impossible".[9] On the contrary, such a dimension is, paradoxically and at the same time, a source of creativity and optimism. It is creativity for Marguerite Duras since she manages to translate this zone of human reality via the power of an imaginary which is not "simple affabulation illusoire", but is "expérimentation, construction, production".[10] And "c'est dans la reprise des temps par l'imaginaire que le souffle est rendu à la vie".[11]

There is creativity for the Durasian reader since an important aspect of the modernity of Duras' texts resides in the fact that, as in the *Nouveau Roman*, such writing,

---

[7]"Produit d'un monde - le nôtre - où domine le doute, la création durassienne, jonchée de démentis, entretient d'étroits rapports avec la sensibilité de son temps" (Marc Saporta in 'Les Possibles Parallèles', in *Marguerite Duras*, L'Arc, p.3).

[8]Marini, 'Une Femme sans Aveu' in *Marguerite Duras*, L'Arc, p.10

[9]Marty op. cit. p.85

[10]Marini op.cit. (L'Arc) p.12

[11]Duras, interview in *Le Nouvel Observateur*, 28.9.84, quoted by Marini op.cit. (L'Arc) p.16

"incomplet dans son dire ainsi qu'au niveau de sa signification (...) réclame la coopération du lecteur pour actualiser tous ses possibles sémantiques."[12]

There is optimism insofar that the politics of the impossible does not obliterate the underlying positivity of Marguerite Duras' prose. This aspect is too often ignored by critics such as Kristeva, Sibony, Makward, Borgamano, Selous and Montrelay, to name only a few. From the anarchic vision of the world and from the very battlefield of gender politics, other symbolic formations appear; hope emerges under the form of love. This love is not to be identified so much with the old romantic project, but is intertwined with the antithetical, lucid interplay of unrelenting libidinal desire on the one hand, and constant unavoidable suffering and absence on the other. Behind the unreason of love lies the tremendous, though unconscious, strength of Duras' enlightened female characters and the 'mad' optimism of the relentless attraction between the sexes.

The underlying optimism of Marguerite Duras' prose stems from a positive view of the unconscious. In Duras' texts, the reader finds a conception of the libido and of the unconscious very close to Deleuze and Guattari's model, with the unconscious viewed as an 'energy' or intensity. This is in opposition to a common Freudian emphasis on chaotic instinctual nature,[13] and even to the Lacanian model based on language. In the notion of love as irrepressible instinct, we see at work the productive force of the unconscious - or desiring-production, as Deleuze and Guattari would call it. The content of such an imaginary formation is indeed "the desire to desire", and what it produces is not only a psychic reality but a social reality. From within suffering, the gratuitous state of love remains the only hope and solution to the 'madness' of human agencies, and actualises what Roger Gentis describes in these terms:

---

[12]Ninette Bailey, '*Moderato Cantabile* ou Comment (ne pas) Lire un Texte', in *La Chouette* no.19 p.26

[13]For Freud the unconscious constitutes a locus of socially unacceptable desires; the unconscious is made out to be something which wants what is forbidden and which pursues aims which need to be repressed. Ashamed of her/his desires, the individual atones by obeying the Law. The unconscious is itself repressed and comes only to represent a repressive apparatus.

"lorsque l'Eros nous possède c'est pour nous conduire en un lieu hors de l'espace, en un instant hors du temps, où ni je, ni tu, n'avons cours. Cette pure plénitude de l'être dont on ne peut rien dire. A son approche les mots éclatent comme cristal et la pensée est entrainée dans une négativité terrifiante"[14]

And indeed it is within this truth of desire, with its constant challenge to established normative order, that the Durasian enterprise is located and acquires its ideological dimension.

Marguerite Duras' texts remain resolutely contemporary and various critics have indeed indicated to what extent her writing shares common features with other modern literature. We find in her prose, for example, a sensibility reminiscent of Tournier or Le Clézio, for instance in the refusal to dissociate body from soul;[15] or there is the search for transgression, an exploration of the "expérience-limite" also to be found in Bataille.[16] Indeed her texts also have much in common with certain aspects of the *Nouveau Roman*, if only in the refusal of traditional logic and in the importance given to the productivity of language.[17] But the most essential and far-reaching sign of modernity in Marguerite Duras' texts resides in my view in the depiction of an uncompromising poetic vision of the impossible to be found at the heart of human existence. The impossible is here conceived of as a path leading to all possibilities, as a source of endless creation and meaning; and if female figures are the collaborators most suited to this new order, it is primarily because, like Lol, Anne-Marie Stretter or the woman of *Le Camion*, they remain in Duras' terms the only possible incarnation of the multiple potentiality of human existence: "Il pourrait y avoir mille possibles, mille autres possibles de cette femme", asserts Duras.[18]

---

[14] Roger Gentis, in *N'Etre*, Mémoires d'un Oeuf (Coll. Flammarion, 1977). The difference is that for Duras' characters the term 'plénitude' does include death and suffering.

[15] Tison-Brown op.cit. p.66

[16] Marty op.cit. p.66

[17] The link between Duras' writing and the *Nouveau Roman* has been stressed by Saporta in 'L'Ecole et le Regard', op.cit. pp.49-50

[18] From an unpublished interview conducted by R.Udris & Sonia Knox at the London Film Festival, November 1977, reported in R.Udris, 'Entrevue avec Marguerite Duras', *La Chouette* no.15 p.5. It is important to note that the

It would remain to be seen how this vision of the impossible is translated by Marguerite Duras in cinemato- graphic and theatrical terms, and how the use of a different medium with another emphasis given to spatiality, sound or images reflects or deflects the underlying optimism of the play of desire at work in her prose. A comparative study of reader and viewer reception, designed to include a wide range of social responses, could usefully examine how this "pratique de la perte"[19] is experienced by both readers and audiences, and determine whether Duras' artistic production is felt to be as relevant, irritating or challenging as her journalistic activities and public interventions.

In the meantime, to dismiss Marguerite Duras' vision as utopian may not be so easy in view of what has been happening in Europe towards the end of this 20th century, when what had remained inconceivable for some generations has suddenly become reality with the unexpected collapse of an ideological empire: "ce pays mégalithique devenu irrespirable".[20] Marguerite Duras has indeed understood that

> "la politique de l'impossible est la meilleure voie pour découvrir la politique du possible qui ne peut être qu'une inconnue à plusieurs solutions."[21]

---

strength given to female characters in Duras' fiction does not reflect an intrinsic utopian quality to be attributed to women, but stems paradoxically from the freedom gained as a result of their position of exclusion from the ideological order: "Je ne crois pas qu'un homme puisse se perdre de cette façon" asserts Duras in the same interview, "parce qu'on l'a pris en charge dès son plus jeune âge, il est doté de pouvoirs immédiatement...donc il est mort, je veux dire il est sclérosé infiniment plus que la femme, dès son plus jeune âge..."

[19]"Je propose une perte du spectateur dès le départ...ou bien on l'accepte très violemment ou bien on le rejette très violemment" (ibid)

[20]Marguerite Duras, in Mariane Alphant, 'La Vie Duras', *Libération* 11.1.90 p.21

[21]Bataille, 'Lettre à J.Lindon', OC III, p.521, in Jean- Michel Besnier, *La Politique de L'impossible* (La Découverte 1988) p.238

BIBLIOGRAPHY

I Works by Marguerite Duras

a) Novels and recits

Les Impudents, Plon, 1943
La Vie Tranquille, Gallimard, Paris 1944
Un Barrage contre le Pacifique Gallimard, Paris 1950
Le Marin de Gibraltar, Gallimard, Paris 1952
Les Petits Chevaux de Tarquinia, Gallimard, Paris 1953
Des Journees Entières dans les Arbres (including *Le Boa, Madame Dodin, Les Chantiers*), Gallimard, Paris 1954
Le Square, Gallimard, Paris 1955
Moderato Cantabile, Minuit, Paris 1958
Dix Heures et Demie du Soir en Eté, Gallimard, Paris 1960
L'Après-midi de Monsieur Andesmas, Gallimard, Paris 1962
Le Ravissement de Lol V.Stein, Gallimard, Paris 1964
Le Vice-consul, Gallimard, Paris 1965
L'Amante Anglaise, Gallimard, Paris 1967
Détruire, Dit-elle, Minuit, Paris 1969
Abahn Sabana David, Gallimard, Paris 1970
L'Amour, Gallimard, Paris 1971
India Song, Gallimard, Paris 1973
L'Homme Assis dans le Couloir, Minuit, Paris 1980
Agatha, Minuit, Paris 1981
L'Homme Atlantique, Minuit, Paris 1982
La Maladie de la Mort, Minuit, Paris 1982
Savannah Bay, Minuit, Paris 1982
L'Amant, Minuit, Paris 1984
La Douleur, P.O.L., Paris 1985
Les Yeux Bleus, Cheveux Noirs, Minuit, Paris 1986
La Pute de la Côte Normande, Minuit, Paris 1986
Emily-L, Minuit, Paris 1987
La Pluie D'Eté, P.O.L. Paris 1990
L'Amant de la Chine du Nord, Gallimard, Paris 1991
Yann Andréa Steiner, P.O.L., Paris 1992

b) Plays

Les Viaducs de la Seine-et-Oise, Gallimard, Paris 1959
Theatre I: Les Eaux et Forêts, Le Square, La Musica, Gallimard,
    Paris 1965
L'Amante Anglaise, Cahiers du Théatre National Populaire, Paris
    1968
*Théatre II: Suzanna Andler, Des Journées Entières dans les Arbres,
    Yes, peut-être, Le Shaga, Un Homme est Venu me Voir*,
    Gallimard, Paris 1968
L'Eden Cinéma, Mercure de France, Paris 1977
Théatre III: La Bête dans la Jungle (after Henry James, adapted by
    James Lord & Marguerite Duras), *Les Papiers d'Aspern* (after
    Henry James, adapted by Marguerite Duras & Robert
    Antelme), *La Danse de Mort* (after August Strindberg,
    adapted by Marguerite Duras), Gallimard, Paris 1984
La Musica Deuxième, Gallimard, Paris 1985
La Mouette de Tchékov, Gallimard, Paris 1985

c) Films, screenplays, television programmes

La Musica (film), coedited Paul Seban, Artistes Associés 1966
Détruire, Dit-elle (film), Benoît-Jacob, 1969
Jaune le Soleil (film), Films Molière, 1971
Nathalie Granger (film), Films Molière, 1972
La Femme du Gange (film), Benoît-Jacob, 1973
India Song (film), Films Armorial, 1975
Baxter, Vera Baxter (film), N.E.F. Diffusion, 1976
Son Nom de Venise dans Calcutta Désert (film), Benoît-Jacob, 1976
Des Journées Entières dans les Arbres (film), Benoît-Jacob, 1976
Le Camion (film), D.D.Prod., 1977
Le Navire Night (film), Films du Losange, 1978
Césarée (film), Films du Losange, 1979
Les Mains Négatives (film), Films du Losange, 1979
Aurélia, Steiner, dit Aurélia Melbourne (films), Paris Audiovisuels,
    1979
Aurélia Steiner, dit Aurélia Vancouver (film), Films du Losange,
    1979
Agatha et les Lectures Illimitées (film), Prod. Berthemont, 1981
L'Homme Atlantique (film), Prod. Berthemont, 1981
Dialogue de Rome (film), Co-op. Longa Gittata, 1982
Les Enfants (film), 1985

Hiroshima mon Amour (screenplay), Gallimard, Paris 1960
Une Aussi Longue Absence (screenplay), in collaboration with Gérard Jarlot, Gallimard 1961
Nathalie Granger, followed by *La Femme du Gange* (screenplays), Gallimard, Paris 1973
Le Camion (screenplay) followed by *Entretien Avec Michelle Porte*, Minuit, Paris 1977
Le Navire Night, Césarée, Les Mains Négatives, Aurélia Steiner, dit Aurélia Melbourne, Aurélia Steiner, dit Aurélia Vancouver (screenplays), Mercure de France, Paris 1979
Vera baxter ou les Plages de l'Atlantique (screenplay), Albatros, Paris 1980

d) Miscellaneous

interview in *Cahiers du Cinéma* no.217, November 1969
Les Parleuses (with Xavière Gauthier), Minuit, Paris 1974
interview, 'Ce que parler ne veut pas dire', in *Les Nouvelles Littéraires*, Paris 15.4.74
Les Lieux de Marguerite Duras (with Michelle Porte), Minuit, Paris 1977
L'Eté 80, Minuit, Paris 1980
Les Yeux Verts (special issue of *Cahiers du Cinéma*, 312-313, L'Etoile, Paris 1980
interview of 10th/11th april 1981 in *Marguerite Duras à Montréal* (S.Lamy & A.Roy) Spirale, Montréal 1981
Outside, Albin Michel, Paris 1981
L'Autre Journal
- 'Entretiens avec Francois Mitterand' nos.1-11 (hebdo) (26th Feb - 7th May 1986)
- 'L'Homme nu de la Bastille' no.4 (mensuel) (April 1985)
- 'L'Excès - L'Usine' no.5 (mensuel) (May 1985)
- 'L'Amant Magnifique' no.5 (May 1985)
- 'Greenpeace, Gorbachev et la Gauche' no.8 (mensuel) (Oct 1985)
- 'La Lecture dans le Train' no.9 (mensuel) (Nov 1985)
- 'Joëlle Kaufmann. Marguerite Duras: Parler des Otages ou ne pas Parler des Otages' no.5 (hebdo) (26th March 1986)

- 'Les Chiens de L'Histoire' no.6 (hebdo) (23rd April 1986)
- 'Moi' no.10 (hebdo) (30th April 1986)
- 'Tjibaou-Duras' no.13 (hebdo) (22nd May 1986)
- 'L'Amant Magnifique' no.16 (hebdo) (11th June 1986)

interview, 'Sublime forcément sublime' in *Libération*, 17th July 1985

La Vie Matérielle, P.O.L. Paris 1987

interview 'Duras Toute Entière' in *Nouvel Observateur* no.1149 (Nov 1986)

interview 'Duras dans les Régions Claires de L'Ecriture' in *Le Journal Littéraire* no.2 (Dec 1987/Jan 1988)

interview 'La Vie Duras' in *Libération* (11th Jan 1990)

interview 'Les nostalgies de l'amante Duras', *Nouvel Observateur* no 1442, (Fuillett 1992)

e) Television Programmes

- *'Les Lieux de Marguerite Duras'*, prod. INA, May 1976, TF1
- *'Savannah Bay, C'est Toi'*, prod. INA (dir. Michelle Porte) 1984
- *'Apostrophes'* (dir. Jean Cazenave), 28th Sept 1984, Antenne 2
- *'Duras-Godard'* (dir. Verhaeghe), 22nd Dec 1987, FR3
- *'Marguerite Duras: au delà des Pages'* (dir. L.Perrot), Feb/March 1988, TF1

f) Radio programmes, records, cassettes

- *'Les Nuits Magnétiques'*, with Marguerite Duras (radio) 1987
- *'Bon Plaisir de Marguerite Duras'*, France-Culture (radio) 20th Oct 1984
- *'Marguerite Duras Parle'* in record series 'Français de Notre Temps. Hommes D'Aujourd'hui'
- *'La Jeune Fille et L'Enfant'*, read by Marguerite Duras, Eds des Femmes (cassette)
- *'Les Petits Chevaux de Tarquinia'*, read by C.Deneuve, Eds des Femmes (cassette)

II Critical work on Marguerite Duras

a) Books

Marguerite ALLEINS, *Marguerite Duras: Médium du Réel*, L'Age d'Homme, S.A.Lausanne 1984

Madeleine BORGOMANO, *Duras: une Lecture des Fantasmes*, Cistre 1985

Jean PIERROT, *Marguerite Duras*, Corti, 1986

Marcelle MARINI, *Territoires du Féminin*, Minuit, Paris 1977

Carol MURPHY, *Aliénation and Absence in the Novels of Marguerite Duras*, French Forum Monographs 1982

Trista SELOUS, 'A study of the novels of Marguerite Duras up to 1971, in the light of contemporary writers and thinkers', PhD thesis (University of London) June 1985 in Senate House Library. Published as *The Other Woman*, Yale University Press, Newhaven & London 1988

Micheline TISON-BRAUN, *Marguerite Duras*, Rodopi, Amsterdam 1984

Sharon WILLIS, *Marguerite Duras: Writing on the Body*, Urbana: University of Illinois Press 1987

b) Articles

Marianne ALPHANT, 'La Vie Duras' in *Libération* 11.1.90

Verena ANDERMATT, 'Rodomontages de Lol V.Stein' in *Locus, space, landscape, décor*, Modern French Fiction no.57, Yale French Studies 1979

Ninette BAILEY, 'Discours social: lecture socio-critique du *Vice-consul* de Marguerite Duras', in R.J. North & C.A.Burns (eds) *Literature and Society: Studies in Nineteenth and Twentieth Century French Literature*, Birmingham University 1980

Ninette BAILEY, '*Moderato Cantabile* ou Comment (ne pas) Lire un Texte' in *La Chouette*, French Dept., Birkbeck College, University of London, no.19, Nov. 87.

François BARAT & Joel FARGES, in contributions to *Marguerite Duras*, Albatros, Paris 1975

Denis BERTRAND, 'Le corps émouvant. L'Absence. Propositions pour une sémiotique de l'émotion', in *La Chouette*, French Dept., Birkbeck College, University of London, no.20 April 1988

Madeleine BORGOMANO, 'Le Corps et le Texte' in *Ecrire Dit-elle*, University of Brussels, 1985

Michel de CERTEAU, 'Marguerite Duras: On Dit' in *Ecrire Dit-elle*, Université de Bruxelles 1985

Hélène CIXOUS, 'Le Rire de la Méduse' in *L'Arc* no.61 (1975)

Béatrice DIDIER, 'Thèmes et structures de l'absence dans *Le Ravissement de Lol V.Stein*, in *Ecrire, Dit-elle*, Université de Bruxelles 1985

Pierre FEDIDA, 'Entre les voix et l'image', in F.Barat & J.Farges (eds), *Marguerite Duras*, Albatros, Paris 1975

Francois PERALDI, 'Les Indes impossibles' in S.Lamy & A.Roy (eds) *Marguerite Duras à Montréal*, Spirale, Montréal 1981

Sylvie GAGNE, 'L'Ombilic des Indes' in Lamy & Roy (eds) *Marguerite Duras à Montréal*, Spirale, Montréal 1981

Sylvia HARVEY, *L'Amour of Marguerite Duras*, MA dissertation, Birkbeck College, University of London 1982

Leslie HILL, 'Marguerite Duras and the limits of fiction' in *Paragraph* vol.12 no.1, Oxford University Press March 1989

Jacques LACAN, 'Hommage fait à Marguerite Duras du *Ravissement de Lol V.Stein*, in *Marguerite Duras par Marguerite Duras*, Albatros, Paris 1975

Elizabeth LYON, 'The cinema of Lol V.Stein' in *Camera Obscura* no.6, Berkeley, fall 1980

Christiane MAKWARD, 'Structures du silence/du délire' in *Poétique* no.35, Sept. 1978

Marcelle MARINI, 'L'Autre corps' in *Ecrire, Dit-elle*, Université de Bruxelles 1985

Marcelle MARINI, 'Une Femme sans Aveu' in *Marguerite Duras*, *L'Arc* no.98, LeJas, 1985

Eric MARTY, 'Marguerite Duras: hypothèses-notations-fragments' in *La Chouette*, French Dept., Birkbeck College, University of London no.15 April 1988

Michele MONTRELAY, 'Sur *Le Ravissement de Lol V.Stein*' in Montrelay *L'Ombre et le Nom*, Minuit, Paris 1977

Andre ROY, 'Ecrire Duras' in Lamy & Roy (eds) *Marguerite Duras à Montréal*, Spirale, Montréal 1981

Marc SAPORTA, 'Les Possibles Parallèles' in *Marguerite Duras*, *L'Arc* no.98, LeJas 1985

Trista SELOUS, 'Evidence of struggle-problems with *India Song*' in *Undercut* no. 3/4, March 1982

Michael SHERINGHAM, 'Knowledge and repetition in *Le Ravissement de Lol V.Stein*' in *The Nouveau Roman*, Romance Studies no.2, 1983

Daniel SIBONY, 'Jeux d'ombre, littérature et mélancolie' in *Nouvelles Littéraires*, July 1987

France THEORET, 'La lenteur, le cri, l'autonomie' in Lamy & Roy (eds) *Marguerite Duras à Montréal*, Spirale, Montreal 1981

Raynalle UDRIS, 'Entre-vue avec Marguerite Duras' in *La Chouette*, French Dept., Birkbeck College, University of London, no.15, Jan.86

Sylvia VENET, 'Femme dans l'écriture- Marguerite Duras' in *La Chouette*, French Dept., Birkbeck College, University of London, no.6, Sept. 1981

III Psychoanalytic theory and clinical literature

Mary BARNES, Joseph BERKE, Mary Barnes: *Mary BARNES: Two Accounts of a Journey Through Madness*, McGibbon & Kee, London, 1971

Michel FOUCAULT, 'La Pensée du Dehors' in *Critique* no.229, 1966

Michel FOUCAULT, *Histoire de la Folie*, NRF Gallimard, Paris 1972

Michel FOUCAULT, *Mental Illness and Psychology*, transl. A.Sheridan, Harper Colopton Books, London 1976

Roland JACCARD, *La Folie*, P.U.F, Paris 1979

Julia KRISTEVA, 'Oscillation du 'Pouvoir' du 'Refus'' in *Tel Quel* no.58 (Summer 1974)

Julia KRISTEVA, *Soleil Noir: Dépression et Mélancolie*, NRF Gallimard, Paris 1987

Maud MANNONI, *Le Psychiatre, son Fou et la Psychanalyse*, Seuil, Paris 1970

Marcelle MARINI, *Lacan*, Paris Belfond, 1986

Ruth MENAHEM, *Langage et Folie*, Les Belles Lettres, 'Confluents psychanalytiques', Paris 1986

Juliet MITCHELL, *Psychoanalysis and Feminism*, Penguin 1974

Emma SANTOS, *La Loméchuse*, Femmes, Paris 1976

Emma SANTOS, *L'Itinéraire Psychiatrique*, Femmes, Paris 1977

Thomas SZASZ, *The Myth of Mental Illness*, Paladin, 1972

Armando VERDIGLIONE, *La Folie dans la Psychanalyse*, Payot,
Paris 1977
Unica ZURN, *L'Homme Jasmin*, Gallimard, Paris 1970

IV   Other theoretical and critical works

a) articles

Homi BHABHA, 'The Other question' in *Screen* vol.24 no. 6,
Nov/Dec 1983
Véronique DAHLET, 'Le Miracle de l'Aveugle - A Propos de
Fable de Robert Pinget' in *La Chouette*, no.19, Nov. 1987
Xavière GAUTHIER, 'Existe-t-il une Ecriture de Femmes?' in *Tel
Quel* no.58 (Summer 1974)
Guy ROSALATO, 'Culpabilité et sacrifice' and 'La folie et le
sacré' in *Psychanalyse et Semiotique*, 10/18, Paris 1974
Armando VERDIGLIONE, 'La jouissance de la matière' in
Psychanalyse et Semiotique, 10/18, Paris 1975

b) Books

Gaston BACHELARD, *La Psychanalyse du Feu*, Idées, Paris 1949
Gaston BACHELARD, *L'Eau et les Rêves*, Corti, Paris 1968
Mieke BAL, *Narratologie*, Klincksieck, Paris 1977
Jean-Michel BESNIER, *La Politique de L'Impossible*, La
Découverte, Paris 1988
Gilles DELEUZE, Félix GUATTARI, *Anti-Oedipus*, University of
Minnesota Press, 1983
Gilles DELEUZE, Felix GUATTARI, *On the Line*, Semiotext(e),
New York 1983
Jacques DERRIDA, *L'Ecriture et la Différence*, Seuil 1967
Shoshana FELMAN, *La Folie et la Chose Littéraire*, Seuil, Paris
1978
Gérard GENETTE, *Figures II*, Seuil, Paris 1969
Roger GENTIS, *N'Etre*, Flammarion, Paris 1977
Stephen HEATH, *The Nouveau Roman*, Elek, London 1972
Jacques LEENHARDT, *Lecture Politique du Roman*, Minuit, Paris
1973
George POULET, *L'Espace Proustien*, NRF Gallimard, Paris 1963
Alan SHERIDAN, *Michel Foucault: the Will to Truth*, Tavistock,
London 1981

Daniel SIBONY, *La Haine du Désir*, Christian Bourgeois, Paris 1984

Philippe SOLLERS, *L'Ecriture et l'Expérience des Limites*, Seuil, Paris 1970

Klaus THEWELEIT, *Male Fantasies*, Polity Press, Cambridge 1987

Jane TOMPKINS, *Reader Response Criticism from Formalism to Post-structuralism*, University Press, Baltimore 1980

Margaret WHITFORD, *Luce Irigaray*, Routlege, London 1991

« Un Barrage Contre Le Pacifique »